Remembering the Past in Contemporary African American Fiction

Remembering the Past in Contemporary African American Fiction

KEITH BYERMAN

The University of North Carolina Press • Chapel Hill

© 2005 The University of North Carolina Press
All rights reserved
Manufactured in the United States of America

Designed by Jacquline Johnson
Set in Bembo by Keystone Typesetting, Inc.

This book was published with the assistance
of the Anniversary Endowment Fund of the
University of North Carolina Press.

The paper in this book meets the guidelines for
permanence and durability of the Committee on
Production Guidelines for Book Longevity of the
Council on Library Resources.

Library of Congress
Cataloging-in-Publication Data
Byerman, Keith Eldon, 1948–
Remembering the past in contemporary African
American fiction / Keith Byerman.
p. cm.
Includes bibliographical references and index.
ISBN 0-8078-2980-3 (cloth: alk. paper)
ISBN 0-8078-5647-9 (pbk.: alk. paper)
1. American fiction—African American authors—
History and criticism. 2. Literature and history—
United States—History—20th century.
3. American fiction—20th century—History and
criticism. 4. African Americans—Intellectual life—
20th century. 5. Historical fiction, American—
History and criticism. 6. Autobiographical
memory in literature. 7. African Americans in
literature. 8. History in literature. 9. Memory in
literature. I. Title.
PS374.N4.B94   2005
813'.5409358'08996073—dc22
2005010242

cloth   09 08 07 06 05   5 4 3 2 1
paper   09 08 07 06 05   5 4 3 2 1

To those who have passed.
You are remembered.

Contents

Acknowledgments

I would like to express my appreciation to the
audiences and panelists at various conferences
where I have presented many of the ideas
expressed in this work. Their questions and
comments helped to sharpen both my thinking
and my writing. I would also like to thank the
staff of the University of North Carolina Press,
and especially Sian Hunter, for patience and
encouragement during the development of
this project.

*Remembering
the Past in
Contemporary
African American
Fiction*

INTRODUCTION

Toward a History of the Black Present

One of the prominent features of American culture since the late 1960s has been the flowering of interest in African American history. Though the quest for a documentable black past goes back at least as far as the pre–Civil War period, its development as a topic of significant national concern really began with the demands of activists in the late 1960s for the recovery of what had been lost or deliberately suppressed. What could have been a relatively straightforward historiographical project was transformed by the controversy over William Styron's *Confessions of Nat Turner* (1967), the modest success of Margaret Walker's *Jubilee* (1966), Ernest Gaines's *Autobiography of Miss Jane Pittman* (1971), and the cultural phenomenon of Alex Haley's *Roots* (1976). Rather than simply an academic field, black history became an institution and a commodity and thus a key part of American culture. While the modes of expression have changed to some extent, the processes of analysis, popularization, and commodification continue unabated.

Within this context, major African American narrative artists have focused their literary efforts on the black past. Gaines, Toni Morrison, Charles Johnson, and Gloria Naylor, among others, have chosen to (re)construct the past rather than tell stories of the present. In this choice, they distinguish themselves from earlier generations of African American writers—the black arts movement, the protest/modernist generation (Richard Wright, James Baldwin, Ralph Ellison), and the Harlem Renaissance. While there has been an interest in historical narrative as long as blacks have been writing fiction, this is the first generation to make it the dominant mode. Part of the reason for present-time orientation among earlier writers was the perception that black writing existed primarily (or at least largely) as a means of "advancing the race." Those writers with a different concern, such as Jean Toomer, Zora Neale Hurston, and

Ellison, were often subject to severe criticism, even though their work itself reflected current issues. The problems of the race were considered so desperate that to use one's skills for anything other than protest, group assertion, or amelioration was considered wasteful, escapist, and perhaps treasonous. Fictionalizing the past was useful only to the extent that it identified sources of present problems or enhanced the image of the race.

While this is an oversimplification of a varied and complex literary history, it can be helpful in defining the distinctiveness of recent African American narrative practice. Present-day authors are neither unaware of nor disengaged from current issues, as the nonfictional writings of many of them clearly demonstrate. They speak in other venues of violence, family dynamics, the criminal justice system, gender issues, and economic and political debates, as these affect black life. But in their fiction, they do not use the stories of the past to comment directly on immediate problems or to promote a positive racial image. I emphasize "directly" because the argument of this study is that these writers do in fact speak out of and to their (and our) moment in history. These are writers who came into their maturity in the 1960s, with all that that era signifies: civil rights, Black Power, Vietnam, popular culture, violence, ghettoization, the emergence of a black middle class. Their fiction began to be published in the 1970s, at the time of Black Studies programs, black history as an academic discipline, blaxploitation films, *Roots*; in other words, the institutionalization and commodification of black experience. They achieved recognition in the 1980s, the period of African American commercial success in the media and athletics, as well as the economic decline of the black working class, police brutality, and the development of a full-blown drug culture and black-on-black crime.

I want to argue that the very choice of history as subject is determined by authors' experiences of the recent past and the present. But the connection is primarily indirect and metaphoric. Such figuration is necessitated by the dominant "racial formation" that shapes the cultural discourse of the present.[1] Because we live in a time in which any discussion of "race" must be framed within this formation, writers have undertaken to speak to, through, and beyond "race" through stories of different eras from our own. This displacement allows both defamiliarization and reinvention of the meanings of black experience. The refusal to make direct connections reflects a resistance to incorporation within the dominant discourse. Stories that seem to be "only" about slavery or the Jazz Age cannot so easily be reduced to current discursive practice.

Crucial to this project is an understanding of how history is being represented in fictional narrative. A key is Toni Morrison's dedication of *Beloved* to "the Sixty Million and more." While this phrase can be read as a recognition of and connection with historic black suffering in the slave trade and slavery itself, it also has intertextual significance. It clearly echoes and signifies on the "six million" victims of the European Holocaust. It multiplies that number and extends it in history from a decade to centuries. It lays claim to precedence and priority in the saga of human suffering and cruelty. If Jewish history is special in the modern world on the basis of loss, black experience is seen as having a greater claim to exceptionalism. And just as the narratives of the Holocaust are gestures at speaking the unspeakable, of bearing witness to an evil beyond imagination, so too this figuration of black history recasts that experience as one beyond the rationalist discourses of historiography and social analysis.[2]

The point here is not simply literary and historical primacy but rather a reconceptualization of black experience as a survivor narrative and thus a rewriting of the American grand narrative. If the African American story is one of extended Holocaust, then the national history cannot be understood as primarily the story of individual achievement and democratic progress. It is instead a story of greed, domination, and violation under the guise of individualism and the rule of law. The "true" story of black life in America is one in which the dominant discourse of race, with its attendant practices, intends the victimization of a group of people distinguished primarily by their color. Moreover, this intention is not limited to some benighted past of virulent racists but continues through time, though in different forms. One of the formal characteristics of these contemporary works is that their narrative presents are located at a variety of points. Some are situated at the time of the action—slavery, the early twentieth century, the civil rights movement, while others are pinpointed at some later point—years after the event, the writer's present, or even the future. Such positioning allows the authors to show the continuity of history under apparent breaks.

Thus, contemporary narratives are trauma stories in that they tell of both tremendous loss and survival; they describe the psychological and social effects of suffering. More important, perhaps, they tell of the erasure of such history and, as a consequence, its continued power to shape black life. The stories told by recent writers are those of ordinary people who are often compelled to live life in extremis. Their tales are often represented as suppressed, hidden, forgotten, or distorted. They are not the sagas of great heroes with clearly definable inspirational value; instead, they describe the compromised, the deformed, the criminal, the disreputable, though these terms themselves must be understood in the context of racial domination.

A key question for this study is why such narratives are being told at this moment in history. If we are moving into a postethnic America,[3] if black achievement economically, educationally, and politically is in fact at an all-time high, then it could be considered pointless and even counterproductive to insist on a race-oriented history. Even if we take into account the deterioration of the inner cities, the explosion of crime in black neighborhoods and the often related police brutality, racial profiling, and the poverty levels of black women and children, it is not especially obvious how stories of black women who kill their children (*Beloved*) or of slave suicide pacts (*The Chaneysville Incident*) speak to those circumstances.

The argument here is that such narratives are motivated in part by precisely a recognition of both current prosperity and deprivation. Both are conventionally understood in the frame of the American grand narrative of individual achievement in defiance of the odds. Those who succeed are thus encouraged to forget; part of what they are to forget are those who have not succeeded. But if the narrative can be disrupted by stories of trauma and survival, then a different set of causes and effects emerges. The fact that the writers themselves are among the successful—educated, professional, often celebrated—adds an element of self-criticism to their work. The very stories by which they tell of a different, more troubled experience become the sources of promotion, income, and publicity.

That is why it is important to return to the narratives themselves. Part of what they describe is the ease with which one can be caught within the dominant discourse. They express the dis-ease of the articulate and successful in the face of holocaust. They tell of the desire of communities not to tell their secrets, even to their children. The compulsion to tell despite the discomfort and despite the probable misreading in the dominant culture suggests a commitment to reclaiming the past specifically as historical. Whether the age is postethnic, it has become difficult to define it in essentialist terms. If writers understand that African Americans are still treated and still conceive of themselves as different despite a "post-race" national discourse, then that difference can be understood as a function of a history in which racial formation may change but continues to exist as a definer of social reality. If American history is understood as holocaust, with blacks as its victims, then present conditions are seen in a fundamentally different way. In a nation that simultaneously engages in and denies the reality of harmful racial practices, policies, and beliefs, both destruction and survival are expected outcomes. Success is as much the product of national denial of history as it is the result of individual effort. Thus, the successful black writer, like the famous athlete or respected politician, is an accident of history and remains connected with those leading traumatized lives in the inner city and the rural South. Toni Morrison achieves celebrity status in part because she is willing to tell horrific stories of black life, stories that allow the American public both to feel pity for the suffering and to replicate black abjection by imaginatively experiencing that suffering.[4] It is the ways authors seek to maneuver through this discursive situation, which potentially implicates them in black suffering, that is a key concern of this study.

The Uses of Theory

Making this argument is possible using the insights and methods of cultural criticism and trauma theory. Cultural criticism assumes that expressive forms, including literature, are the products of their historical contexts, including socioeconomic conditions, ideologies, and cultural practices. No text is generated in some purely aesthetic realm; rather, it is the product (and producer) of the discursive systems and social realities of its time. Cultural criticism collapses conventional notions of the artistic text as a distinct category separate from other discursive practices and emphasizes the role of ideology and other cultural elements in the production, reception, and interpretation of texts. Because such elements are present in any expressive practice, virtually anything can be a "text." Thus, film, fashion, popular literature, advertising, news reporting, and music have all been subjects for analysis.[5]

The present study undertakes to apply these insights in a particular way. While most of my analysis of texts follows the pattern of close reading, the emphasis here is on the impact of social reality, ideology, and discursive practices on recent African American narratives. The analysis focuses on the chosen texts as historical products, as well as discrete aesthetic objects. It assumes that the history in the texts is part of the history of the texts; in other words, that the choice to write historical narratives itself must be understood historically. Thus, my interest, unlike that of most commentators on these narratives, is not so much the history portrayed within the texts as it is the philosophies of history and the ideologies of the present that inform the choices of subjects by the authors. I am interested in the present rather than the past as historical moment and context for literary production. The effort here, in part, is to define the patterns of the last quarter of the twentieth century that have shaped African American narrative practice and to see these texts not merely as embedded in that history but also as shaping practices themselves.

Trauma theory argues for the understanding of narratives of the past in terms of compulsions to tell that are linked to suppressions of what must be told.[6] Such stories seek to speak the unspeakable in the sense that some experiences seem beyond representation, but also in the sense that it is survivors who must do the speaking of occurrences that implicate them in the horrors, if only through the guilt of having survived. As victims themselves, telling forces confrontation with their own humiliation, impotence, and perhaps collaboration. Denial is the easier way. But since the perpetrators of the evil suppress the experience, the only possible narrators are those willing to expose the past. Moreover, as Morrison clearly shows in *Beloved*, the stories will out, regardless of the desires of survivors. What we see in contemporary African American narrative is precisely the recreation of history as a tale of endless black suffering, and it is in fact this sense of history that serves as the meaning of "race" in these fictions. Blackness in America "means," in these texts, living and dying in and through a traumatic reality. Part of that experience, consistent with theory, is the dialectic of assertion and denial of that reality, by both blacks and whites. It is not my purpose to argue whether the language of holocaust should or should not be applied to African American experience. Rather, I am pointing to the patterns of figuration I see in a specific group of writers. I respect the views of those who insist that Shoah was a unique horror and further that efforts at comparison can only denigrate the significance of that reality.[7] Contemporary writers, in a variety of ways and for a variety of reasons, have chosen to narrate black holocaust.

A key reason has to do with notions of "recovery," the therapeutic side of trauma theory. By compelling an examination of the distorted and commodified past, on the level of those who lived the traumas, history can be revealed as having a profoundly different pattern than the one insisted upon within the dominant national discourse. The voices, bodies, and stories of those rendered invisible by oppression can finally be seen, if only in fictive representations. At the same time, such recovery can enable healing, in that the wounds and diseases of the past, if made clear, can be treated for both the nation and the race. But because this is primarily a postmodern literature, such healing possibilities themselves are often problematized. The writing itself often challenges the assumptions of womanist and Afrocentric readings of it as therapeutic.

This study has a somewhat different emphasis from most cultural criticism and, in fact, might not fit that category at all. The texts I choose to examine are "serious literature," not the modes of popular culture. While both areas have received sophisticated critical attention in African American studies in recent years, there has been a tendency to segregate the analyses and methods. Film, rap, sports, and Malcolm X as commodities are written about one way; Toni Morrison, John Edgar Wideman, and nineteenth-century women writers are written about in another. My intent is to bring together this material and these methods. It is my belief that it is "serious literature" that speaks most fully and deeply to both the past and the present; it complicates and problematizes even as it represents. I also understand that such a designation is problematic and probably even tautological. Toni Morrison, for example, cannot be understood as a writer who stands outside her historical moment and produces "transcendent" works of literature. She is a product of her time and her position within a market-oriented culture, and so therefore must be her writings; she must use the discourse available, and she must, in part at least, reflect social conditions and values. But she is not merely a product; she is also an agent, to some extent based on her understanding of and achievements within the culture. As agent, she is capable of critically understanding and signifying upon that same historical reality. My concern is to articulate both the limits determined by our history and the agency that enables writers to speak to that history. It becomes necessary, then, to spell out, within limits, the social realities and discursive practices that define what Michael Omi and Howard Winant have called the "racial formation." My articulation of this history will, of course, be a fictive narrative itself since it must be generalized and selective; moreover, others with much more specialized expertise have written in much more detail on these matters. I am seeking only to stand on their shoulders and present an overview.

This "narrative" will then be followed by a discussion of the representations of black history that formed the discourse that recent writers have chosen to enter. These representations include the practices of academic history that began in the 1960s to challenge the conventional wisdom, especially on slavery and Reconstruction. Associated with this revisionism was the development of Black Studies, which questioned not only the content of the social sciences and humanities but also the assumptions about academic methods. In popular culture, historical novels, films, and television began to depict the black past. Whether these representations were realistic, sentimental, or sensationalistic, they broke down both the notion that blacks were not part of history and the view of blacks previously dominant in the media.

Once these contexts are established, it becomes possible to examine how various writers respond to them and operate within them. I have resisted organizing these discussions by either the chronology of publication or the historical period(s) presented in the texts. To do either would simply replicate previous critical practice. Rather, I have structured the analyses according to modes of historical representation using rubrics of "memory," "desire," and "family." These serve as thematic ways of understanding the operations of history within narrative, especially as the narratives construct that past as trauma and recovery.

Such a critical structure puts into the foreground philosophies and attitudes toward history, the relationships between history and group and individual identities, and the implied and explicit connections writers make to various aspects of American culture. As a brief example, Sherley Anne Williams's *Dessa Rose* has been read as an act of signifying on Styron's *Nat Turner*, which in some sense it is. But that connection does not explain why Williams produced such a work twenty years after Styron's novel, nor why she created a female hero, nor why she emphasized interracial relations, nor, finally, why she produced a story of black triumph, through trickster behavior, over white authority. Not only is her text different from Styron's, but it is also different from the historical projections of black nationalism that were used to condemn *Nat Turner*. Her work enters the discourse of 1986, not 1968, and must be understood in those terms. So it is with all the works being examined here.

The Meanings of "History"

It is necessary, at this point, to inject the various meanings that the term "history" has in this study. It includes imagined or actual events that occurred in the past, based on media accounts (*Jazz*, *Beloved*, *Dessa Rose*), family or community history (*Divine Days*, *The Chaneysville Incident*, the Homewood trilogy, the Appalachee Red trilogy), historiographical accounts (*Middle Passage*, *Cattle Killing*), or hypothetical events that reflect conditions or circumstances (*Paradise*, Gaines's novels). "History" also includes previous and current representations of black history, whether fictional or historiographical, that serve either as points of intertextual reference or as "databases." Thus, for example, the field of social history gives some legitimacy to consideration of the experiences of ordinary people, while Afrocentric interpretations bring attention to the "African" side of African American, a position that opens possibilities for writers, either positively or negatively.

"History" can also be understood as the stories of ordinary people in times of stress[8] rather than hero or victim narratives; but in the all-too-common context in human history of violence, dehumanization, abjection, and invisibility, this experience is comparable to holocaust. The writers in this study are in this sense generating a historical rather than essentialist idea of black experience. That is, it is a shared experience of suffering rather than a genetic or geographical connection that shapes group identity.

"History" here necessarily includes the historical moment(s) of the writers themselves—the question of how this time produces these narratives. Particular issues (for example, male-female relationships, urban life, prison, the continuing reality of racism) can serve as frames of reference for the treatment of the past in some texts. Moreover, this study assumes that contemporary African American writing is fully participant and engaged in American culture and society. Thus, I am not seeking a signifying monkey or a blues aesthetic in the tradition of Henry Louis Gates and Houston Baker, though I believe that such notions can have significant value in understanding African American expressive culture. What links the writers I have selected (and a number of others that could be included) is their desire to understand and explain the American past as it has impacted and continues to impact black people. Thus, I see their work, not in terms of anthropology, nor genetics (African personality), nor a strictly gendered approach, but rather as an aesthetic expression of social and political reality that necessarily incorporates these other elements, but in the specific ways that are relevant to the need to come to terms with contemporary reality. That "coming to terms" involves an effort to grasp the meaning of black life as it is lived today in the contradictions, complexities, and jumble that is American culture. Because this "jumble" seems to have many negative effects on black life, part of the function of the writing is therapeutic.

Trauma theory argues that the confusions of the present are the result of terrible events in the past, events that continue to have impact precisely because their power has been denied. Thus, "history" must take into account a psychological dimension. Historical fiction of the sort discussed here does two things: it assumes that, because of the conditions blacks experienced in the past, their survival offers clues to the problems of the present, thus having a practical value. But it is also potentially therapeutic in that it insists on revealing the fullness of the past, in all its ambiguity and ugliness and complicity, which means that it compels survivors (and we are all its survivors) to face the truth. American blacks, as well as whites, have resisted that truth, as evidenced, for example, in the relative lack of popular success and notice of several of the writers included here and the media productions based on their works, as opposed to works that are either presentist in orientation (Terry McMillan, for example) or more easily embedded in the national narrative of heroes, villains, and progress (*Roots*). Presentist work offers the therapy of gendered anger, of success narratives, of pure victimization, which allows for clarification of motives and explanations for experience in straightforward terms. Other writers, including those discussed here, problematize issues by identifying the historicity of behaviors, motives, and beliefs and suggesting that presentist approaches are part of the suppression of underlying reality.

Finally, in the context of postmodernism, "history" is not straightforward narrative, nor does it offer tidy solutions to the present. The desire for therapy does not guarantee that the constructed reality will serve a therapeutic purpose. Certainly, Morrison, Wideman, and others do not offer simple cures. They suggest some possibilities, but how those might work is not spelled out. Historical fiction for them is not allegory. They often seem to be implying some notion of community, but as something constructed rather than found or revitalized. Resources have been discovered through the long history of black suffering, but those have to be improvised and changed repeatedly. When they become fixed, they often become part of the problem. It is necessary to go through the shame and disruption of remembering in order to begin to forge relationships that can become communities that can make a difference. Constantly working against this is the desire to forget, to create a different history or to reject the past altogether. The possibility for change is in memory, but a memory few want to keep.

Self-Defense

Given the preceding description of my task, a relevant question, now that cultural criticism has problematized the notion of "race," is why a critical study would bring together a group of writers on the basis of their race. The answer has to do with how these particular authors see history. Recent studies of historical fiction have shown that white writers working in this form often display a radical skepticism about the nature, meaning, and value of history.[9] Linda Hutcheon has argued that postmodernism operates as a set of contradictions that both invoke the past and question our access to it (16). It is not a reality easily distinguishable from the inventions of fiction. For this reason, a number of writers of historical fiction emphasize irony and parody in their reconstructions (or inventions) of the past. If, as Hutcheon suggests, postmodernist historical writing both accepts and doubts our ability to engage the past, African American writers are more likely to demonstrate a belief in history as accessible, even if they agree on little else. They are less likely than white writers to be ironic, parodic, or overtly self-reflexive. The past is very real, though its patterns are not necessarily easily discernible. What they give special attention to is the falsity of previous descriptions of black experience, but they tend to assume that it is possible to provide a more accurate account. While they would not disagree with Hutcheon's contention that "both history and fiction are discourses," they seek out or create discursive elements that have been suppressed or ignored (folk material, journals, letters, newspaper stories) that can open up and give voice to that which has been denied or silenced. They are more likely than white writers to privilege these texts as valid ways of knowing the past rather than as simply more texts to add to the mix. The writers examined here insist that the past had and continues to have profound impact on the minds, emotions, and beliefs of individuals, families, and communities. Moreover, as bell hooks has noted, the fragmentation of identity associated with postmodern writing is problematic in the context of society's persistent denial of black subjectivity (*Yearning*, 26–28). While these writers recognize the range of subject positions that can be taken and the role race plays in constructing a black self, they show some resistance to giving up the notion of a core identity. In Wideman's story "Damballah," as one example, he shows the elements that produce a new, constructed African American identity; at the same time, the character Orion is portrayed as a unitary, coherent, complete African self. These writers often reveal how history has objectified blacks and how survival has often required role-playing, but they are less likely than other contemporary writers to revel in that fragmentation.

Telling the stories of the past, even if they are fictions, is vitally important to these writers. (John Wideman has named one collection *All Stories Are True*.) While they may not agree on its shape or meaning, they all see it as central to American and African American experience, identity, and culture. The reason for this insistence has to do with another tendency: the desire for something like closure in the sense of clarifying the meaning of the past for the present. Unlike Thomas Pynchon, John Barth, Don DeLillo, and others, it is not enough to point to difficulties of understanding reality or to reveal the illusory aspects of contemporary society or the constructedness of identity. Because the past in these African American narratives is a traumatic one, healing, love, and empowerment are offered as possibilities, if not actualities. While relatively few of the texts discussed here offer anything like tidy conclusions, certainly works by Morrison, David Bradley, Johnson, Williams, Gaines, and Naylor point in the direction of resolution, intimacy, and community. Though the others are more open-ended, they, too, resist both radical doubt and despair.

Within this general agreement, the authors in this study were chosen because of the variety of their techniques and subjects. They differ in approaches and attitudes toward history, in its meanings and implications, and in its uses. They share neither ideology nor philosophy of history. They also have responded to the racial formation of the present in profoundly different ways. And they do not mark the limits of possibility. With some modifications in structure and claims, it would make perfect sense to include Octavia Butler, Ishmael Reed, August Wilson, or Alice Walker, among others. I have sought to make this analysis representative, not exhaustive. Some writers are included because I felt they deserved more critical attention than they have received; others are here because, though they have received attention, it has not been in the context of writers doing related things. At least one, Toni Morrison, is included because she has become unavoidable. Finally, I think we are past the point where selection in a work like this can be explained in objective or even simply logical ways. The choices, I believe, have some coherence, but more basically these are the writers I like to read and think about, the ones I believe are "serious" in their engagement with American and African American life and culture. And that assessment is, of course, itself ultimately subjective and historical.

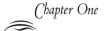

Chapter One

HISTORY, CULTURE, DISCOURSE
America's Racial Formation

It is, of course, impossible to fulfill the promise of the title of this chapter. Major works of the past two decades in various fields have undertaken to explore small parts of the topic. Studies of popular culture, the legal system, media, gender, the arts, economics, politics, philosophy, theology, education, housing, and sports have brought race issues to the forefront of the nation's intellectual and popular awareness.[1] Race, and particularly blackness, seem to be everywhere, both in structural concerns—policies, offices, practices—and in forms of representation. At the same time, however, we have seen attacks on and suppression of serious discussion of racial matters, especially as they directly affect those who have been the victims of racist and discriminatory practices. Alongside stories of "The New Black Intellectuals," we have new versions of the Welfare Queen and the Black Beast. It is this dialectic of affirmation and denial, both in social conditions and in ideology, that I wish to briefly explore in this chapter. This pattern of contemporary racial formation is, I believe, central to the work of recent African American narrative artists. The particular focus here is on how the past has been defined within these discursive practices.

Michael Omi and Howard Winant, in the 1994 edition of *Racial Formation in the United States*, define "racial formation" as "the sociohistorical process by which racial categories are created, inhabited, transformed, and destroyed" (55). They add that "race is a matter of both social structure and cultural representation" (56); more dynamically, "an alternative approach is to think of racial formation processes as occurring through a linkage between structure and representation" (56). Structure encourages and informs racial representation, while representation as ideology validates and shapes a racialized social structure. Such a description implies that race is neither an aberration nor an illusion; it is a deeply embedded part of the social order and the forms of cultural expression. It conditions if not determines virtually every aspect of life, from personal identity, to political discourse, to religious, economic, and intellectual institutions.

But while race is ingrained in the society and the culture, it is a continuously transformed and contested aspect as well: "The effort must be made to understand race as an unstable and 'decentered' complex of social meanings constantly being transformed by political struggle. With this in mind, let us propose a definition: *race is a concept which signifies and symbolizes social conflicts and interests by referring to different types of human bodies*" (55; emphasis in original). By this definition, the tendency to see race in America as simply black versus white is misguided. The emphasis is on body differences as sources of power struggles. Such a definition, as shall be seen, is especially useful in examining African American historical narrative, in which black bodies, both male and female, are the sites of conflict over identity, exploitation, and relationship. While this point is most clear in neo–slave narratives, where control and ownership of the body is obviously at issue, I wish to argue that these works are also concerned with such issues in the present, when black women are stereotyped as sexually out of control and black men as predatory monsters.[2]

One characteristic of contemporary racial formation relevant to this analysis is the dialectic of racism and racelessness that variously manifests itself. This pattern is apparent in several ways: economic and employment status, celebrity and notoriety, education, housing patterns, political rhetoric and power, academic and media analysis, legal standing, and ideological debate. In all these areas, simultaneous claims have been made of major progress toward a race-neutral society and of regression toward segregation and racial oppression. Ronald Reagan's assertion in the early 1980s that we had ended racism was only the most prominent claim that the goals of the civil rights movement had been achieved and that corrective measures such as affirmative action were not only unnecessary but actually detrimental to final achievement of a color-blind society. What remained depended on individuals—both to end now-discredited prejudicial attitudes and to accomplish, through personal effort and regardless of color, their goals for themselves and their children. It was, as Dinesh D'Souza said, "The End of Racism." At the same time, a plethora of works by cultural critics, educators, economists, and social scientists insisted on the reality of ongoing social problems that were strongly associated with race. New fields emerged, such as critical legal studies, critical race studies, multiculturalism, and discourse studies, which built cases for the presence of race as an integral part of American culture, ideology, and social policy and practice. Debates over political correctness, affirmative action, education, and welfare reform, among other issues, have been largely shaped by assumptions about the meaning of race in the history and life of the nation. But because the discourse itself operates within a commodity culture, it is often reduced to ideological packages in the form of best-selling books, television appearances, and sound bites for the evening news. To participate directly is to be trapped within preformed positions. Other forms of speaking become necessary, and this is the situation of contemporary writers. While it is impossible to fully map the current racial formation, I want to suggest in some detail some of the elements that have shaped recent narratives and to which their creators have responded.

Contemporary African American culture as conventionally understood may be said to begin in the last stages of the civil rights movement with the increasing importance of media representation. As images and not merely reports of marches and violence in the South entered the living rooms of America, race took on a different meaning. In her novel *Meridian* (1976), Alice Walker describes the impact of watching televised images of singing activists, bombed churches, and funerals on a group of college students. At the same time, those who offered an alternative to nonviolence found the media receptive to their messages as well. Malcolm X succeeded in part because he was a master of what came to be called the "sound bite," though his actual analysis was much more significant. Somewhat later, the Black Panthers manipulated the imagery of black berets, leather jackets, and rifles to promote their agenda as part of "radical chic." When civil disorder broke out in urban areas throughout the nation, cameras were there to record the violence and implicitly to define it as "riots," thereby building on the traditional representation of black men as savages.

Throughout the 1960s, then, black reality increasingly became image and commodity. Cultural nationalists and revolutionaries sold their writings through major white publishing houses, and African-related materials became commercially successful products. America, both black and white, bought "blackness." The complex history of racial interactions that had shaped the nation since 1619 was largely erased even as it was supposedly being embraced. Slogans, fashion, and fragments of historical information ("the first black to . . .") were offered as substitutes for serious analysis.

At the same time, opportunities emerged in the entertainment field for safe, reassuring representations. Black singers, actors, and comedians, such as Sammy Davis Jr., Sidney Poitier, and Flip Wilson were rewarded richly for projecting integrationist possibilities for the nation. They were followed by Diann Carroll, Bill Cosby, the Supremes, and others, often even more successful. Any scars of the past were magically covered over by beauty, humor, and popular talent. Thus, what was considered the full range of black life was brought within the discursive universe of American culture. That this "blackness" did not in fact include the totality of African American experience and that it did not portend a resolution of racial conflict was irrelevant.

The key event of the 1970s in this context was the publication and subsequent television serialization of *Roots* (1976). By creating a saga of a black family with a heroic ancestor, Alex Haley brought African American experience within the framework of mass culture; by claiming historical veracity for his narrative, he made the connection between the motherland and the New World for blacks. That the story was highly problematic as history generally and as personal history specifically was secondary to its value in bringing into the mainstream notions of ancestry that had largely been limited to nationalist groups. It made a link to African royalty at the same time that it generated the image of the proud individual who is preeminently American in his insistence on rising above the emasculating effects of slavery. Moreover, it subtly undermined radical solutions to the nation's problems by showing that blacks consistently failed to achieve freedom through escape or violence. Rather, they learned to accommodate themselves to the existing oppressive order. While they might retain some elements of African culture, these did not aid in gaining agency in the New World. The lesson for modern African Americans, then, was clear: as long as you adapt to American reality and do not presume to challenge it in any fundamental way, you can enjoy the appearance if not the substance of a meaningful black past.

Roots also enabled whites to come to terms with racial issues by emphasizing the pastness of the past. Since the story locates racist evil clearly in periods disconnected from the present, it becomes possible for everyone to condemn such evil because they do not have to relate it to experiences of the present. All people can admire Kunta Kinte for his resistance and resilience; his color is secondary to his all-American desire for freedom and selfhood. Coming at the end of the civil rights and Black Power eras and during the nation's bicentennial celebration, it provided closure and the promise of a new, color-blind America. Blacks can be strong and proud, can overcome evil and deprivation, just like other groups in the society. And they can do it, as the hero did, on their own, without special programs or government intervention or even white involvement. The book encourages a turning to the harsh past as a matter of genealogical and antiquarian interest, not as a means of raising questions of social justice.

Roots also stimulated and reinforced the commodification of black images. Blaxploitation films, such as *Shaft* and *Superfly*, neutralized concerns about urban unrest by parodying ghetto life. The slave hero was joined by the pimp-gangster as the key representations of the black man; Kunta Kinte was remade into Mandingo, the "black buck" who is the only one who can sexually satisfy the lascivious plantation mistress and who must pay for his prowess by being burned in oil. This new image, in fact, simply repackaged the Black Beast of late-nineteenth- and early-twentieth-century literature and film but, consistent with contemporary racial discourse, emasculated it through exaggeration of costume, violence, and language. Such figures could not challenge the social order because they could not be taken seriously.

The extent to which black power could be trivialized is evidenced by the similarities of these figures to the buffoon characters of television of the time. *The Jeffersons* and *Good Times* on the surface provided distinctions from stereotypes; after all, George Jefferson was a successful businessman and the family of *Good Times*, in part at the insistence of its star Esther Rolle, was a conventional working-class nuclear family. But the dress, manner, and speech of the key male characters reflected, in the case of George Jefferson, the reincarnation of Kingfish of *Amos and Andy*, and in the case of JJ, a minstrel version of urban black youth. Whether "movin' on up" or stuck in the ghetto, such representations reassured white America that black men were not people to be taken seriously in any revision of the social order. The emergence of Bill Cosby as a televisual star in the 1980s provided similar belief, though in a somewhat different way. By creating an upper-middle-class family, he implicitly asserted a claim that African Americans had the same desires, ambitions, and values as their white counterparts. Material success could displace color as the central concern of life, and, moreover, it had already been achieved by those who mattered. The display of expensive artifacts of African and African American cultures on the set also suggested that culture could be defined in terms of objects, not historical engagement. In fact, such representations suggested that there was no black past except as commodities. In the achievement of black wealth and status, there was no need to remember anything unpleasant from either the past or the present. The move into modernity and even postmodernity was represented as seamless. Any contentions otherwise were simply unjustified grumblings from malcontents or from those who had a vested interest in maintaining for their own benefit a racialized order.

If anything, the 1980s and 1990s intensified the neutralization and simultaneous reinvigoration of racial discourse. A key development was "racelessness," the ability of some blacks to appear at least to transcend their color. Cosby was a leading figure as he not only produced and starred in a crossover hit show in which race was largely irrelevant but also became a pitchman for mainstream

American products. He could be seen with America's children of all races consuming the nation's products. At the same time, Michael Jackson became a global celebrity whose talent, ambiguous sexuality, and plastic surgery made him the ultimate nonthreatening mass cultural commodity. He could make use of putatively ghetto settings and sexual gestures in performance without intimating that these were anything other than performance. In athletics, Michael Jordan combined remarkable skills with a nonracial, nonpolitical persona that made him one of the most recognized and respected figures in the world. He perfectly served the marketing needs of his sport and of elements of the corporate world because he not only reinforced the association of blackness with the body but also demonstrated that the aggressiveness associated with the black male body could be profitably channeled and controlled. To "Be Like Mike" was to be carefully bounded, to keep explosions of energy and domination within clearly defined limits.

Thus, the racial formation generated a black imaginary that appeared to establish the terms by which racial harmony could be achieved within the culture. And through the demonization of gangsta rappers and young black men who did not accept these terms, the society demonstrated the discipline and punishment it could invoke to sustain the formation. A parallel discursive move allows black women to be Miss America and entertainment stars (Cicely Tyson, Oprah Winfrey, Whitney Houston) while verbally assaulting Anita Hill and Lani Guinier and depicting welfare recipients as promiscuous young black women so as to destroy the system of public assistance.[3]

While the past and present were being constructed in this manner in popular culture, related developments were occurring in the academy. The demands of 1960s protest led to the formation of Black Studies programs and accelerated scholarship in the field of black history. Black Studies resulted from the admission of significant numbers of African American students into predominantly white universities. While administrators expected these students to be grateful for the opportunity to "improve themselves," the students, many of whom were brought in from poor inner-city neighborhoods, felt isolated and alienated. "Stripped of their identities as black people and forced into a curriculum that denied their heritage by an unconscious conspiracy of silence, black students found themselves completely, irreconcilably alienated within the ivy-covered walls of the white universities" (Fischer, 18).

What was demanded was not only a revised content within established fields and a new interdisciplinary field, Black Studies, but also a rethinking of the function of the university and of intellectual activity: "Black Studies was committed in the first instance of its determination to undoing all prevalent 'authentic' notions of such disciplines as history and English. Hence, at the site of the university, Black Studies presented a hugely unsettling challenge. For even as it sought in its own voice to lay claim to disciplinary status as a normal academic subject, its very conjunctive and stylistically diverse energies eradicated the referential lines of both subjectivity and disciplined academic knowledge" (Baker, *Black Studies*, 12–13). At the time of the creation of these programs, Nathan Hare made explicit their central purpose: "A black education which is not revolutionary in the current day is both irrelevant and useless. To remain impartial in the educational arena is to allow the current partiality to whiteness to fester" (3). Thus, Black Studies originated in the desire to advance a political agenda; one means of doing so was to promote racial pride through the recognition of black achievement. Courses in black history, literature, and other arts initially operated as sites of recovery of those persons, events, and texts that had been eliminated from the subject matter of established fields.

But this function complicated and often obstructed the other function, which was to gain recognition as a valid intellectual discipline with its own content and methodology. The political and inspirational origins of Black Studies limited its credibility in the university, since they were not consistent with the traditions of objectivity and balance that were said to be the underpinnings of modern education and research. This lack of respect among the professoriate allowed administrators to effectively "ghettoize" these programs by underfunding and understaffing them and by using them as a means to demonstrate their commitment to diversity by hiring only African Americans in them and then not making such hires in more traditional fields. In this way, the intellectual and political challenge of Black Studies could be minimized and exploited.

Black history as a specific field has followed a somewhat different trajectory, since it has been practiced in some version since the late nineteenth century. Beyond the amateur work that was produced in the Reconstruction era, W. E. B. Du Bois produced work in the 1890s that met the standards of scholarship and that also took a critical position vis-à-vis those who oppressed blacks. In this sense, his work defined what came to be understood as black history, as opposed to historiography that did not see African Americans as significant or that accepted the stereotypes of the time.

Despite Du Bois's work and that of Carter G. Woodson, major rethinking within the profession of the role of blacks in American history did not take place until the 1950s, when Stanley Elkins and Kenneth Stampp published groundbreaking studies that saw slaves as crucial to the meaning of the "peculiar institution." Elkins represented the enslaved as holocaust victims, trapped within a dehumanizing and psychologically and culturally destructive system; Stampp revised this view by insisting that blacks engaged in a variety of acts of sabotage and resistance that enabled them to retain some dignity and control over their lives. "Slavery studies" was advanced over the next twenty years with the work of John Blassingame, Eugene Genovese, and Herbert Gutman. What enabled this development was the emergence of social history as a distinct field. This method reconceptualized the nature of evidence in historical analysis to include nontraditional materials such as diaries, journals, and plantation records, as well as the more conventional official records. Lawrence Levine extended the method, in his *Black Culture and Black Consciousness* (1977), to the use of folk material produced by the slaves themselves.

In this manner, the historical profession could claim to have moved beyond the bias of the master's view of slavery. Similarly, new areas of research, such as black women's and black labor history could open up with access to appropriate materials. Thomas Holt suggests both the possibility and the responsibility:

> Our task, then, is twofold: to put black people at the center of their history and to put the black experience at the center of American history, by reinterpreting that history in light of that experience. We can write no genuine history of the black experience without attempting to see our ancestors face to face, without straining to hear their thoughts and desires, without groping for the textures of their interior worlds. But having done that, we then must establish linkages between that interior world and the exterior developments and movements in the larger world; for only in that way can history lay any claim to centrality in the national experience. (5–6)

The result of this effort has been the production of hundreds of monographs, as well as a number of prize-winning studies. Virtually every aspect of the black experience has been covered from multiple perspectives.

History has also been engaged, though in a different way, in the neoconservative movement, which has taken race as a central subject. Much of this work has been done in the social sciences—economics, history, and sociology. It is, in part, a response to Afrocentric claims about the centrality of people of African descent in world and American history. Thus, Mary Lefkowitz subtitles her book *How Afrocentrism Became an Excuse to Teach Myth as History*. In *Not Out of Africa*, she attacks Martin Bernal's contention that much of Greek culture had originated in Egypt. More generally, this group of scholars and commentators, whose work has often been supported by right-wing foundations, argues that the racial history of America as we have understood it ended with the civil rights movement, that we are, to cite Dinesh D'Souza's title again, at "the end of racism." Thomas Sowell, John McWhorter, Glenn Loury, Shelby Steele, and Stanley Crouch—all black—have joined D'Souza, Richard Herrnstein, Charles Murray, Stephan and Abigail Thernstrom, and others in reinstating a version of the black pathology argument of the 1960s.[4] The new version argues that so much progress has been made in the past forty years that the only reason debates about racism continue is that blacks are invested in what McWhorter calls a "Cult of Victimology." Instead of going about the business of integrating into American society, African Americans maintain cultural practices, belief systems, and social and political structures that are tied to the past and that deprive them of opportunity in the present. Fear of individuality, personal responsibility, and even success inhibit achievement. In this reading of history, the freedom movement did in fact accomplish its goal of social justice; it is simply black refusal to get over the past and accept the new reality that is the problem. In part, this is said to be the result of the very success of that movement: to the extent that it generated a "civil rights establishment," it produced and encouraged programs of dependence and an ideology of guilt and victimization. Thus, from this perspective, blacks blame whites for problems of crime, poverty, poor education, and discrimination when they themselves are responsible. This revisionist history, in essence, insists on a break in the flow of time while ironically contending that it is the mass of African Americans who have failed to see the truth of history.

Given all these debates over the past, one important question is why it is necessary for contemporary fiction writers to visit history once again. The answer can be found in Thomas Holt's definition of the purposes of historical writing. While it is possible, as Afrocentrists have argued, "to put black people at the center of their history and to put the black experience at the center of American history," historians must do so based on the methodology of the profession, which rejects any version of "attempting to see our ancestors face to face, . . . straining to hear their thoughts and desires, . . . groping for the textures of their interior worlds" as inappropriately subjective. Moreover, as Clarence Walker has indicated, the effort to write such history, especially with the emphasis on "community," is an act of "romanticism" that "obscures more than it reveals and posits community as an unproblematic *summum bonum or summum historicum*" (xv). To problematize black experience as a historian is to enter the current ideological debates over race on the "wrong" side, regardless of one's politics; to assume that experience to be unproblematic is to enter on the unprofessional side. The key difficulty in Holt's position is that he presumes to be able to read the consciousness of the "ancestors," not simply in behavioral terms, but in spiritual and psychological terms as well. But the discourse of the historical profession does not permit such an approach. Thus, what is represented in historical writing, even when it follows this "romantic" model, is abstractions of human experience; to write differently would be to make every historical work a biography. To talk about "black experience" is of necessity to generalize.

Because historians are inherently limited in how to frame the African American narrative, artists must fill the gap of rendering subjective, individual experience. In a sense, there is agreement with Holt's position, but it is artists who can in fact represent the inner life that is the deepest meaning of black life. But it is also necessary to do so with an understanding of the status of literary representation in postmodern America. Postmodernism means, among other things, "the contemporary world as a realm of fragmentation, dissociation, and the post-personal [that] seems to dissolve the cultural continuities of community and individual ego to which earlier artistic egos remained loyal" (Mikics, 297). In much historical fiction by white writers, representation of the past must be questioned even as it is done. According to these writers, the past is unknowable since the sources on which it is based are ideological and self-interested. We see in the work of John Barth, Gore Vidal, and others extravagance, doubt, and parody. History itself is simply a fiction; whether one uses it for serious purposes or for "play" is a matter of individual choice.[5]

In contrast, African American writers, especially those discussed in the present study, find it necessary to question and validate history at the same time. As members of a group whose past has been consistently denied and distorted, they cannot afford radical doubt about a past that has had so much impact on the present and that provides the foundation for claims of moral authority.[6] Whether the choice is to use that experience to reinforce positive group images or to confront the sources of ongoing difficulties within the group or the nation, it is essential to assume the actuality of the past and the ability to represent it. At the same time, acknowledgment must be made of the unreliability of both historical materials and literary devices. Not only is it necessary to question access to the past, as postmodernism does, but distortions of the historical record based on racism or indifference to black experience must be engaged. One device used in these texts is the representation of social science and its practitioners, who claim to be "objectively" examining black life. What is consistently shown is the limits of such an approach at the same time that the novels themselves demonstrate the value of other approaches—eyewitness accounts, journals, folk material, storytelling—which are assumed to tell something like the truth of history. In this sense, black writers differentiate themselves to some extent from others who take a postmodern approach to the past.

Moreover, given the contemporary racial formation, it is easy to get trapped within a discourse that categorizes and thus neutralizes one's vision. As one example, much of the recent discussion of African American writing has been cast in terms of gender conflict. Authors such as Alice Walker and Toni Morrison are said to be engaged in black "male-bashing." Claims that they are simply telling one part of the larger story are met with accusations that they are part of the larger society's effort to destroy black men. The media attention given to these controversies serves the purpose of deflecting discussion of both substantial literary questions and the social issues that might be undergirding such representations. In this way, texts are de-historicized and made part of contemporary ideological battles.

What is crucial, then, is a dialectical sensibility that problematizes as it affirms historical narrative. What is seen throughout the following discussion is the various ways this process is carried out; there is no one way to accomplish this purpose. What these writers share is the need to speak for the historically silenced and to speak in ways that are not themselves distorted by contemporary American cultural and social discourses and practices.

Issues of representation and form are obviously relevant to the shaping of these themes. How is a black past to be constructed that avoids both essentialism and the facile figurations of the dominant discourse? What shape can a story take so that it does not simply fall into an easily dismissible category? While the solutions here are varied, they do tend to fall into certain categories. A common mode is first-person narration used to tell a communal rather than private story. In *Middle Passage, Jazz, Cattle Killing, Divine Days,* and *The Chaneysville Incident,* to name a typical group, the narrators work across time and space to try to construct meaningful stories out of the divergent voices and records they encounter. Their texts often follow a pattern where they assume an order and meaning that subsequently proves inadequate. In this sense, the novels are narratives of discovery in which the speakers uncover their own connection to the past in ways that are sometimes disorienting and sometimes rewarding.

Another pattern is the reconstruction of lost or suppressed elements of history. The most famous case is *Beloved,* but *Dessa Rose, Dreamer,* Wideman's Homewood books, and Andrews's Appalachee trilogy are also based on actual events and people that are reshaped into complete narratives that explore motives, ambiguities, and relationships in ways that historiography cannot. These are generally stories that focus on ordinary people, even when they include the famous or celebrated. Structurally, the authors are less interested in retelling events "as they happened" than in using them as a grounding in "fact" for their fictive inventions. The "real" persons and events often exist as fragments of news articles or parts of family stories rather than as complete narratives. Such incompleteness allows the authors the freedom to construct their own versions of the past rather than be tied to comparisons with the narratives of historians.

Another formal trait is the use of intertextuality in a variety of ways. Some works, such as *Dessa Rose* and *Divine Days*, are deliberate acts of signifying on specific earlier texts, *The Confessions of Nat Turner* and *Ulysses*, respectively. Each engages both the form and the thematics of its referent. Others make use of genre—slave narratives, sea adventures, detective stories, tall tales—as the basis of their own work. Again, the concern is less replication than the use of a frame that gives some structure without obligating the authors to the implications of the genre. As an example, several of the works have been labeled neo-slave narratives, but none of them use the narrative techniques or other features associated with the nineteenth-century antecedents.[7] The use of historical events and earlier genres can be understood as an essentially postmodern device for manipulating discursive practices while claiming the usefulness and even validity of them. All are "texts" and thus problematic in terms of access, reliability, and completeness; but they are also the ways by which the writers can make sense of a past that is too important to ignore and a present that is a part of a different history than that usually offered.

The final feature of these works, and the one most tied to this notion of a counterhistory, is the use of multiple voices within them. Each author finds ways to let the past speak, and each insists that what is spoken is profoundly different from the dominant discourse. Whether the narrative technique is a single speaker who listens to others (*Bailey's Cafe*, *Two Wings to Veil My Face*, *Middle Passage*), or a narrator who seems to have access to the secrets of the community (*Mama Day*, *Jazz*, Appalachee trilogy), or one who reads documents (*Chaneysville*, *A Lesson Before Dying*), or a fragmented telling that moves from speaker to speaker (*A Gathering of Old Men*, *Paradise*, Homewood trilogy), the point is the same. The past is experienced by individuals, even if they are treated as indistinguishable members of a group; at the same time, being black means that experience is a troubled and usually traumatic one. What in fact creates the race, according to the stories examined here, is not some biological essence but rather a past and present that discursively cannot get over the myth of racial difference. And because the society cannot make that discursive move, history is over and over again experienced as holocaust.

PART ONE *Memory*

Chapter Two

BURYING THE DEAD
The Pain of Memory in Beloved

Memory has played a special role in the shaping of African American culture generally and in contemporary literature specifically, as can be seen in the three chapters of this section. It affects the way the individual relates to the group, especially in an environment where both personal and group identity have been denigrated, as in much of the history of the United States. It also affects the group's sense of itself, as the stories of the past are repeated from generation to generation. As will also be seen, in the context of a traumatic history, memory also plays a complicated role as events are both repressed and recurrent. Scenes of violence, humiliation, and dehumanization are blocked out by both individuals and communities, but they cannot thereby be erased. In the works of Toni Morrison, Ernest Gaines, Gloria Naylor, and Sherley Anne Williams, we can see the dynamic of memory's repression and its return, as characters and communities struggle to come to terms with trauma. We also see the ambiguities inherent in efforts to achieve recovery and healing from that trauma.

The dedication of *Beloved* is to the "Sixty Million and more" who were victims of the European slave trade. The number of Africans directly affected by that trade has been variously estimated by historians from fifteen to a hundred million. The choice of sixty million, I would suggest, is an act of signifying by Toni Morrison. The number echoes and multiplies the six million Jews killed in the Holocaust. It suggests simultaneously a connection to and difference from that more recent horror. Both events have been historically contentious in recent years, with arguments made about their realities and effects. Both have also served to create a sense of a special people shaped by a legacy of suffering. Such a legacy is important for group identity in a time when science has discredited biology as the basis for such identity. The trauma of suffering creates a group bond across geography, class, gender, and genetics. One does not have to be an essentialist to claim membership in a group that has a historical experience of victimization. Specialness comes out of the insistence that suffering must have meaning and consequences.[1]

But basing that specialness on a horrifying history generates its own difficulties, as trauma theories have suggested. Since the horror can be overpowering, it can disable any attempt to lead a normal life. Because it is often literally unspeakable, it cannot be controlled or made sense of by the ordinary discursive practices of memory or narrative.[2] The normalizing mechanism, that which enables survivors to go on with their lives, is denial or repression. Negation serves not only the need to escape what cannot be faced but also the need to evade the guilt, shame, and impotence associated with survival. Why, after all, do some continue to live while so many others die? Survivors often feel that they have somehow failed those who were destroyed, through compromise with the destroyers, through lack of courage, through weakness. Survival becomes a personal flaw in this context, one that is itself overwhelming. Better to repress the experience.

Beloved is about repression and its relationship to oppression; it is also about the return of the repressed and about the need to bear witness. After all, if the denial of horror is successful, then the people are not special; without that past, no basis for spiritual kinship exists in the present. This denial of relationship is a claim made by, among others, black neoconservatives.[3] Morrison, along with Ernest Gaines and others, creates narratives that reveal that past by breaking through the repression, by revealing the distorting effects of the "white word," and by reconstituting communities and individual identities based on revelation and witness. They do this through the expansion of individual memory into communal history, which both brings private experience into the public sphere and validates the individual history as a figure of the group history. It creates the possibility for what Benedict Anderson has called "the imagined community." Such figuration repudiates neoconservative individualism and claims of the end of racism.[4] At the same time, those notions are themselves revealed as forms of repression that deny past and present reality.

In *Beloved*, a tension is maintained between victimization and personal agency. By focusing on the experiences of black women, Morrison challenges any simplistic claims about individual heroism. Her female characters are maternal figures and thus have responsibility for children, as well as themselves. In fact, the children are part of the self and thus condition one's choices and actions. Baby Suggs develops her sense of responsibility to the black community around the need to save her children, knowing all along exactly what she has lost. When such saving is no longer possible, she dies. Sethe drives herself on the escape out of the need to get her mother's milk to her infant. Thus, both agency and victimization are linked to maternity. The significance of this point is that the individual must be understood as embedded within a familial and by extension communal reality. Action does not occur in isolation; it implicates and has consequences for others. Thus both the *Roots* model of personal heroism and the neoconservative focus on individualism are challenged by narratives of women.[5]

The horrors that must be repressed are likewise tied to relationships, which is one reason for the repression. Unlike a number of slave narratives, which tended to represent the brutality of slavery in abstract or anonymous terms by describing the instruments of torture or by portraying the suffering of individuals who have no other connection to the narrator,[6] the memories of Sethe and Baby Suggs are tied to personal relationships. In such a case, to remember the horror is to remember oneself as witness and fellow victim. It is also to alienate oneself in that the memory points to the absolute difference between those who died and those who lived. The dead are other; to remember is to witness again the irrevocable move from identity to difference, from connection to separation, from presence to absence. When that loss is associated with cruelty and pain, then the survivor must relive not merely the suffering of a loved one but also her own helplessness in the face of it. Better to forget.

Memory is represented in *Beloved* as insidious and intrusive:

As for the rest, she worked hard to remember as close to nothing as was safe. Unfortunately her brain was devious. . . . [S]uddenly there was Sweet Home rolling, rolling, rolling out before her eyes, and although there was not a leaf on that farm that did not make her want to scream, it rolled itself out in shameless beauty. It never looked as terrible as it was and it made her wonder if hell was a pretty place too. Fire and brimstone all right, but hidden in lacy groves. Boys hanging from the most beautiful sycamores in the world. It shamed her—remembering the wonderful soughing trees rather than the boys. Try as she might to make it otherwise, the sycamores beat out the children every time and she could not forgive her memory for that. (6)

The past insinuates itself into the present unwanted, in moments of pleasant or ordinary experience. Its "suddenness" in fact seems designed to disrupt normality, to displace adjustment to the present. Sethe is compelled to return in her mind to Sweet Home, not so much to understand as to relive the sensory experience.[7] But she is always conscious of that return as a distortion; her memory always chooses the beauty of nature over the horror of brutality, causing a response of shame. Crucial to understanding Morrison's purpose is understanding both the shame and the distortion.[8] Part of the distortion is the renaming of the victims as "children." Those who were hung were grown men; while labeling them as children gives Sethe a maternal relationship to them, it denies them standing as moral agents. It turns them into pure victims, denied the possibility of adult action and choice. The past is sentimentalized and, as such, is an inverted replication of the master's narrative. Both infantilize the slave by denying him/her responsibility within the peculiar institution. These murdered black men in fact engaged in behaviors that challenged their status as "boys"; for this they had to be killed.

Why must this truth be repressed, and why is shame felt for the memory that displaces it? To know the victims as agents is to implicate them in their own suffering and thus to complicate their victimhood. As desiring and thinking beings, they asserted themselves in dangerous ways. Those ways, of course, were dangerous only in the context of an oppressive system that sought to deny them their humanity and their manhood. They sought, in effect, normality; they were not self-sacrificing but rather self-fulfilling. Thus, Sixo keeps returning to the Thirty-Mile Woman he loves; for this he is eventually killed. His actions, however, should not be seen as extraordinary in themselves; in another context, they would represent a mildly interesting romance narrative. Sethe's own horrendous scars are the result of her quite reasonable complaints about the degrading treatment of her by Mrs. Garner's nephews. Her voice is an implicit claim to her womanhood and dignity, a claim the South would have permitted if she had been white. She chooses not to suffer humiliation; for this she must be punished.

The shame that Sethe associates with her memory is tied to the seductiveness of a sentimental understanding of the past. It is not merely that she prefers the beauty to the horror, life to death; it is also that she seeks a purity to the horror. The victims are all innocents struck down by pure villainy. One use of such an image is that it relieves her of responsibility for her own actions in the killing of her daughter and attempted destruction of all of her children.

What Morrison writes here is a deconstruction of the historical narrative, with all that that implies for the present. Black history, and more generally American history, is not a saga of great individuals and democratic institutions, as implied by *Roots*, for example. It is not in this sense the grand narrative of individualism and progress. Rather, it is the story of oppressive and repressive practices engaged in and endured by ordinary people. Their exceptionalism is the product of trying to be ordinarily human in a context that denied black humanity (and, in another sense, white humanity as well). Both heroism and victimization are redefined in this revision. The hero is not fundamentally different from everyone else; to imagine her as such is to free everyone else of moral agency. The hero is simply one who insists upon her humanness, her identity with others as a desiring, expressive being.

Paul D and Beloved represent different ways of understanding the past. It is significant in this context that Paul D runs the ghost of the baby out of the house as soon as he arrives. The past, as a presence, must be evicted, even though, as Baby Suggs has explained, " 'Not a house in the country ain't packed to its rafters with some dead Negro's grief' " (5). In Paul D's view, survival grants one the power to structure the past so that it serves the present. He does not forget; in fact, his recounting of his observations and experiences intensifies the horror of slavery. He is the one who brings to Sethe the information that her husband had helplessly witnessed her sexual humiliation by white men and as a result had gone mad. He also recounts his own suffering, which seems to combine concentration camp and prisoner of war torture. He goes into graphic detail about Halle smearing buttermilk on himself after seeing Sethe being suckled by the white teenagers and also about his own being caged and nearly drowned along with several others.

Just as these narratives speak the nearly unspeakable horror of slavery, the construction of them as narratives relieves the teller of any responsibility for the events.[9] Black history is a story of victimization. In this masculine version, men are released from guilt for their impotence in the face of white domination either through madness or through endurance. There is no guilt because there were no options. Thus, Paul D reads the past as divided off from the present and having only the relevance one chooses to grant it. He will not share the present with an embodiment of the past. He casts out the ghost and refuses to recognize the identity of Beloved.

When he hears the story of Sethe's killing of her child, he initially refuses to believe it and then, when it is confirmed, he accuses her of bestial behavior. Significantly, his comment replicates the view of schoolteacher, the master who seeks "objectively" to determine whether she is human or animal. While Paul D's assertion can be seen as a response to the apparent "cold bloodedness" of an action he did not observe, it is also useful to see it as a response to the assertiveness of Sethe. Such assertiveness calls into question the purity of his narrative of victimization. Her action, terrible though it is, makes a claim for agency and responsibility. Furthermore, her refusal to repudiate (as opposed to regret) her action only adds to the complexity of the problem. Her choice reflects a sense of history in that she knows that her daughter will suffer in the same ways as previous generations of black women. Her killing of the daughter for whom she struggled mightily to escape so as to bring the child mother's milk rejects a deterministic history that insists on black submission to white power. Murder, in this sense, becomes an affirmation of black life.[10]

For Paul D, such an action implicates the victims in history; it proposes the reality of choice, even if it is negative. Death is not the worst option; it is only the most troubling one. Unlike others, Sethe, having acted by escaping, refuses to surrender the meaning of that act by submission to white power, not only of her self, but of the future she has been nurturing. She takes responsibility for that future by destroying it. In doing so, she enters history as a flawed human being, not a pure victim. For Paul D, this role calls into question his self-definition; because he has only reacted, though courageously, he is made guilty of acquiescence to the system of domination. He has *done* nothing, and that is exactly the problem.

If Paul D argues for the rejection of the past, Beloved insists upon absolute acceptance of it. She demands not only witness but also guilt. The present and the future must be sacrificed for the past because the suffering must be atoned for in some way. Taken as the embodiment of the killed daughter, she offers Sethe an opportunity to do penance for her hurtful action. In a sense, Sethe is offered the possibility of erasing history by living in it. She can undo her "crime" by devoting her life to the nurturing of the ghostly presence. By neglecting the present in the form of Paul D and the future in the form of Denver, she can purify herself. But of course the past is insatiable, as symbolized by the vampire images in the text. Nothing can make up for death; to try to "fix" the past is to be consumed by it.

The past has other attractions as well. For Denver, Beloved is the possibility of gaining a relationship that was lost before it began. She can "claim kin" with this older sister and gain from her a connection that was sacrificed by their mother's violent action. By accepting Beloved, Denver can erase the psychological damage of having a mother who kills daughters. The restoration of the sister means that Sethe's threat is removed. A "normal" domestic order is now in place. The problem for Denver is that no such order is possible. The past, as embodied in Beloved, is about itself, not the present. The present, in fact, must be destroyed if the past is to prevail, for the present is what came into being as a result of the destruction of the past. The killing of the girl child made possible the continuing freedom of Sethe and Denver. To recover the past is to recover slavery, which is the effect Beloved has on Sethe. It is only when Denver breaks free of the grip of her sister that she is able to reclaim the present. She must reenact the struggle for freedom by going out into the community and calling on it to recognize its responsibilities to one of its members.

Morrison's purpose can be understood by noting the importance that she gives to the internalization of the past by her black characters. Baby Suggs, who has lost all of her children to slavery, urges the newly free community to respond to suffering by loving themselves, their bodies, and each other. They fail to do so. As a result, they betray Sethe by their silence, leading her to kill her child, leading Beloved to return to get the life that should have been hers. At the end, Beloved is forced to leave, but Sethe has barely begun her return to the present. And the community has returned to repression: "It was not a story to pass on."

This is not to suggest that the realities of slavery are ignored. The stories of the men of Sweet Home, the schoolteacher's ledger book of Sethe's human and animal characteristics, and the text that is Sethe's scarred body all are part of the narrative of white cruelty and domination. But Morrison, as always in her works, is most interested in the psychocultural effects of such history, especially on African Americans. By giving the novel the form of a ghost story she suggests that it is possible to be seduced by horror either by believing that the past can be manipulated to one's own ends or by believing that the past is so powerful that one has no responsibility to the present.

The first of these positions is taken by whites generally, by black conservatives, and often by those whom conservatives label "professional Negroes." The mainstream position is that the past has little meaning other than as a commodity. It does not explain present reality in a society that is not only postslavery but also postracist.[11] The past is useful in providing material for movies and best-selling novels (including *Beloved*), but it is a separate reality from the present. Whites do not have responsibility for what occurred in some distant time (any time before the mid-1960s), and blacks cannot expect the government, the society, or individuals to recognize claims based on history, no matter how painful or tragic that history was. We are at the "End of Racism" in an era of Personal Responsibility. Moreover, as Randall Kennedy has argued, given the end of "race" as a viable concept, it is no longer necessary for African Americans to identify with each other. Social background, class status, and geographic location are now much more viable elements of community than skin color or any mistreatment associated with skin color. Morrison, by representing the past as an integral part of the culture, challenges this position.

Ironically, her view of history also leads to questioning of some aspects of Afrocentricism, specifically those that imply that history can be used to invert Western notions of superiority/inferiority. The claim is made that black history is noble, including as it does Egyptian civilization, sub-Saharan empires, and major figures of American invention and intellectual achievement. Moreover, African-based cultures are fundamentally different from the West in their emphasis on family, community, respect for ancestors and spirituality, and artistry. History, in other words, contained an African golden age, the remnants of which can be seen in New World cultural survivals.[12] The "break" in this history comes with the slave trade. Under the evil influence of whites, transported Africans lost their knowledge of the past and will remain a lost people as long as identity is primarily constructed in reference to Western values and culture. Molefi Asante, for example, has argued that his pride in family is based on its refusal to develop a Du Boisian double-consciousness; instead, it has maintained in America an essentially African identity ("Racism, Consciousness, and Afrocentricity").

In *Beloved*, even those elements that could be labeled African, such as Baby Suggs's rituals of cleansing, are of limited value. Not only do they fail to prevent tragedies from occurring, but they offer little in the way of comfort when bad things do happen. Even Baby Suggs herself cannot be saved by her wisdom and human sympathy. Moreover, her generosity seems itself to contribute to suffering. Because the community is disturbed by the richness of her feast of celebration for Sethe's successful escape, they hesitate when the slave catchers come, and their silence enables Sethe to be found. Thus, the very elements in the text that critics have identified as African work against black freedom and happiness.[13]

The second version of black history reads it as a narrative of victimization. According to this interpretation, black identity, family, and community have been shattered by the horrors of slavery and racism. All of the negative aspects of African American life are the result of this holocaust experience. It is the responsibility of the government and white society to face the consequences and effects of the past and to rectify the wrongs that have been done. In a sense, this view, in whatever form it takes, is the opposite of the view that the past counts for nothing; here it counts for everything. But the positions are similar in that each denies agency and responsibility to some key component of the society. Here it is the victims who are represented as passive sufferers whose actions cannot be judged; whatever irresponsible or violent behavior, whatever malfeasance, whatever falsification of reality occurs, it is the result of a legacy of racism. The misdeeds of Clarence Thomas, Marion Barry, Mike Tyson, or sometimes of gangs or drug dealers, to mention only the prominent recent examples, are exempted from any notion of individual culpability.

Beloved suggests the costs of living in the past. As Sethe becomes more and more absorbed in living with and for the dead daughter, she becomes less and less capable of living in the present. Beloved consumes her existence, and she surrenders herself to this ghost. She neglects Denver in order to make amends for the past. The heroic imagery of her escape to feed the infant mother's milk is made grotesque in the vampire imagery of her emaciation and Beloved's obesity. She effectively destroys herself, her home, and her relationships through this obsession. Similarly, Paul D, when he discovers the truth of Sethe's past, leaves her to the designs of Beloved. This man who had previously cast out the ghost is rendered ineffectual and ultimately homeless by what he has learned. In both cases, failure to act in the present is justified by the assumed power of the past.

Possible alternatives in the face of history are provided by Denver and Stamp Paid. It is worth noting that they are of different generations and come at the past from different perspectives. What they share are a refusal to be paralyzed by history and an engagement in community as a means to change the present. Denver, too young to bear witness to the trauma of slavery or the horrific consequence of the killing of her sister, must gain her knowledge through the stories of others. A kind of sponge, she soaks up narratives from the community, her mother, and her grandmother. She must deal with the contradictions implicit in the story of her own birth in the wilderness with the aid of the white young woman Amy Denver and its apparent moral opposite in the story of the killing of Beloved and very nearly herself. From a child's perspective, the contrast of the mother as heroic and villainous could not be more stark. As a result, Denver constantly demands her mother's attention and affection. She is jealous and troubled when Paul D comes into their lives as a powerful force from a past she cannot know. Her narcissistic tendencies are only reinforced when she realizes that Beloved is the lost sister. This presence apparently allows her to complete her identity by filling in the gap. The older sister potentially is another mother to love her.

The initial achievement of a restored family gradually turns to frustration as it becomes clear that Beloved demands all of Sethe. The innocence of Denver's earlier similar demands becomes grotesque and threatening as it becomes clear that this older sister will accept nothing less than the mother's life and, moreover, that Sethe feels compelled to surrender it. She cannot accept the price that she paid for survival; it is better to join the dead than to remember the dying and to take responsibility for some of it. Denver, whose interest is in living, finally comes to see that fascination with the past is ultimately a death wish. She reenters the community that had shunned her and seeks its aid. The community, which had been complicitous in the tragedy of 124 Bluestone, responds for its own reasons to her pleas. Together they ultimately drive out Beloved and restore some semblance of order and life to the neighborhood.

Through these narratives, Morrison suggests the complexity of engagement with the past in the present. She differentiates between recognition and acceptance of the harsh realities of history and obsession with it to the exclusion of engagement with the issues of the present. Thus, Stamp Paid's insistence on facing the whole truth of the past is linked to his acceptance of responsibility both individually and communally for the present. The past is explanation for the present, not rationalization for or escape from it. Likewise, Denver chooses life over death, practicality over nostalgia and guilt, and forces the community to do the same. In this process, it is important to be able to identify the true threats and true allies. Sethe's confusion of the helpful white man with the schoolteacher is a mark of her illness, not a measure of legitimate racial suspicion.

The tendency among reviewers and critics has been to read *Beloved* as a searing historical text that recreates the holocaust of slavery largely for its own sake.[14] In this view, it offers a counterpoint to the heroic, sentimental narratives of Alex Haley and Margaret Walker. It reminds Americans, both black and white, of a terrible past they would prefer to ignore, if not erase. Morrison herself has encouraged this view of the novel.[15] But to read it in such a way is to limit its force, for, ironically, such a horrible past permits by contrast the claim of a far less troubled present. But, in fact, white enemies, often in the form of disinterested observers, still scar black lives; black men are still killed and caged, black children still die, black women still suffer anguish, pain, and guilt. But if the answer is only to assert victimage, then the present is hopeless, the only reactions Baby Suggs's turning her face to the wall or Sethe's resignation to self-destruction. Paul D presents a different possibility. Damaged and humiliated, he tries escape and despair when he learns Sethe's secret, but he is restored by Stamp Paid and by Denver's return to life. While recovering himself, he undertakes the healing of Sethe: "You are your own best self," he tells her as a way of beginning the process.

But it is not clear that the author is optimistic about the therapeutic value of her text or, by implication, other efforts to "heal" the trauma of African American history. Sethe, after all, responds to Paul's assertion with doubt: "Me? Me?" In addition, the repeated line at the end of the text suggests suppression of reality: "It was not a story to pass on." If the community and the individuals refuse to tell, then there can be no healing since the nature of the injury cannot be known. And thus it may be that *Beloved* is a cautionary tale to help us understand continuing troubles rather than a narrative of healing. In this sense, it would come closer to the understanding of Holocaust narratives, not as granting meaning to the incomprehensible, but as reminders that the unimaginable has been part of our history.

For Morrison, in this text, the solutions, if there are any, for each generation's troubles are internal, both personal and communal. The past should be neither ignored nor indulged; to do either is to disempower action in the present. Harm continues to be done, so one must recognize its sources. But both the self and the community have always chosen life over death; the past contains models for healing as well. From the center of pain and guilt must come the resources for healing and self-affirmation. It is the only way to honor the ancestors.

Chapter Three

BEARING WITNESS

The Recent Fiction of Ernest Gaines

Just as *Beloved* offers both white enemies and white allies but sees black people as ultimately the key to their own survival, so *A Gathering of Old Men* and *A Lesson Before Dying* locate recovery in the African American community. Gaines's stories, however, take place much more in the public sphere. In each case, the law plays a central role in shaping the narrative, suggesting that notions of justice and legal practice are key to the African American experience. In both novels, the law represents the historical failure of the larger society in that racism contaminates claims of fairness and equality. At the same time, however, law provides the opportunity for personal and communal reclamation in that individuals and groups come to stand for and articulate the nation's violated ideals.

The narrative of *A Gathering of Old Men* is itself communal, made up of the voices, both black and white, of Gaines's mythic part of rural Louisiana. In a sense, all of the history presented also belongs to the community; it is its significance to individuals that is private. These individuals have been unable to speak their experience and, in their silence, have lost their sense of self-worth. In this sense, the author is refusing any sense of an erased past. Rather, he is concerned with the continuing effects of impotence and cowardice in the face of past (and present) oppression. This is a narrative concerned with the meaning of black manhood in a world hostile to its existence. Here, as elsewhere in his fictions, Gaines examines the challenges to such manhood, both external and internal. Unspeakable in this text, as opposed to the scenes of violence recovered in *Beloved*, are the moments of humiliation and frustration for the survivors. The purity of suffering that informs Morrison's narrative is not so evident here; while Gaines also catalogs the injustice and brutality of Southern experience and gives names and faces to the victims, their stories are not so vividly told. Nor are the survivors themselves victims of much physical violence; rather, they are the sons, brothers, husbands, and fathers who were unable to prevent the harm done to their loved ones. Much more than Morrison, Gaines is interested in the psychology of survival as a compromised state.[1]

He makes use of the mystery formula as an element for breaking silence. In this genre, the past is crucial to the uncovering of truth. By manipulating the device of detection, the author can trigger revelations of personal and group history.[2] What makes the past speakable is the inversion of conventional racial violence; in this instance, a white man has been killed. The harshness and racism of the murdered man is not in question; any black *man* on the Marshall plantation could claim justification for wanting him dead. The problem is that only one of the men in the quarters is believed to have the courage to actually commit the act. All the rest are seen as emasculated by their experiences. The stories that are told are Gaines's effort to suggest both the desire to act in defense of the family and the psychological castration that results from failure to do so.

A Gathering of Old Men comes at the cultural moment of the wide popularity of African American women writers. Several of these, including Alice Walker and ntozake shange, have been accused of attacks on black masculinity. Attention to male sexual irresponsibility and abuse, along with violence and drug use, produces an image of the black man as predatory. At the center of this controversy was a struggle over the meaning of black identity. Was that identity essentially masculine, as had been indicated by much of the literary and ideological practice in black America?[3] Were black men, in other words, the key victims and warriors in America's racial holocaust and the battle against it?[4] The challenge of women's writing was not simply a complication of the conventional portrayal of black experience; it was a fundamental questioning of the nature of that experience.

What Gaines does in this context is attempt to refocus the gender issue. First, he changes the time frame from the slavery era to the early and mid-twentieth century. The effect of this shift is to make the psychological damage he describes an experience of the present, not simply an inheritance from the past. This repositioning obviates any essentialist debate, since it situates the effects of racism among the living and does not require that suffering somehow be inherited. It is not merely a cultural artifact but a social reality. History in this sense is continuous, and its effects are neither symbolic nor indirect. At the same time, he assigns these effects to an older generation, thus implying that they can be overcome under different conditions.

The second shift in Gaines's emphasis is on the central role of white racism in the everyday lives of his black characters. Unlike Morrison, Walker, shange, Gloria Naylor, and others, Gaines locates his story in a rural South in which whites, especially Cajuns, are a regular presence and the law supports white power and violence. While a black culture exists in his fictions, at least in the sense of a common set of understandings on key concerns, neither the Big House nor the quarters are fully segregated spaces. In this environment, the attitudes and behaviors of black men cannot be isolated and judged but are constantly mediated and staged in varied contexts. This setting is in contrast to those of Walker in *The Color Purple* and Naylor in *Linden Hills*, two texts in which black men are powerful and brutal forces. Gaines sets up a more complex arrangement of power and agency.

The third element in his version of black narrative is the communal expectations for black manhood. Walker, Naylor, and to some extent Morrison, represent sexual violence as part of a patriarchal narrative of domination passed from father to son. Gaines suggests, in contrast, that the meaning of manhood is generated and perpetuated by the entire community, women and children, as well as men, and whites, as well as blacks. Through the use of multiple narrators, the author reveals the terms by which the old men have been judged and deemed failures. In some instances, the definition is constructed by negation, as when white racists punish black assertion. In other cases, it is the admiration offered by liberal, paternalistic whites for a certain kind of black strength. Black women and the old men themselves comment publicly on their weakness and ineffectiveness. The meaning that is constructed out of these various commentaries is one that says little about sexual abuse or in-group violence or even about hard work and economic responsibility. In these senses, all of Gaines's characters are "good" men. What constitutes black manhood is something more; it is a self-respect that enables one to stand up to the threats of racism even if that requires facing harm. Passivity and submission in the face of humiliation and danger is unmanly. Such a definition does not value recklessness and violence; it does not, in other words, grant heroic status to the "bad man" figure of African American folk culture.[5] Rather, it insists on maintaining dignity in the face of both everyday insults and acts of racial violence.

The story is organized around this principle. When a Cajun overseer is shot to death in the quarters, everyone, both black and white, assumes that only Mathu would be capable of such an act. Candy, the white owner of the plantation, seeks to protect him by ordering all the old men to fire their guns, thus making it impossible for the sheriff to conduct a successful investigation. The weakness of the men, and even the limited power of Mathu, is made clear by their initial obedience to this white demand. The sheriff assumes that there is no mystery about the shooting, but as a transitional figure himself, he feels some compulsion to follow the rules of justice rather than those of racial domination. Though willing to use methods of intimidation against black men he does not respect, he nonetheless is committed to establishing the truth in the case. He seeks to avoid racial trouble in his jurisdiction and knows that he can only do so by convincing those whites willing to use violence that he has in fact gotten at the truth. The law, in other words, must be able to demonstrate the legitimacy of its authority, and order is becoming a higher value than white supremacy in its exercise.

The narrative is situated at a moment of transition, a moment at which the social order itself must pay attention to black experiences so as to sustain itself. For the purposes of his novel, Gaines locates that moment in the period of the 1970s, around the time of the publication of *Roots* and similar works, including his own *The Autobiography of Miss Jane Pittman*. But like Morrison, he is interested not in conventionally heroic narratives but in the stories of ordinary people. These stories, he implicitly claims, rather than those of exceptional figures, will be truly transformative. The focus is on coming to terms with a past filled with suffering, humiliation, and self-effacement. Only by acknowledging such a past will it be possible to construct a future.

The mechanism of public confession becomes the means of such reconstruction. The old men may initially act at Candy's behest and may be acting on the same assumption that she is, that the law can be tricked. But the legal necessity to speak, in fact, empowers the men to face oppression and their complicity in it. Each man is called on to justify the firing of his gun, and each discovers sufficient reason to kill. Each lives with survivor's guilt and believes that he could have done something, if not to prevent suffering, at least to have obtained justice. The firing of the guns is the symbolic assertion of a manhood defined by protection of the community and self-respect. The stories they then tell are the acknowledgments of their failure to do so. By narrating failure, they shed its power over them. They exorcise the demons that have held them in thrall for most of their lives. By pretending to have killed Beau Bontan, they kill the fear and the anger that has kept them immature and irresponsible.

The ritualistic and even religious language of the previous paragraph is consistent with the healing and cleansing effects of their narratives. The stories themselves are tales of the sacrificing of the innocent for the perpetuation of evil, usually with the support and contrivance of the legal system. So it becomes symbolically important to use the rituals of law to come to terms with that history. Gable tells the story of the false accusation of rape against his retarded son that leads to a farce of a trial and to the boy's execution. But this all-too-common experience is rendered obscene when the electric chair fails to work properly, and the boy, who believes that he has died and is in heaven, is forced to wait while the executioners first strike and curse the chair and then bring in a repairman. All this time, Gable has had to wait at the back of the prison to receive his son's body. When the execution finally takes place, it is a trivial moment for the white officials: "They wasn't even talking about it. It wasn't worth talking about" (102). White silence becomes an important tool of oppression. Speaking is only used to encourage a similar black response: " 'They said at least he was treated like a white man. And it was best we just forgot about it and him' " (102). For Gable, who cannot forget, though he has seldom spoken this story, such treatment makes all whites the same and provides adequate motivation for murder.

While Gable presents himself simply as a victim of racism, other narrators claim a more troubling role for themselves. Tucker, for example, tells the story of his brother, who insisted on continuing to sharecrop using traditional methods, despite the competition from Cajuns, who had tractors and the best land. In a version of the John Henry tale, Silas, with his mules, races one of the tractors in a plowing contest and wins. Because his victory implies the equal if not superior ability of blacks, he is beaten to death, and the law declares his death an accident. More important for the narrative is Tucker's response: " 'And they beat him, and they beat him. And I didn't do nothing but stand there and watch them beat my brother down to the ground' " (97). Even more, he goes along: " '[I]n my fear, even after I had seen what happened—in my fear, I went along with the white folks. Out of fear of a little pain to my own body, I beat my own brother with a stalk of cane as much as the white folks did' " (98). His silence in the face of abuse becomes the defining experience of his life; his survival is the mark of his shame. What he seeks from the community is nothing less than condemnation, but they are in no position to condemn him: "He looked at all of us, one after another. He wanted us to pass judgment over him for what he had done. Us judge him? How could any of us judge him? Who hadn't done the same thing, sometime or another?" (98).

While Gable's narrative tells of victimization and Tucker's tells of survivor's guilt, Johnny Paul suggests the erasure of history itself as the ultimate effect of racial practices. He talks about what the black community "don't see," and what the sheriff does not even know is not there. What he refers to is the reality that had been created by previous generations of both slave and free blacks that was reaching its final destruction. He describes the flowers that grew in various places,[6] the everyday life of men moving into and through the fields with their mules, and the sounds of church services. He also points to the cemetery, which is threatened by the Cajun insistence on putting all of the land under cultivation, even if this means desecration of the place of the dead. By calling forth the flowers and pointing to the graveyard, Johnny Paul enables the community both to "rememory" its past and to measure its loss.

The men must not only speak of the horrors so that the suppression of that history can be overturned; they must also seek, through confession of their complicity, the forgiveness of the dead and of themselves. They simultaneously force the white part of the audience to face the truth of the past and the black part of the audience to reconsider their own role in that past. By refusing to be simple victims, they effectively reclaim the possibility of black agency. The narratives themselves, though stories of impotence, are paradoxically empowering in that they place the speakers in history. Moreover, these acts of testimony within a legal process grant the stories an authority they would not have if kept within the confines of family or even the black community. By entering the public sphere, they fill out the historical record in a manner that cannot be erased or repressed.

Aspects of these male narratives indicate that Gaines is concerned with more than the nature of black manhood. Repeated reference to the tractor and its devastating effects on the black landscape and on the economic order, as well as accusations against the system of law and justice, suggest the pervasiveness of a racial formation that has black emasculation as one of its effects. Everyone in the novel is caught within the formation and can only speak in terms of it. Thus, Candy, the plantation owner, despite her sympathy for "her" people, especially Mathu, still must think of them as hers. The members of this black community cannot escape the association of true black manhood with acts of violence, including guns, because these are the emblems of power within a framework of domination. The failure to resist is therefore the failure of manhood. Moreover, they understand African American life as associated with the past, with the land and mules. The new technology of tractors is "white," and thus the future in some sense is given over to whites.[7] In this sense, they are caught in nostalgia for the past even as they face its terrors.

The last confession, that of the actual killer, brings the empowerment of confession into the present even as it speaks to the changes in the racial formation. Charlie Biggs was the weakest of the men, the one most intimidated by white authority. Even when he finally reacted and killed Beau Bontan, he ran away, leaving Mathu to take the blame. But he returns, refusing to live any longer in fear. The connection of that effort is signified by the sheriff, who after hearing the confession, calls him by his name: " 'After you, Mr. Biggs,' Mapes said, and nodded toward the door. 'What's that you called me, Sheriff?' Charlie asked him. Charlie grinned—a great, big, wide-mouth, big-teeth grin. It was a deep, all-heart, true grin, a grin from a man who had been a boy fifty years" (193). While it can be argued that recognition here comes from white authority and therefore reinforces existing power relationships, in fact, the sheriff's use of a title of respect is a recognition of what is changing within the existing racial and legal order. If Charlie, of all men, is capable of resistance, then the South must be changing, a change both desired and resisted by the black community.

As the sheriff points out, that community had prayed and struggled for justice and equality, but it also wanted whites to remain a simple embodiment of evil. It could not have it both ways. The people look forward to the apocalypse of Fix Boutan's attack on them, an attack they can now defend themselves against. But the historical change they sought robs them of revenge. Fix's youngest son, a university football star, asserts that his opportunities for a future will be tainted by any connections with racial violence, especially since his success is linked to that of his black teammate. Fix and his family must bow to modernity, even though it violates their desire to maintain power. Thus, a new racial formation is seen as in the making, but one that cannot be made by the old men, because they are transitional figures.

Gaines rejects violence as an aspect of black manhood by turning the racial conflict that does occur into carnival. When whites associated with Bontan's family come to the plantation, a gun battle breaks out that is played largely for comic effect. Neither the old men nor the drunken whites can shoot straight. The only two killed are the white instigator of the violence and Charlie. Their deaths seem to symbolize the end of a historical era. Luke Will demanded confrontation even though the Bontan family itself had conceded that the old methods were now counterproductive. In addition, while everyone pays respect to Charlie's transformation, his death is presented as justice served in that no one claims that his killing of Beau Bontan is the source of that respect. He is the necessary sacrifice for the healing of the past.

Thus, Gaines proposes a different understanding from Morrison of the function of the past. While she suggests that memory and history are terrors that perhaps cannot be faced by survivors, he indicates that wounds continue to fester as long as they are not exposed. That exposure, no matter how difficult, makes possible recovery. His comic ending announces the success of the purging and in that sense the end of history. While the resolution is not neat (after all, Fix has been defeated, not converted), it does imply a new beginning for the community. It is not the act of violence but the acceptance of responsibility that marks the transition from boyhood to manhood. Even if this generation must pass away, it has at least told its stories, come to terms with its own fears, and passed its experience on to a new generation. Morrison, in contrast, offers some possibilities for personal and communal healing but at the same time asserts that they will be accomplished through repression, which means that they will not truly be done at all. In a ritualized narrative of confession and purification, Gaines proposes that claiming the past empowers the future.

A Lesson Before Dying (1993) revisits the concerns of the earlier novel in the context of a younger generation. While it can be read as a commentary of sorts on the Rodney King case, which began a year before the book was published, it is more deeply about how a black community responds to the injustices that it must endure. Gaines sees injustice and exploitation as inherent in American society, especially when it comes to African Americans; this helps explain why he keeps coming back to their traumatic encounters with the law. He reads such experiences as a product of historical choice and contemporary practice and thus as evil to be witnessed and challenged. By situating the novel in the period just before the civil rights movement, he can engage the question of how much conditions have changed in the modern era of race relations. Implicitly, his text speaks to life in the American South before, during, and after the movement, especially in matters of justice and the law.

Important to this process for Gaines, as it is for John Edgar Wideman, Charles Johnson, Leon Forrest, and David Bradley, is the black intellectual. This figure serves a different purpose from that of outsiders such as Raymond Andrews's Appalachee Red, who enters the community as a stranger and maintains an aura of mystery. Gaines's intellectual, in contrast, is something of a known quantity, one who has consciously and deliberately left the community but is drawn back into it, often unwillingly. His (the character is virtually always male) status is usually ambiguous. On the one hand, he is admired for his education, his ability to acquire and manipulate the knowledge of the larger world; on the other, this very achievement has led to a questioning of communal values and practices. Moreover, especially in Gaines's oeuvre, such knowledge has given the character Hamlet-like qualities of indecisiveness and cynicism.

Thus we have in *A Lesson Before Dying* the figure of Grant Wiggins, the local schoolteacher who desires to leave his family home but is unwilling to do so without his lover, who is attempting to get a divorce. By setting the story in the late 1940s, Gaines can emphasize the repressive aspects of life in a small community that prevent open expression of affection and diversity of attitudes and behaviors. From Wiggins's point of view, the folk world is a dead end in itself. His frustration is intensified, but not created, by the presence of an oppressive racial order. His goal is escape, not change.

For Gaines, as for the other writers, a central concern is the reestablishment of relationships between the intellectual and the community. And while he is setting the narrative a half century before the present, the problem is a version of the one faced in various ways by contemporary intellectuals such as Cornel West, bell books, and Henry Louis Gates Jr. and writers such as Wideman, Alice Walker, and Toni Morrison. Each has achieved a privileged status in society, a status far exceeding that of most whites, to say nothing of blacks in inner cities and rural areas of the South. The simple fact that Wiggins has mobility, can choose to stay or go, marks him as different from the others. The question is how to bridge that status gap in a manner that is meaningful and "authentic." The response of Gaines and others is to locate the bond primarily in the memory of suffering. Regardless of differences in education, occupation (or lack of it), and social position, all black people (and especially, in Gaines's case, black men) share the experience of racism and suffer because of that experience. Even if the individual experiences are of quite different intensities, they constitute a community of suffering.[8] Though Wiggins endures primarily social affronts while Jefferson must lose his life, the text brings them together as brothers in spirit if not fact.

Gaines works hard in this narrative to limit Wiggins's options and thus create a sense of his imprisonment within the social order. He lives in the house of his aunt in the quarters, though he resents the lack of privacy and the "rustic" conditions. He once lived in California with his parents but, for reasons that are never made clear, chose to return to the plantation to teach, a profession he claims to hate. Finally, Vivian, his lover, cannot leave because she is in the process of obtaining a divorce and fears losing custody of her children. None of these elements quite explains why he has chosen to remain for six years in a place he purports to hate; he has no use for religion, he does not believe that education is doing the children any good, and he is deeply resentful of the arrogance and racism of whites. He stays, it would seem, out of spiritual inertia. In this sense, he is the latest in a line of world-weary young black men that Gaines has incorporated in his fiction since his first novel, *Catherine Carmier* (1964). Disconnected from the life of the folk, he cannot return home and yet seems to have no other place to go. The overcoming of this malaise is brought about by immersion in the lives and suffering of the people, who compel him to bear witness to their experience.

He is a man who has no use for the past represented by the South in which he lives but who lacks the resources to move into any kind of future. As shall be seen, Gaines sees immersion in that past as a way to the future. By entering the communal memory more fully, even if not sympathetically, Wiggins begins to understand the human dimensions of this world and thus to be open to meaningful action to change that world. Moreover, the text suggests that refusing the past in fact serves to reinforce the racial domination that Wiggins so hates. By living only in the present, he fails to connect personal affronts to social oppression and remains passive in the face of ongoing suffering. In the novel, it is refusing to forget that is crucial to his moral development.

The rejuvenation of the intellectual is thus the central theme in a narrative that, on the surface at least, seems to tell a very different story. That other story is the one of the criminalized black man suffering within a white supremacist system. It is crucial to Gaines's purpose that readers know from the beginning that Jefferson is innocent of murder and robbery, unlike Bigger Thomas of *Native Son*, one of the texts on which this one is signifying. Jefferson is guilty because of the color of his skin, not because of any actions he has taken. Like Bigger, though, Jefferson is assumed even by his defense attorney to be less than human:

> "Look at the shape of this skull, this face as flat as the palm of my hand—look deeply into those eyes. Do you see a modicum of intelligence? Do you see anyone here who could plan a murder, a robbery, can plan—can plan—can plan anything? A cornered animal to strike quickly out of fear, a trait inherited from his ancestors in the deepest jungle of Africa—yes, yes, that he can do—but to plan?
>
> . . . Gentlemen of the jury, be merciful. For God's sake, be merciful. He is innocent of all charges brought against him. But let us say he was not. Let us for a moment say he was not. What justice would there be to take this life? Justice, gentlemen? Why, I would just as soon put a hog in the electric chair as this." (7–8)

By situating the story prior to the civil rights movement, Gaines can present such commentary as unremarkable; within a fundamentally racist legal system, it can even be taken as a reasonable defense. The gaze called for by the attorney serves to objectify and dehumanize, not recognize, Jefferson. Guilt or innocence is secondary to racial designation; the attorney places himself fully within a racist discursive universe even as he "challenges" its conclusion. Regardless of the outcome, white privilege will be maintained. The law will serve whiteness regardless of how it works; there is simply no place within its discourse for black humanity. Unlike Bigger Thomas, whom Richard Wright represented as individually guilty, even if racially victimized, Jefferson is pure victim. He is the emblem of a racial formation and social practice that makes the African American man guilty by definition, in part because of his presumed bestial nature. In the particular comments about the character's inability to "plan," Gaines would also appear to be criticizing a whole body of recent commentary in sports, business, and social science, about the superiority of black physical over mental abilities. Black men cannot be coaches, quarterbacks, or decision-makers based on this presumed lack; nor can they be expected to do well on measurements of intelligence.[9] In this sense, Gaines is suggesting that changes in discursive practices from the pre– to the post–civil rights era is only at the level of surface statements, not deep structure.

By making Jefferson a victim, the author is freed from addressing the question of personal responsibility. Jefferson's fate is determined by forces over which he has no control; the only question for him is the quality of his dying. Even the motivating idea of the narrative, that he must be made to see that he is not a hog, reflects the thoroughgoing racial conditioning in his life. He is, in essence, the sacrifice for the salvation of Wiggins, who must learn to value community by helping to create it. Although folk community can be said to exist at the beginning of the novel, its effectiveness is clearly questioned. Not only can it not save Jefferson from a racist legal system; it cannot save him from taking on the bestial identity generated by that system. Despite strong traditions of family and religious faith, it cannot make connection with him in his time of greatest need. In this sense, Gaines refuses to sentimentalize folk culture, as is often done in contemporary African American literature and criticism. It is, in his view, a culture constructed to endure oppression, not to end it. Its resistance takes the form of subterfuge and dignity in the face of overwhelming white power. When that power is turned against one of its own, the folk can do little to prevent destruction. What it can do, as seen in *A Gathering of Old Men*, is hold onto the memories of what happens until such time as someone is prepared to act. In addition, the very insistence on remembering can be a condition for the emergence of that person.

Likewise, the community can do little to nurture those with larger ambitions and skills. It is noteworthy that Gaines makes little effort to explain why Wiggins returns to the plantation and stays for several years. Its conservative mores and religious beliefs offer little to a man who has lived in the larger world and who has been taught to value self-assertion and rational thinking. As he has done in earlier works, Gaines suggests that this folk culture is reaching a historical dead end. The plantation community is primarily made up of old people and a few children; representative of this is the fact that neither Wiggins nor Jefferson has parents in the community. The text presents us, then, with an opening vision of suffering and disintegration with little in it that is either noble or hopeful.

What makes change possible is, ironically, the potential within despair. The old people realize that their ways can no longer be of direct use to Jefferson, and so they turn to Wiggins precisely because he has a knowledge of the world they lack. In other words, they have a sense of their own historical situation and its limitations. Their appeal to him works because he maintains remnants of loyalty to their way of life. His education has produced frustration and cynicism, in part because he understands more clearly the oppression that all of them, including himself, have had to endure. But their way sustains them, even if not to a hopeful end in this world. This is in part because theirs is a transindividual perspective, while his focuses entirely on the self. He is able to achieve a meaningful identity as a black man by practicing their methods. He puts up with the petty humiliations that whites impose because they are part of the means to the communal end. He must wait in the white man's kitchen and be repeatedly searched and not called by his name. He submits despite his anger because the community needs his efforts. And in this struggle, they can be of help to him because they remember that humiliation and have learned how to survive it without bitterness.

Moreover, he continues the effort without believing in its efficacy. He makes it clear to everyone, both black and white, that nothing he does will affect Jefferson's life or his death. But this very skepticism creates possibility. Because of it, both blacks and whites know that he does not see this as a cause that will lead to social disruption; he acts out of loyalty to old black women, not out of political belief. In addition, his skepticism makes possible a relationship (eventually) with Jefferson, who rejects the false hope of any belief system. In contradistinction to Raymond Andrews, who locates a network of relationships under the accretions of history, Gaines sees community as something to be created out of the disintegration caused by history. Black families, belief systems, and interracial connections have been broken by racism, escape, and failure to adapt. Conscious effort must be made to establish ties across the ruptures.

Because Wiggins does not believe that Jefferson can be psychologically saved (that is, made to die as a man, not a hog), he undertakes his tasks by adopting the clichés of reclamation. He wants the condemned man to do this for Miss Emma, if not for himself. He carefully avoids engaging the underlying terror of death. In effect, he mouths the words of other people as a way of remaining disengaged from the difficult realities. Much of the first half of the novel is devoted to the pointlessly ritualistic encounters at the jail and with Wiggins's self-pitying responses. Relatively little of the narrative to this point, which is presented by Wiggins, addresses directly the encounters with Jefferson. Instead, he describes life in the quarters and his relationship with Vivian. Most of this material strengthens the aura of frustration, humiliation, alienation, and self-hatred. In effect, it justifies the narrator's initial attitude and approach to Jefferson. Wiggins represents himself as the true sacrificial figure, compelled to live in such a backward community, frustrated in love, and forced daily to endure insult, ignorance, and pointless activity. He steels himself for such a life with alcohol, books, and dreams of escaping with Vivian.

In this portrait, Gaines continues the African American intellectual and literary tradition of criticizing middle-class blacks, including intellectuals, for their failure to engage the significant struggles of the black masses. While the most direct assaults were made in the black arts movement by Amiri Baraka and others, the pattern can be traced back to Charles Chesnutt, W. E. B. Du Bois, and E. Franklin Frazier. The critique, which runs down to the work of Alice Walker, Toni Morrison, and David Bradley, focuses on the desire to evade the consequences of racism through status-seeking, wealth, and often education. It is an attack on individualism to the extent that self-interest separates one from the moral obligations of racial community. This criticism is often accompanied by a romanticizing of the masses, either as folk culture or as urban community.[10]

As suggested above, Gaines generally avoids this latter impulse. What changes Wiggins and leads him into his role as builder of community is, first, his resignation to his commitment to Miss Emma and, second, Jefferson's insult of Vivian. The first of these Wiggins presents as simply an extension of his world-weariness: "I could never stay angry long over anything. But I could never believe in anything either, for very long" (125). His turning away from hostility, while differently motivated, replicates the black folk emphasis on endurance, and it produces a similar possibility. But, though he does not acknowledge it, his resignation also gives him a link to the past and some sense of rootedness that otherwise does not exist for him. Moreover, Miss Emma uses her own ties to the past to make possible Wiggins's work with Jefferson. While meeting with the white man who has the power to decide, she keeps reminding him of the work she has always done for his family and the loyalty she ought to receive in return. Her efforts eventually succeed.

Wiggins then can go about the business of being helpful to Jefferson. His resignation to his role also opens him to the first real interaction with the condemned man. Significantly, the moment comes in the center of the book. Jefferson has been complaining that Grant is "vexing" him with his visits and expresses the desire to be left alone. Then, to provoke the visitor, he insults Vivian: "'Her old pussy ain't no good,' he said. My heart suddenly started pumping too fast. I made a fist of my right hand. If he had been standing, I would have hit him. If he had been any place else, I would have made him get up and I would have hit him. I would have hit any other man for saying that. But I recognized his grin for what it was—the expression of the most heart-rending pain I had ever seen on anyone's face" (130).

This is the first moment of authentic response for either man in the story, and in a narrative about masculine identity, it is not surprising that it involves conflict over the defining of a woman's value and that it is initially a moment of verbal and almost physical violence. They are tempted, in their mutual frustration, to fall into stereotypical combatants over a woman. But they manage to resist that ritual. Jefferson expresses the deep anguish of the condemned, and Wiggins finally is forced to value something beyond himself. Nonetheless, Gaines does not move directly to communication between the two. Rather, he focuses on the gradual shift in Wiggins, who, for the time being, continues to play a dominant role. While Jefferson remains largely silent, Wiggins lectures him on the need for responsibility to others, especially Emma.

At the same time, however, Wiggins facilitates greater contact between Jefferson and the black community. He dedicates the children's Christmas program to the imprisoned man, and he delivers a gift from the children. He takes up a collection in the town to buy a radio to keep in the jail cell. This gesture expands both community and Jefferson's frame of reference by making the outside world available to him. It can also be seen as an enhancement of self, since the radio is the first thing that Jefferson ever owned. But possession is also problematic; he refuses to go to the visitors' room if he has to leave the radio behind. Its one-directional communication, which nonetheless he can control, is easier to tolerate than encounters with people that he knows. Actual dialogue under the circumstances is simply too painful.

The cumulative effect of Wiggins's efforts to create community around Jefferson results in the change from hog to man. It also shifts the focus of attention and authority. Wiggins urges the doomed man to speak and to write, with the outcome that Jefferson's voice becomes central. While Wiggins attempts to maintain some control by "grading" the prison notebook, he is effectively reduced by it to a secondary role. In a scene reminiscent of Bigger Thomas's meeting with his lawyer, Jefferson explains his role in the world:

"Me, Mr. Wiggins. Me. Me to take the cross. Your cross, nannan's cross, my own cross. Me, Mr. Wiggins. This old stumbling nigger. Y'all axe a lot, Mr. Wiggins. . . . Whoever car'd my cross. Mr. Wiggins? . . . Yes, I'm youman, Mr. Wiggins. But nobody didn't know that 'fore now. Cuss for nothing.

Beat for nothing. Work for nothing. Grinned to get by. Everybody thought that's how it was s'pose to be. You too, Mr. Wiggins. You never thought I was nothing else. I didn't either. . . . Now all y'all want me to be better than ever'body else. (224)

The insight renders Wiggins largely silent. None of the soothing clichés can stand against this truth, which is not only personal but also historical and racial; it is the larger truth that education, alcohol, and self-pity have helped Wiggins suppress. He can only bear silent witness to the transformation in Jefferson that has taken place; none of his training or reason prepares him for such a moment, for it is the voice of black history itself that has spoken.

The narrative shift is pressed as Jefferson's notebook becomes the text and then the voices of the community bear their witness to what has happened. The notebook combines observations about the community with Jefferson's own concerns. In this way, it subverts a simplistic understanding of that community. It reveals, for example, the presence of religious doubt; God is said to be "for" the white folks, since he allows blacks to suffer injustice. Jefferson is led to speculate on the meaning of dreams and the behavior of whites. Although he claims not to understand Wiggins's urging that he go deeper into himself, he clearly articulates an understanding of the dynamics of the world around him. He offers evaluations of both blacks and whites and notes acts of decency that had not been imagined before. He details the attention he receives from the community while noting that it had never previously acknowledged him. Thus, he becomes the opportunity for the people to recognize both his and their own humanity. He also becomes the validator of Wiggins's virtue and endurance, even as he points to the other man's weakness: Wiggins refuses to be present for the execution. The power of Jefferson's writing is such that the sheriff feels compelled to ask him to note that his treatment has been good, and the deputy Paul agrees to deliver the notebook to Wiggins.

The implication here is that the black text is both humanizing and empowering. Expressing the truth of black experience changes both the writer and the world around him (her). It offers a countermemory to dominant history that both reveals and judges. It also is a counterpoint to both intellectual skepticism and simple folk faith. Jefferson doubts God, but he knows love. He changes the gaze of hate into one of respect and thereby creates the possibility of a community that transcends race, class, and gender. The black male word generates a transformed world.

The measure of this possibility is the narrative return to Wiggins at the end. He continues, in many ways, to be self-absorbed. He doubts that he has made any difference. At the same time, the quarters are silent at the moment of Jefferson's death, a gesture that would not have happened if the people had not seen him as a man, a status produced in part by Wiggins's efforts. Wiggins refuses to believe in either God or justice but also knows that there is a price to be paid for unbelief: "They [the folk] must believe, if only to free the mind, if not the body. Only when the mind is free has the body a chance to be free. Yes, they must believe, they must believe. Because I know what it means to be a slave. I am a slave" (251). The recognition of his own enslavement to despair is, of course, ironic. He is, after all, the one who felt that his mind had in fact been freed by knowledge, by a larger experience of the world. But his liberation must come from another source, Jefferson. In the final scene, Paul, the white deputy, drives to the quarters to deliver the notebook and to bear witness to Jefferson's manhood. In this moment, it is the white man who plays the subordinate role. He pays respect to Jefferson and then compliments Wiggins for his skill as a teacher. It is a comment that is discomforting because it carries with it a responsibility. He must accept his ability to teach, to make a difference; and he must accept his role as witness himself to the possibility of transformation. He must now be a believer, in himself, in learning, in love, and in the community they can engender. His manhood depends on it.

In *A Lesson Before Dying*, Gaines suggests a constructive role for artist-intellectuals such as himself. He appeals for a renewal of belief in black community and a larger American community, including a system of law that accepts black humanity. He is a witness to a troubled history, a history of suffering and dehumanization, and he understands the deeply ingrained cultural and social structures that perpetuate that history and does not believe in radical change as the means to a different end. In this sense, he holds an essentially conservative view of the folk world he recreates. But he also says, as he did in *A Gathering of Old Men*, that out of this traumatic history can come a different future. That change, however, requires witnesses to both the past and the possibilities for transformation. *A Lesson Before Dying* is an assertion that people like himself must be part of the community being created.

Chapter Four

TROUBLING THE WATER

Subversive Women's Voices in
Dessa Rose *and* Mama Day

Sherley Anne Williams and Gloria Naylor may be counted among those writers that Alice Walker labels "womanist." By this she means that they are primarily concerned with the lives and experiences of women of color: "A black feminist or feminist of color. . . . A woman who loves other women, sexually and/or nonsexually. Appreciates and prefers women's culture, women's emotional flexibility (values tears as natural counter-balance of laughter, and women's strength)" (ix). But Williams and Naylor are also concerned with the question of history and its relationship to both gender and race. In *Dessa Rose* and *Mama Day*, they create memory texts in which the voices of African American women are central to explanations of the past. In this conjunction of issues, they could be considered as adding to a tradition that includes Margaret Walker's *Jubilee*, Ernest Gaines's *Autobiography of Miss Jane Pittman*, and Walker's own early novels. They could also be considered, in another sense, part of a longer tradition of black women's writing that Mary Helen Washington, Barbara Christian, and others have so carefully traced.[1]

What is different in these two works is the extent to which tradition is problematized in the process of extending it. While each work serves at one level the ideological purpose of specifying the harm done to black women and more generally to black people and the ways they have survived their experiences, each one also suggests the price that must be paid for survival. In different ways, both must do violence to the recovery of truth and the healing that are their principal themes. Even as they appear to reveal heroic stories of suffering and endurance, they suppress part of the tale that complicates and potentially invalidates the meanings so carefully constructed. Memory thus becomes subversive of the very truth sought through it.

Dessa Rose has been read as an act of signifying on William Styron's 1967

Confessions of Nat Turner.[2] Styron's novel was attacked because it presented what many considered to be a distorted view of its central black character; thus, it was said to exploit black experience in order to discredit black history. Williams herself has suggested the textual relationship in her author's note: "I admit also to being outraged by a certain, critically acclaimed novel of the early seventies that travestied the as-told-to memoir of slave revolt leader Nat Turner" (ix). It can and has been argued that Williams, through the device of a neo–slave narrative, presents a challenge to Styron's conception of the rebellious slave.[3] By portraying first an incompetent white writer and then a brave and successful rebel, she inverts and subverts white control of the word and of history. Her Adam Nehemiah is a parody of both T. R. Gray, the original recorder of the "Confessions," and of Styron and his biased narrative masquerading as "a meditation on history" (Styron's phrase).

But there are problems with too much focus on this intertextual connection. One is a matter simply of time: *Dessa Rose* was published almost twenty years after *Nat Turner*. Major changes in the historical study of slavery and African American life generally had occurred in the interval. As Albert Stone has pointed out in *The Return of Nat Turner*, the paradigm that shaped historiography when Styron was researching his novel had fundamentally shifted within ten years (299–329). The Elkins model of the concentration-camp victim had been replaced by the Genovese model of negotiation among active agents. Thus, by the time Williams wrote her novel, Styron's representations were passé, at least in the literary and historical professions. To grant much influence, even of a negative sort, to the white writer is to put the black one in the position of reacting rather than creating.

A clue to another purpose behind the asserted connection can be found in Williams's own play with the historical record. First, she dates Styron's book "in the early seventies," fully five years after its actual publication. This displacement is important in that it dehistoricizes the novel by removing it from its context of black nationalist activities, Vietnam protests, urban civil unrest, and racial-political assassinations. It also takes away its significance as the first of a series of novels by major white authors—Saul Bellow, John Updike, Bernard Malamud—that use black male characters as emblems of that unrest. She places it instead in the frame of Nixonian policies of "benign neglect" and of the commodification of blackness through products such as blaxploitation films.

A *Nat Turner* relocated to a time of the retrenchment of civil rights can then be read as a text of revitalized racism and its renewed discourse. This creates the space for a *Dessa Rose* that incorporates a white writer who is racist to the point of parody. From his first appearance, Adam Nehemiah is portrayed as arrogant, egocentric, and uncomprehending. The white who presumes to understand and explain black life from a position of privilege is not only doomed to failure; he is also a fool and an apologist for white supremacy. By identifying Styron as a negative source and then denigrating his efforts through her own character, Williams is able to position her work as a subversive liberationist text.

One question would be the need to do this at all. After all, as Stone has pointed out, the controversy over *Nat Turner* had largely been forgotten by the mid-1980s (382–86). The historical profession had moved on in slavery studies, and black writers had become successful in representing different racial images in both the popular and literary cultures. After *The Autobiography of Miss Jane Pittman*, *Roots*, and *The Color Purple*, why should William Styron's Nat Turner matter? One answer is that the very success of such black narratives threatens the status of a special black history and of the very meaning of blackness. If the nation can so readily accept images of black suffering as one aspect of its past, if these verbal and visual products so easily "sell," then it would seem that the larger culture has effectively absorbed into itself one of history's most recalcitrant elements without undergoing any significant moral, social, or political debate. On the surface level of the culture, the struggle simply is declared over. Black suffering sells, black entertainers and athletes become wealthy and beloved, black history enters the textbooks, black writers become celebrities.

This process suggests the emptying out of the meaning of blackness. This absorption is occurring simultaneously with the intensification of economic and political attacks on the poor and minorities. How is the black writer supposed to tell the story of oppression without having it become simply more of the "white noise" of the culture? Albert Stone suggests an answer:

> If they wish to participate in the contemporary political struggles to liberate the oppressed . . . , fiction writers must deploy their "lying" (that is, their symbolizing) imaginations upon new historical subjects. By all sorts of devices—including legends and myths, displacements and condensations, jokes and tall tales—they must invite into their narratives the disguised figures from official history, as they must also recapture forgotten or unknown people from the past. Thereby they can challenge official explanations and silences. (19)

Williams needs *Nat Turner* not so much as a text to react to or resist but as a version of "official explanation," in part because Styron does to Turner, using psychoanalysis filtered through 1950s historiography, what contemporary social science and public policy does to blacks, especially those in the inner cities.

By identifying figures from history who contradict this discourse and by constructing a narrative about them, she offers not merely a counterhistory but also, by implication, an alternative present reality. This narrative carries messages of the foolishness of white intellectual analysis, as suggested above; the value of communal rather than individual endeavor; the centrality of women's actions and beliefs; the importance of interracial cooperation; and the legitimacy of subversion of the society's racial formation. If Williams had chosen simply to retell the story of Nat Turner, she would have entered a discursive practice whose rules were established. She chose instead to refer to Styron's novel, thus inviting comparison without engaging it directly. Her claims that his work "travestied" black history and that "literature and writing" often "betray" black people suggest that there is a righting of the story that her writing can perform. Such a text will be neither travesty nor commodity. She lays claim to a difficult but necessary truth-telling.

The way to this truth is, in historiographical terms, another travesty. Williams admits to taking significant liberties with the historical record in her own project: "*Dessa Rose* is based on two historical incidents. A pregnant black woman helped to lead an uprising on a coffle . . . in 1829 in Kentucky. Caught and convicted, she was sentenced to death; her hanging, however, was delayed until after the birth of her baby. In North Carolina in 1830, a white woman living on an isolated farm was reported to have given sanctuary to runaway slaves. . . . How sad, I thought then, that these two women never met" (ix). The novel, of course, corrects this missed opportunity of history. Deborah McDowell insists that in doing so, Williams is not engaged in some form of literary hypocrisy by which she holds Styron to a standard she herself ignores. McDowell makes the case that *Dessa Rose* presents multiple versions of history that raise questions about the nature of truth in representing African American experience ("Negotiating between Tenses," 144–45). This observation must be qualified in the sense that one voice, Dessa's, is privileged in the text. As indicated above, Adam Nehemiah's voice is subverted from the beginning of the narrative. Rufel, the white woman sheltering slaves, is initially presented as immature and self-centered. Only as she gains understanding and takes risks for slaves is she taken seriously. Even so, at the end of the novel, she is made to disappear in a brief paragraph. One implication of the statements by Williams and McDowell, including the latter's observation that the book "bears the proud mark of a resolutely propositional and polemical novel" (145), is that it is ultimately a monologic text, with the title character's voice (and thus that of the black woman) being the one that counts.

Such privileging accomplishes at least two purposes. It points to a suppressed history, that of strong black women who both endured and resisted slavery.

They were raped by masters, abused by mistresses, separated from spouses and children, and denied the most basic human and legal rights; nonetheless, they were not simply passive victims. They nurtured families, created communities, worked at hard labor, passed along a culture based on hope, justice, and freedom, and fought back when it was possible. Such a representation moves beyond those of Toni Morrison's *Bluest Eye*, Alice Walker's *Color Purple*, and Gloria Naylor's *Linden Hills* in that those works portray the black woman primarily as victim. It moves even further past black male narratives, both autobiographical and fictional, in which women are barely characterized at all, except as bodies assaulted by slavery and racism.

Dessa Rose also offers a different version of the trauma of history. By refusing both the concentration-camp paradigm informing Styron's work and the simple heroic model found in *Roots*, Williams must construct a version of history that allows for heroic behavior but also recognizes the power of oppression. Her novel values heroism but insists that such behavior, in the context of slavery, is both costly and damaging. Slavery not only demands the physical submission of the enslaved so that the work of the plantation and thus the wealth of the master can be accomplished; it also requires that the slave accept, at least publicly, the denial of her/his own humanity. The qualification here is important. Both victimization and heroic narratives imply that no distinction exists between the public and the private self. A work such as *The Autobiography of Miss Jane Pittman* suggests that such a distinction exists but that the selves can be compartmentalized; Jane can go on being the good servant in the view of whites while repeatedly nurturing rebels. *Dessa Rose* offers a more complex view, in which the proud, rebellious private self erupts into the public realm.

The memory of Dessa focuses, especially early in the text, on Kaine, her beloved. Unlike Gayl Jones's *Song for Anninho*, where time is dissolved repeatedly so that Almeyda seems to be with Anninho when thinking about him, Kaine is more clearly in Dessa's past. He functions as the noble and ennobling past that enables integrity and survival in the present. In this sense, Williams's novel is more linear than Jones's poetry. The novelist is concerned with progress from slavery to freedom, from past to present to future. In such a pattern, it is important to represent the past as both heroic and painful. The past must be seen as traumatic but also as worth claiming. Victimization alone cannot empower action in the present and creation of the future. Kaine's attractiveness and his loss emerge from the same source. He refuses to accept the condition of dehumanization as natural or normal. He consistently asserts his manhood in a public manner. When his banjo is destroyed by the master, he strikes out at him and is killed for his action. Significantly, the banjo is the emblem of his connection to Africa. He is the link to a brave and creative past, but his very courage requires his death. Openly expressed black manhood, defined in terms of resistance, cannot be tolerated in a white supremacist society.

What can succeed is something more subtle, represented by Harker. With the same commitment to black freedom, he chooses maneuvering within the existing system over directly confronting it. His special skill is understanding white thinking; such understanding could be turned to the advantage of the oppressed. He has such confidence in his insight that he devises a scheme whereby the group sells various of its members into slavery and then, after they escape, resells them a short time later. Such a plan depends on blacks knowing how to behave like slaves, the white woman being coached in her role, and other whites being tricked because of their assumptions about slavery.

Such an approach is diametrically opposed to the principles by which Kaine lived and died. For the purposes of this text, pragmatism ultimately is valued over idealism. Dessa compares the two men:

> And here he [Harker] was promising hisself to me talking about a future he wanted for us, and this frightened me. Kaine hadn't done this. You know, the future did not belong to us; it belonged to our masters. We wasn't to think about no future; it was a sign of belliousness if we did. So it scared me to hear Harker talk this way. I felt sometimes that if I hadn't pushed Kaine to think about running, he never would have hit Master. What was that banjo compared to us? He could've made another one. Now here was Harker showing them same signs. Oh, Harker knowed the laws and rules was set against us, but he act like that was just so he could sharpen his wits on them, make doing what he wanted to do more interesting, you know, a little exciting. And this was how he went at that scheme, like all our fears about slips and what-if's was just something to make everybody think a little deeper, a little faster. (210)

The future, which is Harker, assumes knowledge of the existing order and skill to operate within its framework. The issues are not so much moral as practical. Assuming a desire for freedom, the point is not to die for it but to achieve it. One's identity and integrity are not at risk; they are taken for granted. By contrast, Kaine sees the future as closed; the only morally acceptable responses to the situation are escape or death. One's identity is daily at risk because the master determines the rules of existence.

Significantly, Dessa positions herself by not recognizing the importance of the banjo in Kaine's worldview. It is for her nothing worth dying for, especially since it can be replaced. From his perspective, the instrument is less an object than a symbol. It is an extension of Africa, of that ancestral past of dignity and freedom. The power to destroy the banjo is the power to destroy that past, which is his only source of identity. Unlike Harker, who constructs himself in relationship to the present, Kaine must have the past or be nothing.

Dessa, positioned between these perspectives, signifies the need of the race to know and accept the past, with all its suffering, but then to move beyond it. What it means to "know and accept" is to absorb the values and qualities of that past and to adapt to changing circumstances. In this sense, Dessa's role is similar to that of several characters in the works discussed in this study. That role is to experience the transition from past to future, whether that is seen as slavery to freedom, "Old Negro" to "New Negro," folk to modern, Africa to America, or mythic to historical. This is one sense in which these texts speak to the present: in our own fluid moment, what should be kept and how should it be preserved? What will enable African Americans to endure whole in this time?

The vehicle for Dessa's transition is her relationship to Rufel, the white woman who provides a refuge for runaways. What is first established is Dessa's distrust of whites, based on both personal experience and cultural training. This common wisdom is tested at key moments in the last two-thirds of the book. Initially, the characterization and self-representation of Rufel resemble that of Adam Nehemiah. She is patronizing, naive, and rather foolish but more basically racist in her interactions with blacks. The fact that she provides sanctuary for runaways is qualified by the lack of charity in her motives for doing so. The initial conflict reflects the attitudes of both women. As Dessa recovers from her escape, Rufel rambles on about "Mammy." As the black woman slowly regains full consciousness, she is momentarily confused about what seems to be a reference to her own mother. She lashes out in anger at this violation of her own memory, knowing "even as she said it what the white woman meant" (124). For three pages they contend about the truth of "Mammy," each claiming ownership of the designation for her own remembrance while knowing they are talking about two different people.

The first significant point about this confrontation is that it concerns control over the past.[4] Both Dessa and Rufel have deep connections to personal experience captured by the term "Mammy." For Dessa, it is a story of a mother who raised her and nine others while working in the fields. The word conjures up a black history of children lost to illness and the auction block. In the memory is also the mother's command to recall all the names and fates, "lest her poor, lost children die to living memory as they had in her world" (126). In contrast, Rufel's memory is the validation of her privilege. Her Mammy is the woman who devoted her life to Rufel's happiness. Though her life is otherwise troubled, especially in her relationships to her husband and her parents, Rufel is convinced that Mammy loved her unconditionally until the day she died. In this sense, she legitimates a version of history that puts whites at the center of black experience and defines black feeling in terms of relationships with whites.

When Dessa challenges this memory, she is striking not only at Rufel's personal history but also at the cultural order through which the white woman has structured her identity. When she says that " 'Mammy' ain't nobody name, not they real one" (125), she calls into question a history that designates people by their roles or by the whims of masters, not by the human individuality of the person. She proves her point by naming her "Mammy" and telling why the name was appropriate. She then recounts the story described above, naming in the process Rose's progeny, both living and dead. All have names given by their mother, whose own designation as Mammy comes from her children, not her master.

This scene is important because it begins the process of change in Rufel, though not in Dessa. Confronted with the challenge, the white woman feels compelled to reconstitute her own memory. She feels required to recall Mammy's real name, Dorcas. The recovery of name leads directly into a process of the correction of memory: "Pappa had not given her Mammy as a birthday present as Rufel sometimes claimed" (130); "No, Rufel corrected herself" (131); "She blinked away angry tears, seeing then the loved features, the coffee-black skin and cream-colored head-scarf, the full lips, but subtly altered so the face seemed that of a stranger" (133). Part of this historical reconstruction is the recognition for the first time that Dorcas might have a life distinct from her relationship with Rufel: "But Mammy might have had children and it bothered Rufel that she did not know. . . . Had she a sweetheart? A child?" (136). Within a page of this acknowledgment of ignorance, she is led to doubt Dorcas's real feelings toward her: "Had Mammy minded when the family no longer called her name? Was that why she changed mine? Rufel thought fearfully. Was what she has always thought loving and cute only revenge, a small reprisal for all they'd taken from her? How old *had* Mammy been? Why had they gone to France? Rufel never asked. Had she any children?" (137).

The status of children is obviously crucial in this memory and for the text in general. The presence or absence of black children shapes the meaning of "Mammy." If Dorcas is in fact a mother, then Rufel's naming of her and claiming of status as her child is a mockery of the black woman's experience and a daily insult added to the injury of the loss of real children. If Dorcas was mother, as well as "Mammy," then her life was in fact much like that of Dessa's

Mammy, a life of separation and loss. This insight, incompletely developed as it is at this stage of Rufel's life, makes possible her movement to connection with and even love for members of the black community that has been created on but not as her property.

It is significant that Williams insists on change in the central white character as a precondition for the development of Dessa Rose. It is also significant that Rufel's shift in awareness occurs rapidly, whereas that of Dessa takes much more textual space. On the one hand, the author is making the claim that racial problems are fundamentally the problem of whites, even though it is blacks (and others) who are so clearly adversely affected. As the emblem of whiteness, Rufel must recognize the falseness of her position and the harm that it has caused. On the other hand, the change in Dessa is more complex. The insight that Rufel struggles to, after all, should not be an insight at all; it should simply be part of human awareness. Her ignorance and the privilege that both supports and is supported by it, make her unreliable from the black woman's point of view. Dessa's distrust is supported not only by personal experience but also by generations of family and group history. Because of years of training in their own superiority, whites have become incapable of behaving and thinking like ordinary human beings. This false consciousness, because it is linked to power, requires a dialectically structured black consciousness, which is simultaneously aware of this power and aware of the need to maintain a self not submissive to or seduced by this power. Dessa has successfully developed such a "double-consciousness," and displacing it cannot be easy. To cast it aside readily would be foolish and would betray the experiences of Kaine and Dessa's mother.

The black woman's revised perspective depends on the white woman's sharing of black experience. This sharing is itself complex and problematic. It is not sufficient for Rufel to join the slave-selling scheme. Her risk is the least among the participants, and her involvement can be motivated by nothing other than greed. Her need is for money, not freedom. Only when she narrowly escapes rape by a "Southern gentleman" is her potential victimization realized by Dessa. Skin color does not necessarily protect white women from assaults on their humanity. In fact, because desire is both prescribed and proscribed in the signifier "Southern Woman," Rufel is necessarily at risk in a way roughly analogous to those designated "Black Woman." Dessa's realization of the situation creates sympathy if not identification in the relationship.

Rufel's sexual desire produces another conflict that contributes to understanding. When Nathan and Rufel become lovers, Dessa feels outraged and betrayed. Her response is carefully shown to be the product not of jealousy but rather of group betrayal. This view is justified in part by Nathan's own story of a previous white lover who saw sex with black men both as a validation of racial stereotype and as an opportunity to exercise power. Unlike white men, black ones can be controlled and silenced; the woman who is herself subordinate within Southern patriarchy can use her position to manipulate others.

But this does not seem to be the case with Rufel. If anything, she is the one manipulated in that one motive for Nathan's interest in her seems to be getting her involved in the slave scheme. Beyond this point, he seems to be attracted to, though not obsessed with, her whiteness. In telling of his earlier experience, he emphasizes the importance of the forbidden and dangerous to his sexual excitement. But he is also concerned with Rufel as an individual who attracts him; as the relationship develops, this, in fact, becomes the principal explanation. It also would seem to be her motivation. Lonely, isolated, and disillusioned, she turns to the person who is most understanding and sympathetic. She is humanized by the experience, a point even Dessa comes to understand.

What Williams does with this love story reveals a key to her underlying concerns. Although Dessa saves Rufel from rape and later Rufel does everything she can to save Dessa from reenslavement through Adam Nehemiah, racial boundaries are ultimately left in place. In the epilogue, set many years after the events, Dessa tells the young children of the community that Rufel ended up in the Northeast. There is no effort to describe the ending of the relationship with Nathan. The story that had considerable importance in the development of characters, relationships, and plot is simply dropped. This happens after Dessa has said: "I wanted to hug Ruth [Rufel]. I didn't hold nothing against her, not 'mistress,' not Nathan, not skin" (256).

While Williams clearly refuses any simple white claims of knowledge or understanding of black experience, she also appears to be unwilling to grant the possibility of cross-racial community. Adam Nehemiah has become a crazed shell of his former self by the end of the narrative, suggesting the essential lunacy of white intellectual claims to knowledge of black life. But he was a fool from the beginning. His obsession with the scars on Dessa's body as the evidence of her criminality nicely symbolizes the 1970s and 1980s attacks by policy makers and social commentators on "welfare queens" and their promiscuous lives. His indecipherable notes (and blank pages) recording his research satirize the academic establishment's claims of exhaustive knowledge of African American experience.

But Rufel (Ruth) is different, and that difference is ultimately problematic. She has gained understanding, she has taken risks, she has shared the lives of black people. And, I would argue, it is because of that experience that Williams must get rid of her. "The people" (as Dessa refers to her community) must be preserved, even at the cost of individuals. The special meaning of being black is in the great suffering that Kaine and Dessa's mother endured and that lives in the memories of the community. Ruth represents the possibility of forgetting that past at some point in the future. Ironically, "going west," as the black characters do, requires holding onto the South. Freedom in this text means never forgetting slavery. If "the people" are to retain their identity, it is crucial to remember what made them special. A Ruth in their midst says implicitly that the future does not require such a memory, that it is possible to forge new identities and communities.

The threat here is not that history will be erased or that blacks will be seduced into false alliances. It is, after all, Ruth who moved into identification with her black companions. Rather, the threat of contemporary society is that it is possible for some black people in some places to live much of their daily lives without reference to their race. Education, occupation, and status in some instances can be more important factors than skin color. The point is not that this situation is widespread or is coming about without struggle. Nonetheless, even the intimations of a different social order challenge fundamental identities as they have been constructed throughout American history. If "blackness" and "whiteness" can be imagined as anachronisms, then what relationship should there be to the past? In *Dessa Rose*, Sherley Anne Williams evades the question.

In *Mama Day* (1992), Gloria Naylor also constructs a woman-centered black community concerned with maintaining the special character of "the people." She sets the present time of the work in 1999, thus suggesting a connection to her readers' near future, though most of the action takes place in 1985. She also creates in the title character a figure already complete in herself and in her understanding of human life. While she is ancient, she is burdened, not by time, but rather by the most effective uses of her considerable powers. The concern of the novel is not whether she is right or effective but rather whether those accustomed to other ways of thinking can be brought around to a proper appreciation of her power and wisdom. Her qualities and abilities are grounded in the past and in folk culture, and it is difficult for those educated in conventional science and reason to accept her authority. But all those who resist Mama Day are shown to be foolish or venial or dangerous.

In addition to reconstituting the sense of the present through forward projection, Naylor also loosens her narrative from conventional boundaries of space and history. Willow Springs is said not to be within the borders of any state; it is a Sea Island that falls exactly between Georgia and South Carolina but does not belong to either one. It is also repeatedly said to be a timeless world, where there are no seasons but rather annual rituals. Moreover, the introductory narrative voice points out her own absence from the world of the reader: "Think about it: ain't nobody really talking to you. We're sitting here in Willow Springs, and you're God-knows-where. It's August 1999—ain't but a slim chance it's the same season where you are. Uh, huh, listen. Really listen this time: the only voice is your own" (10).

The world created is a timeless inner landscape, but one that ironically requires a sense of history and of difference from the reading self in order to sustain its force. The reader is an outsider but, at the same time, the only insider. Willow Springs is a site of memory,[5] but it is also a site of the black collective unconscious. The reader, like the modern characters in the novel, must learn to turn away from contemporary America if she hopes to find the true self and the real family. Naylor, in effect, constructs history as myth so as to make possible the creation of a racial kinship network.

One means of achieving this end is to make the site of memory also a site of loss and mourning. Each of the major characters is in some sense an orphan. George, the young professional from New York, was raised in an orphanage, his mother a prostitute and his father unknown. Ophelia, also known as Cocoa, lost both her parents, though she was raised by her grandmother and great-aunt. Even Mama Day has to deal with the madness and death of her mother. The breaking of generations in this manner makes the connections to the past easier to establish and maintain. Without the direct influence of parents, especially mothers in this text, the individual must rely either on the self or on whatever links can be established to the ancestors. In the moral universe of this novel, the latter choice is the only valid one.

This choice is also important because it is a racial choice as well. Willow Springs is a black space; the black people of the island have always owned the land, an anomaly for a location in the Deep South. How they obtained it is a crucial part of the legend/history of the island. By some means, Sapphira Wade, a slave, married Bascombe Wade, the owner, bore him sons, and secured for them title to the island in perpetuity. Exactly how she did this has become confused over time, and, in fact, her name is never spoken. She represents a suppressed narrative of black resistance and conquest that the residents tell neither to outsiders nor to themselves. The story exists in traces, such as the Candle Walk or the phrase "18 & 23," which is a local expression referring to any important or difficult effort but is also presumably the year in which Sapphira gained control. Thus the power of history and the secret of black success is enhanced by the concealment of historical reality. Naylor effectively generates a fantasy of black achievement that must be placed outside reality in order to be fully imagined; even then, parts of the story must remain unspoken.

What is required of the modern black man and woman, then, is faith in the possibility and tradition of black power. Significantly, Naylor does not require belief in nonrational or magical forces as a counter to the conventions of rationality. Mama Day delights in exposing the deceptions and claims of Dr. Buzzard; but she herself operates within a cloak of mystery. In fact, however, she is shown to make use of a folk equivalent of the scientific method. She is a careful observer of both nature and the physical and psychological conditions of her patients. She has developed over the years a wealth of knowledge of herbal medicine. Even the doctor who comes to the island on occasion has trust in her diagnoses, especially since she knows the limits of her skills. While she uses a variety of conjurer's tricks, these are intended to get patients to submit to her care, not to actually effect a cure. Even such apparent voodoo as placing a curse that results in two lightning strikes is explained by one of the modern characters in terms of physics, though he does not believe that anyone on the island has such knowledge.

This pattern of explanation of mysterious phenomena suggests that Mama Day is a modern woman as rational and insightful into human psyches as any of the more contemporary figures in the novel. Black power, and more specifically the power of black women, is thus shown not to be some occult reality but rather a product of commitment to the past and to human understanding. In part, the special rituals serve as means of gaining authority and faith; mystery encourages faith in the practitioner so that her advice will be followed. But that advice itself is based on knowledge about human desire and behavior. Thus, Mama Day can shift Bernice's attention away from flawed ideas about marriage and motherhood by giving her ritualized tasks to perform that in fact make her more attentive to the real needs in her life and so better able to achieve her goals. But none of Mama Day's (Miranda's) skills can save the life of Bernice's child during the storm.

In one sense, the novel may be said to be Naylor's attempt to imagine a golden age of black power and freedom. Mama Day represents a link to the ancestors that allows her to achieve meaningful authority within the community. Even if her knowledge is practical rather than magical, it is nonetheless connected to the understanding of people and nature that has developed over generations in Willow Springs. It is the kind of power that enables the community to maintain its independence from white political and economic domination. Through the representation of George's and Cocoa's lives in the world of New York, the author can demonstrate the shallowness and alienation of contemporary society. By showing George's interest in the neighborhoods of the city, she can reveal the communal impulse that Willow Springs would seem to have perfected. She creates, in other words, a black utopia.

The fact that she establishes the island as a liminal space beyond time, however, may suggest despair rather than possibility. Such a place can only exist as "no-place," outside of history, a mythic state. This positioning would seem to suggest that black power is an imaginary condition, a desire that signifies a lack, an absence, an emptiness that cannot be filled. Mama Day herself has no children, no one to whom to pass her knowledge and wisdom. The mysteries will not be revealed, and the insights cannot be translated into the world of New York. George and Cocoa can be transformed by going to Willow Springs, but they cannot live that changed life elsewhere. Naylor would seem to be saying that this is a beautiful dream, but it cannot exist in historical reality.

The Shakespearean references in the text reinforce this idea. The novel is built in part on *The Tempest*, with its magician, befuddled lovers, location, and storm as key elements. But it is a tragic version of that drama, one that requires human sacrifice to achieve its effects. Bernice's son and George are only the most recent to die on the island in ways that suggest the malevolence of the world. Moreover, the deaths themselves are part of what is suppressed by the residents of the island. Repression of memory becomes a means of constructing the island as utopia, because the realities in fact reveal the devastating effects of time and human frailty. History is not overcome; it is denied.

The origins of the repression can be located in what seems to be a peculiarity of the narrative. The very name of Sapphira Wade, the founding mother of the island, is never spoken, though all the people appear to know it. Yet, given her achievement, producing sons and gaining an inheritance for them in the time of slavery, one would expect her story to be told in detail again and again, and her name to be on everything. Moreover, she could be expected to be the heroic figure in a womanist tale of the struggles, suffering, and sacrifices of women that constitute an important part of the novel.

The silence about her suggests a deeper concern at work. The legends of Sapphira, whatever their variations, all imply that she was somehow implicated in the death of Bascombe Wade, the man who freed her, fathered some or all of her seven sons, and left them the island. Black freedom, then, is grounded in the killing of the father, a crime that the community cannot acknowledge. But the murder must nonetheless be atoned for, and that becomes the curse of Mama Day's family.

All the versions of the Wade legend involve the murder of Bascombe by Sapphira once she had gotten what she wanted. Why his death was necessary is never made clear; certainly it is not established that he failed in any of his commitments to her or that he was violent or domineering. The implication then is that his whiteness is the problem that can be overcome only through his death. Like John Wideman in *Damballah* and Sherley Anne Williams in *Dessa Rose*, Naylor seems to refuse belief in interracial love. In her case, however, the human sacrifice necessary to black power must be paid for with black death. Each generation of the Day family must repeat the sacrifice. So Abigail and Miranda's mother, Ophelia, goes mad when her child Peace dies; eventually she commits suicide. Abigail tries to make up for the mother's loss by naming her own child Peace, but it, too, dies in infancy. Abigail's daughter Grace also attempts to defy fate by naming her child Ophelia, a name that signifies within the family a "woman who could break a man's heart" (151) and expresses Grace's desire for vengeance, since she had been left by her husband. Not only does Grace die, but the anger associated with her daughter's name comes literally true. George, who has a congenitally weak heart, dies from the strain of saving Ophelia's (Cocoa's) life. Moreover, Mama Day, knowing instinctively that he must die to save Cocoa, sends George on the errand that leads to his death. The perfection of the young lovers' relationship comes, not in life, but in Cocoa's communing with his spirit when she returns to the island after his death.

Thus, a cycle is completed in which the sacrifice of a man for the benefit of a woman is paid for with the sacrificing of women and then finally the death of a man to save a woman-child of the family. Except perhaps for the first, none of these deaths are intentional; they seem rather the result of some cosmic operation of bloody justice. Each generation loses that which it values most, and attempts to defy that fate only lead to greater losses.

The key question, then, is why it is necessary to the narrative to insist upon the painful deaths of women and the men who love them. Other writers (and Naylor herself in earlier works) have shown female suffering as a result of male cruelty and domination, either individual or cultural. Toni Morrison, Alice Walker, Gayl Jones, and ntozake shange are among the most prominent in constructing narratives of victimization, and in *Women of Brewster Place* and *Linden Hills*, Naylor has offered her own vivid stories of such suffering. But in *Mama Day*, neither patriarchy nor racism is evident as the cause of loss. Even though the island people identify themselves with a subversive matrilineage, Sapphira's violence and perhaps arrogance seem to be at the heart of the troubled generations. The Day family acquired its name, according to legend, from a statement made by Sapphira after the birth of her seventh son: " 'God rested on the seventh day and so would she.' Hence, the family's last name" (x). She claims equality with God and then, through murder, displaces the father-master. While the island's community and the Day family specifically can claim its inheritance from the black mother, her story and very name must be repressed in order to avoid engagement with the primal crimes (murder and blasphemy) creating that heritage. The full meaning of Sapphira's rebellion must be obscured and displaced into phrases and watered-down rituals from which the violence has been removed. The meaning of her story is that history (and perhaps even justice) emerges from blood and death and that those events, given the tortured racial history of America, occur within the family, though one may not acknowledge or be acknowledged by the ancestors (especially if they are white). Despite this denial, history demands its due and sacrifices must continue to be made.

What, then, is Naylor saying to the present moment and to current gender issues? She points to the centrality of love, though it must be understood in the context of suffering and sacrifice. Naylor seems to be offering an Old Testament version of black experience that emphasizes justice over mercy. The sins of the fathers (and mothers) must be paid for by generations of sons and daughters. Love cannot save anyone; in fact, it quite often produces more trouble. The first Ophelia cannot simply grieve for the loss of Peace and move on through her life. She is driven mad and effectively causes the suffering of her remaining children. Mama Day's love of Cocoa leads her to the destruction of Ruby and the sacrifice of George. Love produces madness, obsession, pain, and death. In this depiction of human relationships, Naylor is consistent with the views of Toni Morrison, Gayl Jones, and Alice Walker, among other women writers. Neither within families nor between lovers is there any assurance that love will improve the lives of individuals or groups.

What is clearly essential, however, is the *desire* for love, which emphasizes its frequent absence. This text, like other contemporary fictions, is anhedonic, though in its conversations between Cocoa and George's spirit and between Miranda and Abigail, it appears to demonstrate the value of affection. But precisely the point is that George must be dead for Cocoa to communicate with him, and the elderly sisters exist in a discursive universe that carefully evades much of their history together and in which even the simplest phrases carry the burden of the past. Love becomes the veneer that conceals the unspeakable truth of history. Thus, one comment that the novel makes on the gender issues of the present is their embeddedness in the violence of history. Love, as either personal or racial, cannot resolve conflicts soaked in ancestral blood. Instead, it must produce either the falseness of romance and repression or the recognition of violent and troubled origins.

But both options make love virtually impossible. Naylor's refusal to assign blame specifically to either racism or male domination suggests the internalization of a variety of destructive elements. Absorption in death and suffering makes it difficult to focus on the needs of the living; death and the dead become the principal context for relationships with the living. Sapphira Wade creates a future for her sons through killing Bascombe Wade. Ophelia denies affection to her living children in order to focus on the dead Peace. Mama Day must sacrifice George to save Cocoa from Ruby's obsessive jealousy, itself caused by a need to express love through the destruction of competitors (real or imaginary) for the beloved. It would appear, then, that a history of deprivation, oppression, abuse, and death creates impossible conditions for the life-affirming expression of love. Thus, contemporary conflicts between men and women and within families are simply the latest version of an ongoing black experience. Because risk, loss, and mourning are the expected circumstances of life, love must always be either tentative or obsessive. It cannot be separated from death and so must always be a form of melancholia.

It is for this reason that *Mama Day* stresses the need to listen to voices, especially those of the dead or disreputable. The quality and effectiveness of voices is central to the structure of the novel. George and Cocoa struggle in their relationship in large part because of assumptions about expected or experienced speech acts. Moreover, each conceals from the other (and to some extent from the self) essential information about the past and about beliefs. Thus, George's obsession with professional football, which Cocoa takes as simply an exercise in masculine desire, in fact represents a deeply felt need for order and connection lacking in his early childhood. It gives structure and focus to a life that would otherwise exist in emotional chaos. Cocoa generates her persona and speech out of the necessity of appearing independent and sophisticated, so as to conceal her own deprivations. Willow Springs represents to her both a wellspring and a site of unpleasant memory and thus a place to be simultaneously denied and returned to.

In conjunction with her perceptions of home, the community is one in which the voices of the dead blend with those of the living. Mama Day literally hears the voices of her father and grandfather, though they died many years before. The voice of Sapphira Wade is dimly echoed in the ritual words of the Candle Walk. The daily greeting between Mama Day and Abigail carries in it the memory of the death of their infant sister and, by implication, the madness and suicide of their mother. Beyond all this are the voices in the wind, the spirits of all those who have died, that enable Mama Day to have a sharpened sense of what will happen and must be done. Her life-affirming and healing efforts are contextualized by the constant presence of the dead.

Moreover, it is the presence of the dead that gives the community its character and strength. Seen as peculiar and simple by outsiders, the members of the community are able to sustain their independence through the unspoken connection to Sapphira Wade and her act of defiance. But since that inheritance is itself ambiguous, they do not escape the vicissitudes of life. Literal and, more important, emotional storms batter their world and their lives. Even in this apparent paradise of black tradition and authority, pain, suffering, and death are inextricably joined to life and joy. Always below the surface can be heard the haunting voices of the dead, and new voices are constantly being added.

What Naylor speaks to, then, is the danger, in matters of both gender and race, of calling forth the ancestors. The reclaiming of black women's voices as an aid to contemporary life necessarily is more complex than the summoners imagine.[6] For all her healing efforts, the powers Mama Day uses require human sacrifice, no matter how much she wishes this not to be true. Likewise, references to Zora Neale Hurston, Nella Larsen, and African goddess figures cannot be restricted to the effects desired by womanist artists and intellectuals. They bring with them stories not simply of healing and endurance but also of blood and anger. They cannot be confined to the uses of nostalgia or ideology. The present is not so different from the past that we are free from the full consequences of both history and the present. We, too, live in a world of the suffering and dying, and our own delusions can conceal the blood that (seemingly) must be shed. What Naylor suggests, then, is that the recovery of the past, in its various forms, requires us to face a complex history that is neither victimization nor brave defiance, though it may include both, but some complex combination that troubles today's waters rather than calming them.

PART TWO *Desire*

Chapter Five

A SHORT HISTORY OF DESIRE
Jazz *and* Bailey's Cafe

With the emergence of feminist criticism in the past quarter century, desire has become a focal point of theory and critical commentary. It has, of course, been present in literary discourse for much longer, as long as there have been stories of love, greed, and power. But recent emphases on bodies, sexual identities, and repression have sharpened the discussions. Within African American literature and the criticism of it, there has been a reluctance to fully engage these issues, in part because the dominant racial formation has used the language of desire to subordinate black being through representations of the licentious black woman and the black rapist. What can be seen in the works examined in this section is the continuing ambiguity about desire. Toni Morrison, Gloria Naylor, and Charles Johnson problematize the expression of physical desire; none of the characters in the novels considered here find contentment in their bodies or their sexuality. Raymond Andrews, while more playful in presenting sexual experience, takes a moral position (through satire) on other forms of desire, such as greed and power. In his case, the erotic serves the purpose of this moral positioning. Thus, even in contemporary texts where black bodies (and sometimes white ones) are central to narrative, the authors experience dis-ease in their representation.

The late 1980s marked the end of a decade in which gender issues among African Americans had been especially contentious. One marker of the beginning of this era was the publication and performance of ntozake shange's *For Colored Girls Who Have Considered Suicide . . . When the Rainbow Is Enuf* (1977), with its depictions of the frequently violent nature of men and the need for bonding among black women. Two years later came Michele Wallace's *Black Macho and the Myth of the Black Superwoman* (1979), which sought to deconstruct the images of the sexes operating among both blacks and whites. Within five years, Alice Walker had published *The Color Purple* (1982), Gloria Naylor had written *The Women of Brewster Place* (also 1982), and Barbara Smith had edited *Home Girls: A Black Feminist Anthology* (1983) and co-edited *All the Women Are White, All the Blacks Are Men, But Some of Us Are Brave* (1982). The Walker and Naylor works became a successful movie and a television drama, respectively, and thus even more firmly established gender issues as a part of racial discussions. In her essay collection *In Search of Our Mothers' Gardens: Womanist Prose* (1983), Walker spelled out the need for black women to develop a feminism appropriate to their own experience and to identify themselves with other black women.

The response to these articulations of the concerns of African American women was often vociferous and sometimes hostile. In his book *Writin' Is Fightin'*, Ishmael Reed accused womanists of reinforcing negative stereotypes of black men and of cooperating with white men in these negative portrayals. He was especially concerned with how *The Color Purple* was filmed by Steven Speilberg (145–57). Charles Johnson, in *Being and Race* (1988), argued that women writers generally took too narrow a perspective on matters of race. But the battle was not simply between the sexes; Trudier Harris, in "On *The Color Purple*, Stereotypes, and Silence," argued that feminist praise for Walker's novel made it nearly impossible to offer a serious critique of the work.

A signal event in the year 1992 was the simultaneous appearance on the *New York Times* bestseller list of three novels by African American women writers: Terry McMillan's *Waiting to Exhale*, Alice Walker's *Possessing the Secret of Joy*, and Toni Morrison's *Jazz*. At the same time, Gloria Naylor's *Bailey's Cafe* was mentioned as "new and recommended." Different as these fictions were in terms of style and subject matter, they all took as a theme the role of desire and sexuality in the lives of women. The most popular of them, *Waiting to Exhale*, focused on the frustrations of young, successful women when men failed to meet their physical and emotional needs. At the other end of the spectrum, Walker took on the cause of African female genital mutilation as the physical emblem of the suppression of women's sexuality. Morrison and Naylor constructed historical novels that spoke to the ways female desire is distorted and violated within African American communities. While the latter two narratives work within the patterns of black women's writing of the past twenty-five years, to which these authors made significant contributions, *Jazz* and *Bailey's Cafe* problematize some of the issues of that emergent tradition.

In these two novels, while women are represented as victims in almost every instance, desire itself seems to be part of the reason. Especially in Naylor's work, female characters are complicitous in their own suffering. Their expressions of desire are often shown to be inappropriate, if not perverse, and their response to victimization is often self-mutilation or obsessive reenactment of the primal scene of violation. Virtually all of them fail to affirm their own desires, preferring to construct selves as sexual objects and victims. In *Jazz*, the two central female figures try to reinvent themselves in the images of the existing popular culture and act out roles found in romance narratives. In both novels, moreover, the narration is structured to emphasize the subjection of the characters to the gaze of the narrator. Their own voices are thereby subordinated to the explanations of them offered by this external voice. They are seen first as objects assigned meaning and only then heard in their own terms.

Another crucial difference played out in these texts is the central role of male characters, not as victimizers, but as witnesses and victims themselves. *Jazz*, for example, belongs in many ways to Joe Trace more than Dorcas or Violet. His struggles in both childhood and adulthood are virtually *the* story of the novel. To an even greater extent, Naylor focuses on male concerns. The narrator is "Bailey," the proprietor of the cafe, and the one who introduces all of the characters and their stories and does so actively rather than passively. That is, he makes his opinions of them very clear and determines how they will be received by his audience. The longest section of the novel is devoted to Miss Maple, a man who prefers to wear dresses in the summer and works as a housekeeper but whose manhood, we are repeatedly assured, is never in doubt.

In addition, these are urban narratives, in that they describe strangers in the city who form fragile and temporary communities. All of the characters, including the narrators, are from some other place, and they know about each other only what they learn from self-revelations and gossip. They are all survivors of those other places, brought together by chance or some design unknown to them. They all seek refuge or opportunity; in other words, they operate in the context of desire in the sense that the past, as both time and place, signifies an absence, a lack, or a violation, and the present signifies the fulfillment, redress, or repression of that need. Morrison's Harlem and Naylor's street are the sites at which the needy come together to seek satisfaction. They are also fugitive places, in that the characters have escaped to them, and so cannot be the locations of fulfillment, since the source of desire is located in the past. Thus, resolution can never be achieved, as Bailey acknowledges (228). These, then, are stories of survivors unable to recover from the traumas of personal, gendered, and racial history. Rather than simply telling the stories of suffering, Morrison and Naylor in these texts explore the displacements and deferrals that such suffering generates in the present time of the narratives.

Finally, one reason to tell the stories in such a way is that, by 1992, the public discourse had shifted to make desire and its urban expression central. Gangsta rap, with its narrative of "bitches and ho's," the framing of welfare's destruction in terms of promiscuous black teenagers, the Anita Hill–Clarence Thomas confrontation, and other events suggested that stories that "merely" portrayed rural life, including slavery, or women as purely victims could not speak to the present moment. Taboos—political, racial, and personal—were being widely broken, in the sense that they now entered the public sphere in the form of media exposés, salacious narratives in film and print, sensationalized acts of violence, and rhetorics of disparagement. Literary expressions that sought to address underlying cultural concerns risked being lost in the "noise" of this discursive universe.

In response, Morrison and Naylor displace their narratives to a different time and build repression, as well as oppression, into those narratives. In this way, a version of Jacques Derrida's *différence*, as both difference from the dominant discourse and deferral of the social meaning of the texts, is achieved. In addition, the thematics of repression suggest that the culture's apparent willingness to leave nothing unspeakable is itself a form of suppression of the racial and sexual traumas that constitute a significant but hidden part of the national narrative.[1]

Set in Harlem in the year (1925) in which the Harlem Renaissance anthology *The New Negro* was published and in which F. Scott Fitzgerald's *The Great Gatsby* helped define the Jazz Age, Morrison's novel is structured as gossip, with a narrator who claims to have knowledge of the secrets of her neighbors. One purpose of such a device is to problematize forms of desire and knowledge based on racialized and gendered assumptions.[2] These assumptions commodify and dehumanize their objects. It is this discourse that Morrison examines for its implications for that time and for ours.

Harlem Renaissance writers offered variations on two versions of black life: the folk and the black bourgeoisie.[3] Depending on the author's stance, the folk could be primitive or simple and good or lost in the city or resilient through their accumulated wisdom. The middle class might be worthy strivers or nightlife sports or versions of Jean Toomer's Rhobert carrying a house on his head. Primitives, prostitutes, tragic mulattoes, and the talented tenth, either artistic or economic, are all part of the worlds created by both the major and minor writers associated with the Renaissance.

What is missing from this apparently substantial catalog is simply the vast majority of African Americans who moved to Harlem and other Northern urban areas in the early twentieth century. This majority was made up of working people who migrated for largely the same reasons as other immigrants—greater economic opportunity and social and political freedom.[4] By focusing on those excluded from the discourse, Morrison can explore the essentializing practices that helped "sell" the Renaissance to its largely white audience. By creating a Renaissance narrator bent on telling a certain kind of tale, she can foreground the false images of blackness that persistently were projected. By creating a Jazz Age narrative, she can explore the constructions of the exotic and the Other that shaped American attitudes on race and gender in the 1920s. In doing so, Morrison offers not only a historical critique but also an analysis of the present.

One means by which this is done is the narrator's effort to turn the story of Joe, Violet, and Dorcas into black melodrama.[5] It can be noted in passing that her success in doing this is probably one source of the problems reviewers had with the novel. If the novel is defined generically as part of the romance tradition, then certain expectations about plot and character have to be fulfilled or the work "fails." Thus, Dorcas could be read as Rudolph Fisher's girl in a red dress, Countee Cullen's and Langston Hughes's jazz dancers, Toomer's Avey, Fitzgerald's Daisy, or Faulkner's Candace Compson. Golden Gray is everybody's tragic mulatto. Joe is the good country man deceived and seduced by the city woman. Violet is the simple country woman confused and finally driven to madness and violence by a world too sophisticated for her. The cast is completed with the stern older woman whose values are ignored by the young, the mother so primitive her name is Wild, and the coldhearted, vain urban hustler. By the rules of the melodramatic love story, when these elements are combined in the context of the city, the results are inevitable. Women will be concerned with appearance and will act irrationally, and men, especially black ones, will necessarily reveal their animal nature hidden beneath a sympathetic or sophisticated surface.

The novel appears to present such a version of urban life. Dorcas, like the young women of the 1920s represented in the media and literature of that time and later, is totally absorbed in appearance.[6] Her clothes, her hair, and her presentation of self get most of her attention. Repeated mention is made of the flaws in her skin, as well as its "yellow" color. Violet works as an unlicensed hair stylist, and her public appearance and behavior are commented on by virtually all the other characters. She is often said to act bizarrely and admits to having a kind of split personality. Joe is a supposedly trustworthy man who, when his love affair goes bad, hunts down and shoots his lover and can offer no clear explanation for his action. Such a story, with variations, was told by Zora Neale Hurston, Eric Walrond, Willis Richardson, Toomer, and Nella Larsen, as well as a number of white artists, in the 1920s and 1930s.[7]

Morrison interrogates this narrative in several ways. The first is by interrupting, in the middle of the novel, the voice of the narrator with those of key characters, including Joe, Violet, and Dorcas's friend Felice. These violations of the monologic structure permit alternative narratives that offer other explanations for the actions that occur and the experiences that the characters have had. Central to these stories is the role of family, especially mothers, in the shaping of character. What had been tales of individuals become much more relational in their meaning. In fact, it can be argued that the narrator's patriarchal story is changed into one of the loss and quest for mothers. Not merely different stories but different kinds of stories compete for control of the text.

Joe does not seek to dominate or possess. He seeks the truly loving touch of a woman. Like the other major characters, he is an orphan. Before coming north, he searches for the woman he believes is his mother, the one the community names Wild. He finds what he thinks is her shelter; in clear echo of the spiritual, he locates her home in that rock. He fails, however, to ever touch or even see her. She is ever elusive, that origin always out of his reach. In representing her as an absent presence, Morrison subverts notions of a nurturing unproblematic Southern past. It is Joe, not Wild, who generates a maternal source for his being. But this created source in fact makes him a man to be trusted by women. In Violet, he finds someone strong and decisive, someone not to be his mother, but to fit the image of woman reflected in his version of his mother. When Violet herself, for reasons discussed below, loses touch with him, he turns to Dorcas, who he believes he can make into that kind of woman despite her limitations. She evokes in him the intensity of feeling associated with Wild and the young Violet. When the girl tires of his love, his despair at being thrice abandoned drives him to forget the admonition of the Hunter's Hunter: "Never harm the young or the female." He makes the sentimental error of believing that he can have the love without the beloved. Dorcas has become an object for him, though an object of his love. Only after killing her does he realize his error and the true nature of his crime.

Dorcas facilitates his tragedy. She seeks to construct herself in the image of the good-time woman. But, as Morrison suggests, such a desire is a death wish. Dorcas seeks only to be possessed by the man that other women desire. But such self-fashioning is demystified in *Jazz*. Unlike Toomer, Hughes, and Cullen, Morrison shows the mystery only to be an emptiness based on cultural constructions of black womanhood. It is a category defined by promiscuity, submissiveness, and possession. What Joe seeks for Dorcas and from her, according to his story and Felice's, is a self that is hers. He would have her make herself new, just as he has done himself repeatedly. But she rejects subjectivity in favor of the object status of Acton's girlfriend. She associates such a condition with power and control. But its self-destructiveness is evidenced by Felice's assertion that Dorcas willed her own death, that Joe's shot would not have killed her. By refusing medical attention and bleeding to death, she created herself as the doomed heroine of her own melodrama.

Morrison goes even further by historicizing the choices Dorcas has. In the deaths of her parents in the riots of East St. Louis, in the antilynching march depicted in the novel, and in the moralistic repressiveness of her Aunt Alice Manfred, the young Dorcas is presented with no image of black womanhood that validates her emerging sensuality while granting her dignity. Both in style-conscious white New York and in modern Harlem, the calculating gaze of men defines her value. Alice tries to inculcate in her niece a version of female identity largely associated with an earlier era in which middle-class black women defined themselves in negation of stereotypes of promiscuity dating back to slavery.[8] But the city does not value such probity. Joe offers her the thrill of a dangerous liaison, but when he expects her to be a self rather than play a socially determined role, she repudiates him. The only part she can script for herself is one that has already been written, one that urban modernity both generated and reflected.

Violet is the character bearing the greatest weight of Morrison's cultural criticism, for she is the one in whom the constructions of race, gender, and region are most complexly embedded. Her orphanhood is distinct in that she sees her mother humiliated and psychologically destroyed years before she loses her through suicide. Her father's absence was forced through his political activism but then seems to become something more like irresponsibility. He makes sudden appearances bearing extravagant gifts but does nothing to relieve the poverty of his family. The grandmother, True Belle, comes back to care for the children and thus serves as a model of female strength, but she also tells stories of Golden Gray, the white-black son of her white mistress whom both mother and servant worship. In his golden-skinned beauty and arrogance, he becomes the idealized child that no dark-skinned child, especially a girl, can ever hope to equal.

Violet herself initially fails at even that most "black" of occupations: picking cotton. She nonetheless shows resilience and determination through first physical labor and then establishing a relationship with Joe. She appears to be perfectly adapted to the country, an image of the simple strong black woman at home on the land, an image beloved by American writers of all races and regions. But she dreams of the city, pulled in part by the stories of Golden Gray and his city manners, appearance, and sophistication. Despite her initial success, she soon develops "cracks" in her being, erratic behavior and increasing depression and self-absorption that pull her away from Joe. This alienation is in fact the reason Joe offers for his attraction to Dorcas.

Violet's behavior and condition are never clearly explained in the text. Both implicit explanations offered by the narrator fit the pattern of discursive conventions. One is that she is displaced in the city, that as a part of some essential folk, she cannot psychically function in an urban environment. This city-country dichotomy, so central to Harlem Renaissance literature, erases black history by creating essentialist types: the homeboy and the zoot-suiter, mammy and the good-time woman. Such images efface the re-creations and transformations of self and community that mark the African American experience. They also deny black subjectivity and agency. Thus, Violet must be "lost" because she made the naive error of moving out of her culturally assigned place.

The second explanation is that she has suffered emotional deprivation because she has had no children. Though childlessness was a choice both she and Joe had agreed to, this explanation suggests that when she has become too old to become pregnant, she realizes the folly of that choice. But her feelings about children seem to have more to do with her own childhood than with biological necessity. Having been deprived of happiness during her early years, she experiences a lack at the center of her being that nothing, not even her success at self-creation on her own terms, can satisfy. Filled with the stories of Golden Gray and the manufactured images of feminine beauty necessitated by her profession as hairdresser, she cannot accept herself. She fractures her being in trying to come to terms with her failure to be "woman." Children, the mysterious allure of Dorcas, and beauty are all puzzles she wants to solve, feels she must solve in order to be a real person. The image the narrator projects of her is that of an ugly, rather bizarre person. We learn only in Felice's comments near the end of the book that Violet is in fact physically beautiful.

The coming together of Joe, Violet, and Felice at the conclusion is the invention of the family that all of them have lacked. Each nurtures the other by providing some of what they felt secretly deprived of. It is not clear that this is a tidy resolution, but it does perhaps point the way to solution. Like Leon Forrest, Morrison uses a gathering of orphans rather than a family reunion as the best that can be hoped for. Even the narrator must finally acknowledge that she got it all wrong, and the reason was that she preferred conventional stories to human reality: "So I missed it altogether. I was sure one would kill the other. I waited for it so I could describe it. I was so sure it would happen. That the past was a abused record with no choice but to repeat itself at the crack and no power on earth could lift the arm that held the needle" (220).

The insistence on a master narrative, especially a patriarchal one, is central to American modernism as it emerged in the 1920s. When that narrative was told to please a white patron, or a white audience, or a black audience itself trained in believing the narrative rather than the experience, it produced the key texts of the Harlem Renaissance. The failure to deviate from the current version is also the failure Morrison is critiquing in our time. While the images may be somewhat different, contemporary discourse insists on the "reality" of irresponsible black men, immoral teenage mothers, wilding children. The media, both black and white, portray a black bourgeoisie safely striving in a nonracist world of suburban homes, good educations, celebrity, and wealth bought and paid for by affirmative action, bootstrap endeavor, and athletic and entertainment talents.

Thus, the dichotomized melodrama of Harlem in the 1920s is a parable of 1980s and 1990s America with its own narrative of good and bad blacks, of beasts and beauties, of romantic love and violent death. It is a narrative that serves various social and political purposes, such as validating the powerlessness and poverty of significant numbers of African Americans, dividing the loyalties of black men and women, evading responsibility for the moral and academic training of a generation of black children, and keeping African Americans out of any positions of significant power.

As she did in virtually all of her fictions before *Beloved*, Morrison here examines the negative role of social and cultural images in the shaping of black identity, especially with her female characters. The focus on the meaning of beauty, which in *The Bluest Eye* (1970), *Sula* (1973), and *Tar Baby* (1981) was centered on imitation of whiteness, becomes here, as it did in *Song of Solomon* (1977), the perfecting of appearance so as to satisfy perceived male demands. Dorcas meets Joe as he goes door to door selling cosmetics as a second job. But what he sees as merely a way to make money and as an irrelevancy to his desire for her, she understands as the very truth of herself. She eventually turns to Acton, whose demands she feels can in fact be met through manipulation of her appearance. Thus, for her, desire and its gratification must be understood in terms of what can be consumed, including the self. She can gain power only by becoming the object of Acton's gaze and his possession. Because he is seen as the dangerous man, the gangster, she must fashion herself to complement his status. Under such circumstances, she disdains Joe, who is truly dangerous in that he seems to require only that she truly become a self. But to do so in a world in which being black and female inhibit self-realization is to risk failure and powerlessness. Dorcas would in fact rather die than undertake that project.

Through this character, Morrison challenges cultural projections of black womanhood and forms of desire associated with it. She implicates all the central characters in the distortions that are produced and thus points to the internalization of such cultural activity and values and not just its imposition by the dominant society. Parallels to contemporary culture are readily apparent in this critique; emphasis on image, on style, and on the appearances of power often supplant concern for substance. It is important to note, for example, that Morrison edited a collection of commentaries on the Clarence Thomas–Anita Hill conflict, in which the truth of allegations was clearly secondary, in the nation generally and black communities specifically, to images and expressions of black desire.[9] She is consistently concerned with the possibilities for the shaping of black female selfhood, especially in a postmodern world in which, it would seem, "Image Is Everything." The effects of such conditions, the novel appears to say, are devastating.

But underlying these effects, in Morrison's terms, is the need to discredit black desire, the refusal to acknowledge substantial absences that generate such desire, and the resistance to satisfying legitimate desire. Such desire is not merely sexual, though as in the Hill–Thomas hearings and the welfare debates, the erotic serves as the focus. The discrediting of Anita Hill's testimony, like the attention given to the putatively irresponsible sexual behavior of young black women in the debates over public assistance, serve to render silent the voices of black women in representing their experience.

In this sense, Morrison, like other contemporary African American writers, does not fully accept the claims of postmodernism. Through the characters of Joe and Violet, she indicates that there is a core self that needs to be nurtured, that can be fractured and perhaps reconstructed. Meaningful education and work, a fair justice system, and media and marketing practices that accept the diversity and legitimacy of African American concerns need to replace images of black criminality and promiscuity that effectively undermine debates about poverty, affirmative action, and other aspects of black reality. Black success, in fields such as athletics and entertainment, in fact reinforces the problem by providing prominent examples of apparent racial transcendence.

Self-criticism is also implicit in *Jazz*. The title and the historical setting implicate cultural producers in the shaping of images of black life at that time and thus, by analogy, in ours. Just as Hughes, Cullen, Hurston, and others succeeded not only in creating but in marketing a version of blackness that emphasized good-time women, hustlers, and "the folk," so contemporary writers, including Morrison, have succeeded by emphasizing black suffering, victimization, and folk wisdom. Slavery, domestic abuse, and racial violence have been highly marketable since the early 1970s, in the larger society, as well as among blacks. A key question, then, is the relationship between speaking some important, uncomfortable truth about black experience and American culture and marketing a product in which that truth becomes simply more consumable goods. Legitimate needs and desires become conflated with the exploitative necessities of a market economy.[10] Race is confronted as an issue, not by engaging in a serious dialogue about the present, but by agreeing that the past was terrible. At the same time, no one has to take responsibility for that history, and it in fact can be used to rationalize the problems of the present. Consumer desire for stories of black suffering enables the refiguration of a racial Other that can be accepted without being engaged; it thereby also enables nonengagement with current African American experience except in manufactured media terms. At the same time, African Americans can embrace those produced images of past and present and not confront their own deepest desires. In this sense, it is telling that the movie version of *Beloved* was not a financial success in either white or black communities. Its suggestions that history is not completed, that some choices are permanently troubling, and that examination of the past is not necessarily therapeutic simply do not satisfy the desires of popular culture. It implies ongoing, insatiable lack, not simple gratification.

At the end of *Jazz*, when the narrator admits that she preferred the logic of a narrative form over the confusion of the experience itself, she is pointing to the key problem for the contemporary African American writer. Given postmodern culture, how is it possible to construct narrative in a manner that has some chance of being understood as the truth of experience? After all, each of the characters in the novel constructs both a self and a version of the world in an effort to satisfy basic needs; each of them, including the narrator, discovers the error of the construction. In fact, each effort seems to aggravate rather than ameliorate problems. Unlike Naylor, who in *Bailey's Cafe* appears to reinscribe rather than erase the master narrative, Morrison seems to suggest a possibility through a gathering of those who have suffered and a sharing of their perceptions. It is in both hearing and telling that recuperation can even be imagined. Significantly, this dialogic model requires the participation of the narrator, who must be willing to give up control of the story. And this surrender may be the model for the writer, though perhaps an impossible one, and a model for society, though probably even less possible there. In both arenas, a basic need is for order, completeness, and closure. Even in postmodern expression, irresolution tends to be seen as a construction by a knowing artist. *Jazz*, of course, is itself such a construction, but it implies its own unfulfilled desire: to be an ongoing conversation among those who have suffered and those who describe that suffering, with the unreachable goal of complete understanding and thus healing.

If Morrison's text concerns the social images of desire that can control human experience, Naylor's is about the violations of desire. If *Jazz* defines a place where the hopeful and deluded seek fulfillment, *Bailey's Cafe* creates a space where the lost and violated gather. As she did in *Mama Day* with Willow Springs, Naylor constructs Bailey's Cafe as a "no place," as a site only in the geography of the imagination. While the characters come from very specific locations, the cafe itself exists at some edge of the world: the back door opens into an empty space from which some never return. The text makes it very clear that Bailey's exists for reasons having nothing to do with business:

> They don't come for the food and they don't come for the atmosphere. One or two of the smart ones finally figure that out, like I figured out that I didn't start in this business to make a living—personal charm is not my strong point—or stay in it to make a living—kind of hard to do that when your wife is ringing up the register and it's iffy when and how much she'll charge.
>
> No, I'm at this grill for the same reason that they keep coming. And if you're expecting to get the answer in a few notes, you're mistaken. The answer is in who I am and who my customers are. (3–4)

The cafe exists for the sake of the stories, which are narratives of suffering, especially those of women. But the telling has little to do with either the creation of community or the amelioration of pain. Bailey (which is not his actual name, adding another level of concealment) introduces the characters by telling what he knows of their background and personality. After this frame, the voice of the character takes over in most instances, but it is not clear whether what is spoken is heard by anyone. Given the intimate and usually humiliating nature of the experiences, it is improbable that they would be spoken. In the liminal space of the cafe, they simultaneously are and are not speech. Naylor uses this device as a means of speaking the unspeakable. What is rendered as dialogue is seldom significant in itself; only in the context of the interior monologues does it carry much meaning.

This method of voicing the stories also allows for development of the theme of muteness.[11] Bailey is the most voluble of the characters, but much of his talk is about the pointlessness of oral discourse or the keys to understanding silence. Thus, he discusses his wife Nadine's preference for silence, suggesting that talk for her has always been unnecessary; his story of their relationship largely concerns his frustration with her quietness, in part because he understands verbal expression as the principal means of validating the self and relationships. Virtually the only time she speaks in the novel is when she tells the story of Miriam, a story that Bailey is reluctant to tell, apparently because it is simply too much of a "woman's" narrative for a man to speak.

But Nadine's silence is different from that of the others in that it appears to be a matter of choice, not compulsion, and a form of power over Bailey and others. She can remain mysterious, even in her ordinariness, and can have an aura of wisdom and profundity without having to articulate any insights. In a sense, she validates a notion of female muteness that Naylor approves, in that it represents choice, normality, and sanity. Consistent with this view, the relationship of Bailey and Nadine reflects an approved mode of desire in that their history together appears to be a straightforward heterosexual bond that in no way exceeds convention.

Setting this standard allows Naylor to intensify the experiences of silence and desire that shape the other narratives. These other stories thus become distortions almost to the point of parody. It is not enough for a lower-class woman to be subjected to the destructive hostility of her husband's upper-class family; she must also become a heroin addict and apparently be "driven" to lesbianism. It is not enough for a young woman to suffer genital mutilation; she must also be pregnant through immaculate conception and have somehow arrived at the cafe from her isolated Ethiopian village. Through these extremes, Naylor breaks the boundaries of contemporary black women's narrative, as though that pattern had reached a dead end. The work of ntozake shange, Alice Walker, early Toni Morrison, and Naylor herself is pushed in the direction of the outrageousness of talk shows and tabloid journalism. Pushing the stories back fifty years does not conceal this emphasis; rather, it lays claim to its pervasiveness and historicity.

A crucial question is the reason for such displacement: if Naylor is constructing tales that could fit within contemporary discourse, why not set them in the present? One reason would appear to be her implicating of women's desire in narratives of suffering. Such a claim would find little acceptance within current womanist and feminist thinking. Locating such views in the past permits misdirection of responsibility onto the oppression of an earlier patriarchal social formation. Society at that time, goes the argument, made the victim guilty of desire, and the narrative is simply representing that reality. But, as shall be seen, this is in fact a concealment of textual antagonism to desire itself.

Each of the stories of women is built on a distortion of female desire. Either the initial desire itself or the response to punishments or perversions of it is shown to be abnormal in some way. At the same time, the narratives clearly indicate the destructive effects of mistreatment of these characters by either men or women who accept a patriarchal vision of women's reality. Assuming that the novel has as its intended audience women conditioned to think in womanist/feminist terms,[12] oppression will be assumed and female guilt ignored. But the exaggerations of experience, the neurotic/psychotic responses, and the centrality of male voices subvert such a reading.

The story of Eve provides one of the milder examples. An orphan, she has been taken in by a man she refers to as Godfather, whose reasons for such generosity are never made clear. What is clear is the severity of his moral views and his almost sadistic nature. He appears to delight, for example, in refusing to give accurate information about her birthdate. He also hates her sexual development and the doubts in the community about his motives for taking care of her. In many ways a Faulknerian character, he finds desire, especially in women, to be morally reprehensible. Nonetheless, Eva claims that the community, with its lecherous men and self-righteous women, is more responsible than he is for what happens to her.

When she discovers the pleasures of the body through a form of masturbation, she becomes obsessed with intensifying the experience; part of the intensification includes performing the act in ever-more-public venues. Her behavior requires the participation of a mentally defective boy, who must be compelled and bribed to continue involvement in a practice he does not understand. Thus, Eve, who claims to understand the meaning of the looks she gets from men and the attitudes of the community's women, does not represent herself as an innocent, and thus her behavior cannot be seen as that of an unknowing child. She courts discovery and punishment, and it is not surprising that it is severe. But part of the reason for her punishment would seem to be her ingratitude; Godfather does everything for Eve, including cooking and laundry.

Godfather's response depends on Naylor's exaggeration of a literary type in portraying him. He is self-righteous, angry, and capable of great cruelty, in the tradition of Maceachern in Faulkner's *Light in August* and Brownfield in Walker's *Third Life of Grange Copeland*. In this case, after finding her, he strips her, burns all the clothes he has provided her, gives her purgatives to clean out all the food and drink she has had from his generosity, and sends her literally naked and penniless out into the world. The extremity of behavior here, which again Eve blames more on the community than the man, cuts close to the edge of parody as a response to female desire. Simple physical abuse or suppression will no longer do as a means of denouncing patriarchy; the cruelties must be grotesque. The result is equally inflated: after walking from the Delta to New

Orleans clad only in a burlap bag, she leaves the city ten years later a wealthy and powerful woman. Since she thanks Godfather for the toughness that enabled her to survive the journey and attain the success, it is hard to read this narrative as a clear-cut parable of male evil. It would seem to argue at least as much as an indictment of sensuality.

What Eve becomes by the time of Bailey's narrative only reinforces this notion. She owns what is variously called a boardinghouse and a brothel. The text evades revealing its real function. Eve chooses the women who will live there very carefully and provides them with what might be taken as refuge. But it is a refuge that offers little in the way of solace or healing. Each of the women whose stories we hear has undergone a version of Eve's experience. In every case, desire ends in horrifying behavior with devastating effects. But Eve does not attempt to make life better for them in any conventional sense. Rather, she gives them the space to play out their troubles in whatever manner they choose, including endless reenactment of their violation. While it can be argued that Eve simply insists on attention to and respect for the women as they are (she requires male visitors to purchase very expensive flowers of the woman's choice), what happens in the rooms seems to only reinforce the suffering they have had to endure.

Thus, for example, Esther, who had been the child-bride victim of a husband who purchased her in order to use her in sadistic sexual practices in his dark cellar, lives in the unlighted basement of Eve's house where such practices apparently go on. What happened during her childhood experience and what happens now at Eve's is not made explicit. Esther, like Celie in *The Color Purple*, is specifically forbidden by her husband to speak of his behavior, and she continues this prohibition in the narrative present. But speaking *about* the unspeakable rather than actually speaking of it has the effect of continuing to mystify it and perpetuating Esther's suffering through endless repetition of the initial violation. Both Bailey and Eve describe Esther's hatred of men, but the narrative suggests her need of such men to sustain her identity as victim. She effectively keeps alive the memory of pain precisely by refusing to speak of it; she constructs a self that does not seek healing, and Eve is complicit in helping her keep alive the trauma.

This story and those of Jesse and Mary (Peaches) can be read as elaborate parables of the historical traumas suffered by black women. They are stories of exploitation, of physical and mental abuse, of sexual violation by black men and white, within and outside families. But they problematize the black feminist narrative model by showing the women to be self-destructive, resistant to healing, and locked in continuing exploitative practices. Unlike the narratives of Walker, shange, Morrison, and McMillan, and even to some extent Naylor's own *Women of Brewster Place*, *Bailey's Cafe* does not suggest that a sisterhood of color can provide healing through self-expression and the laying on of hands. Both Eve's place and Bailey's only provide spaces within which characters can bear witness (sometimes silently) to the suffering they have endured. The suffering itself must go on.

The contrast within the novel is significant. The one traumatized figure who manages to move beyond his troubles is a man temporarily disguised as a woman. What distinguishes "Miss Maple's" chapter is not only the gender of the central character but also the emphasis on public rather than private concerns. While Maple's narrative does give attention to the psychological effects of his experiences, the experiences themselves involve racial violence, war, job discrimination, and an emergent positivist culture. Moreover, Miss Maple's "abnormality," cross-dressing, is seen as a product of rational conscious choice that can be changed and is not essential to his personality or identity. In addition, at the time he is introduced by Bailey, he has devised a means of overcoming the problems he faced and has largely, in his terms (and terms generally accepted within the text), achieved success.

Miss Maple provides Naylor with the opportunity to explore notions of black masculinity, both historically and in the context of contemporary culture. The saga of Maple's family is itself an American multicultural success narrative. His grandparents, a never-enslaved black man and a Yuma woman, move to the California desert, where they endure hardship for many years until water is finally brought to the Imperial Valley. They then become wealthy by raising cotton. Their sons receive educations at the Indian missionary school and themselves become successful farmers. The eighth son,[13] Maple's father, is different in his interest in sophisticated urban style and high culture. He is called "butter britches" by his brothers and is the target of insult among whites who consider him "uppity." It is through him that Maple comes to a different understanding of black manhood. First, he gives his son a long name linked to racial history:

My name is Stanley. My middle names are Beckwourth Booker T. Washington Carver. The T. is for Taliaferro. Most people don't know that's what the initial stands for in Booker T. Washington's name, and they don't know that James P. Beckwourth was a scout who discovered the lowest point for wagon trains to cross the Sierras, getting the Beckwourth Pass and the town of Beckwourth, California, all thrown in for the effort. Someone like Sugar Man, who thinks he has the right to ridicule me for my choice of clothes, doesn't even know where the Sierras are, or that colored pioneers like Beckwourth existed, or that George Washington Carver did a lot more for the world than refine peanut butter. Whenever he licks a postage stamp this season to send out those misspelled Christmas cards to whoever has the misfortune of his knowing their address, he gives no thanks to Carver for it not falling off the envelope. That's because he's only been taught what we call American history. (165)

Thus, even the apparently pretentious naming of his child is the father's effort to subvert assumptions about what it means to be black, though the son does not initially understand this. In fact, it is only through a traditional masculine experience of physical violence that the father's power becomes apparent. The son has always been somewhat ashamed of his parent, in essence agreeing with the brothers' evaluation. This is only reinforced when the father endures the humiliations inflicted by whites. The crisis comes when, significantly, father and son go to pick up the child's graduation gift, an expensive collection of Shakespeare. A group of racists, infuriated by the father's style and envious of such an extravagant gift, strip both of them and lock them in a freight room. After the son's explosion of anguish and anger at yet another degradation caused, he believes in part, by his parent's "effeminate" manner, the two of them don the only clothes in the freight room, women's dresses, and break out of their prison. The father then proceeds to single-handedly beat his attackers senseless, all the time proclaiming that violence is inappropriate.

The effect is that the son adopts his own version of the father's approach. He becomes a Stanford Ph.D. in statistical analysis; he chooses prison over service in World War II; and he submits to sexual abuse in prison rather than risk his life. In place of the father's high culture, he takes refuge in numbers, probabilities, and pragmatic action. When he applies for professional jobs, he is offered janitorial positions; but instead of anger, he responds with analysis by testing whether racism is in fact the cause for his lack of success. His efforts parody the work of social scientists who seek to quantify obvious injustice and offer elaborate and obfuscating explanations for it. What is significant in Maple's case is that he never questions his own abilities or selfhood and thus contradicts a model of victimization. He eventually adopts dresses in part because his appearance (in terms of clothes, not skin color) clearly has no bearing on his job prospects and because women's styles are more comfortable in hot weather, when he suffers rashes. He finally takes a position as a maid for Eve, because the work is easy and he has time to make investments for her, as well as himself, and because it provides him with the opportunity to analyze consumer culture and to profit from it. He specializes in advertising slogans, which he constructs from his analyses of what leads women to purchase products.

Through Miss Maple, Naylor is able to comment on several aspects of contemporary culture in ways she seems unable to do through her female characters. She addresses in some manner affirmative action, consumerism, and constructions of black masculinity. Most deeply, she raises important questions about desire. First, by presenting Maple as a "model Negro," she undermines claims of African American lack of qualification. What he does, at the time he does it, is absolutely essential to the emergence of a positivist, consumerist postwar society. The text repeatedly points to the accuracy and value of the kinds of analysis Maple does; his ability is never questioned by those who refuse to employ him. The elaborateness of his self-study points to the pervasiveness of racism even when it works against the self-interests of those discriminating. The narrative necessity of developing variations within the pattern suggests all the nuances of racist practice and the costs to a society that sustains that practice. The displacement in time protects Naylor from entrapment in late-1980s/early-1990s ideological discourse on affirmative action, while the nature of her character's skills and efforts reflect her strategy of engagement with the issue.

Similarly, Maple's "way to wealth" through advertising slogans reveals the exploitative practices of consumerist culture. He literally calculates the verbal mechanisms by which desire for goods can be generated. The fact that corporations are willing to pay him well for these media products but not hire him to do the work for which he was trained suggests a linkage between consumerism and race. An invisible "Miss Maple" who sends in ideas that will profit the company is valued, while a visible "Stanley," a black man on whom the company might become dependent because of his knowledge, must be rejected. "He" would force a rethinking of fundamental assumptions about racial differences, while "she" fits the model of woman's role as strengthening consumption.

The ambiguity associated with gender in the Miss Maple section allows the author to examine the meaning of black masculinity. She posits an alternative to the social construction of African American men as "Monster," to use the title of an autobiography of the early 1990s.[14] This image, as a product of both white media and gangsta culture, in conjunction with the valorization of the black athlete, reinforced the idea of the black man as what Eldridge Cleaver in the 1960s called the "Supermasculine Menial," an aggressive figure whose physicality was his defining characteristic. Naylor, in effect, speculates about what a black man who was freed from fulfilling that combined race and gender role might be capable of. Being highly intelligent, he sees the limitations of violence and other aspects of conventional masculinity. Guided by reason, he does not see the logic of fighting in a war, or of resisting sexual assault, or, at a more superficial level, of adopting usual fashion standards. And because his sense of identity is associated more with his intellect than his gender, his choices do not cause him to question his sexual identity. He is capable of physical action, as his role as Eve's bouncer indicates, but he understands it as only an insignificant part of his being. His flexibility and confidence enable him to find success and relative comfort even when the world appears to reject him, as it does the other characters in the novel. Through him, Naylor simultaneously posits the narrowness of contemporary constructions of black manhood and the possibilities of a more open approach to identity.

A crucial issue is why the author chooses a male character as the one who is able to transcend the oppressions and violations that form the plots of the individual narratives. The only other figure who comes close to Maple's achievement is Eve, but as already indicated, her "house" is as much a prison as a refuge. While it reconstructs the space of sexuality as woman-controlled, it continues to construct woman as an essentially sexual being. Miss Maple is able to sublimate his masculine desire into the accumulation of wealth by moving beyond bipolar gender identities, but the female characters seem to be locked into their roles of women as sexual victims, doomed to either reenact their violations or make choices in reaction to those violations.

Thus, Naylor, ironically, reinscribes female essentialism within a text that undertakes to demonstrate the ongoing exploitation of women. Her female characters do not appear to have selves or possibilities different from those determined by their suffering. Moreover, she proposes that it is sexual desire itself that is the source of suffering. The male characters in the women's stories are monstrous in their behavior (and thus contradict Miss Maple), but the women are also guilty, primarily of desire. Thus, Naylor offers a cautionary tale that validates suppression of desire, especially in women, at the very time that other writers, such as Walker and McMillan, are calling for greater freedom.

Chapter Six

THE COLOR OF DESIRE

*Folk History in the Fiction of
Raymond Andrews*

The novels of Raymond Andrews are primarily stories of black men in the South in the early to mid-twentieth century. They concern themselves with the struggles for a strong masculine identity during the time African American men were commonly referred to by whites as "boys" and the time when those same whites selectively used racial violence as a means of political and social emasculation. In this sense, the texts, like those of Ernest Gaines, "bear witness" to the struggles for black manhood in a context in which such an identity was presumed by many, primarily but not exclusively whites, to imply danger and criminality. But in its religious sense, such witness has always linked hope with suffering, and so it is with these texts. Manhood can be achieved, for some in death and for others in a reshaping of their relationship to the social order.

In offering possibility within a framework of trouble, both Gaines and Andrews speak to the present in the framework of narratives of the past. Recent representations of the black man as "endangered," as "monster," or as "gangsta" are challenged by exposing how such constructions operate in the larger culture and by showing the varieties of actual black male experience. Narratives that use folk methods—storytelling, legends, tales, folk religion, and ritual—suggest that oral tradition reveals a version of black life profoundly different from that of "official" history. Gaines and Andrews also signify on literary history to force a reconsideration of its role in the discourse of the South and of the nation. While the modes of narrative are different—Andrews is essentially comic and Gaines tragic—the underlying aim is the same: to reconstruct the image of the black man in a way that more accurately reflects his experience. In Andrews's Muskhogean County trilogy (1978–83), the focus is primarily on sons who first feel victimized by the lack of fathers and use this condition to justify their own failures, but then father themselves, often with the help of female figures, into some new notion of masculinity. Through this pattern, Andrews can speak to both the external and internal forces that shape maleness and can suggest alternatives to essentialized and destructive definitions of race and gender. As Andrews says in the preface to *Appalachee Red* (1978), "In our lives we have our daily soap operas of religious fanatics, intellects, prudes, materialists, radicals, conservatives, murderers, philanthropists, racists, dancers, cowboys, and all the other 'characters' any race of people offers. But sadly, because of television and the cinema, most people now regard Afro-Americans chiefly in terms of the inner-city ghettos with their crime, drugs, and poverty. Such a world exists, but it is one I never knew" (x).

In this sense, Andrews can bear witness to both the past and the present. The references here are to blaxploitation films and to 1970s television programming, where, whether in comedy or drama, black life was limited either to the urban hipster/gangster or to variations on the *Roots* family saga. His catalog of the options for black subject positions serves to emphasize the narrowness within which representation has been confined by the media. Similarly, Nixon administration policies of benign neglect and Southern strategy, which were extended into the Reagan administration, made use of similar images in order to justify such racist programs. By shifting the emphasis from white racism to black failure to take advantage of opportunities provided by a now "color-blind" society, government policies enabled a white backlash against the achievements of the civil rights movement.[1] Black men (and women) were presumably no longer under attack because of their skin color or genes but because they had deep character flaws that made them lazy and often criminal. As Robin D. G. Kelley notes:

Lest we forget, Richard M. Nixon was in the White House, attacking black welfare mothers and blaming the black poor for their own poverty. Nixon's domestic advisor, Daniel Patrick Moynihan, passed on a confidential memo proposing that "the time may have come when the issue of race could benefit from a period of 'benign neglect.'" Much of the white middle class agreed. They believed that African Americans received too many government handouts. They were tired of "paying the bill," especially now that racism had allegedly been eliminated with the Civil Rights movement. (5)

Raymond Andrews responds to the historical moment by suggesting that things change less than they might appear to, that blacks had in fact always been energetic in pursuit of their own interests, that race has always been secondary to money, sex, and power, and finally, like many in the tradition of satire, that everyone in the society is deeply flawed and thus subject to comic deflation.

Moreover, the pursuit of ideology to the neglect of underlying human desires generally produces an ironic inversion of what the ideologue seeks.

A clue to Andrews's specific purpose can be found in his preface to the second volume of the trilogy, *Rosiebelle Lee Wildcat Tennessee* (1980). In it, he describes a reunion of his wife's family in their native village in Switzerland. The occasion is a celebration of the eighty-fifth birthday of the patriarch. When Andrews has an opportunity to talk to the old man, he learns of the pride associated with having a family history. In a moment of insight, "it came home to roost that one didn't have to be Swiss, foreign, rich, or even old, to have a family history. . . . Even *I* had one!—one, it occurred to me, just as important as anyone's and certainly as interesting as most, if not more so" (xiii–xiv). This passage can be read as an act of signifying on James Baldwin's "Stranger in the Village," in which the author describes his isolation in a Swiss village where he feels himself a freak and contemplates his difference from the villagers in that they, unlike him, have automatic connection to the achievements of Western culture. Far from his birthplace, Andrews sees the way back to his "postage-stamp of native soil" and, like Faulkner, begins the creation of a historic, imaginary landscape. But the story Andrews can tell as a result of this revelation changes not only the Baldwinian perspective but also the Faulknerian one. The focal memory is of his grandmother, "a black-Indian maverick who met and mated with a white maverick": "Rather than conform to the Code of the Old South by marrying a white woman and keeping a Negress for sport, he dared to have only *one* woman, a black one, Jessie Rose Lee Wildcat Tennessee, whom he put up in a fine house and on land considered at the time befitting a 'white lady.' So pissed became his peers at this white man of their own class upsetting the existing order that they, the ruling class, disowned him, automatically making him open game for the Ku Klux Klan" (xiv–xv).

Thus Andrews offers a narrative of transgression that draws its energy not from the tragic aspects of the color line but from the ironic and comic aspects of boundary-crossing. He does not have brooding Joe Christmases or Ike Mc-Caslins trying to come to terms with their "blood." Instead, he explores the universality of human desire—sexuality, greed, pride, power—that both constructs and transcends race as a delimiting category. Andrews offers instances of the oppressive uses of racial difference, often in graphic violence, but he also suggests that victims who understand the underlying sources of their oppression can manipulate the social order to their permanent advantage. Oppressors are vulnerable precisely because their need to dominate reflects desire and therefore lack. Victims can gain power through apparent, self-conscious gratification of that need.

The strong characters in Andrews's fiction are those who understand this fundamentally flawed human nature and their own desires. In his universe, strength and weakness are not defined necessarily by race or gender; these simply establish the conditions under which strength or weakness is displayed. Thus, Andrews can also be seen as challenging any claim that blacks are limited to a life and a world defined by their oppressors. The possibilities that his characters develop show a reluctance to accept any version of a culture of poverty or victimization. His stories signify on the dominant culture's manipulation of racial representation, especially about black men; ironically, he does this by constructing images that in fact validate conservative values of individualism, self-help, and flawed human nature. His point is that African Americans now and always have embodied these values. The joke, for him, is on all those, whether white racists or black nationalists, who have insisted on racial difference as a fundamental, biological truth.

While the trilogy is in some sense the saga of two families whose patriarchs are white, and while two of the novels are named for key black female characters, it is nonetheless the stories of black men that are central. The distinguishing feature of Andrews's work is that those men construct their identities largely in relationship to white fathers, either literal or symbolic. Other characters—especially white sons or black daughters—define themselves in the context of this core relationship. In his narrative, matters of race are secondary to patriarchy in shaping identity and fate. By making this story a comic one, Andrews in essence creates a parody of the black narrative popularized in *Roots*, the television version of *The Autobiography of Miss Jane Pittman*, and Margaret Walker's *Jubilee*. Each of those works attempted to construct a noble black history that was also racially essentialist. Black fathers (and sometimes mothers), with no white ancestors, suffered for the sake of future generations, with a special emphasis on achieving freedom. Theirs were stories of endless sacrifice; any characters who focused on material benefits or compromise with the ideal were portrayed as lesser beings. Andrews largely turns this story upside down, by showing persistent interracial sexual activity and constant pursuit of material well-being.

Appalachee Red opens with the story of fathers black and white. In a tone approaching that of the tall tale, Andrews tells the World War I–era story of Big Man Thompson, a black man imprisoned for being in the wrong place. Justice is swift and sure in his case, and he ends up on a chain gang for a year. Within a few paragraphs, Andrews has established the racial oppression operating in the early-twentieth-century South. The basic unfairness of the system and the effective silencing of the black man caught in that system echo Richard

Wright's narratives about the same time period. But the more recent author's interests are not primarily racism and injustice. He takes these as givens and focuses his attention on the modes of survival under such conditions. He does describe the horrific conditions of the prison and chain gang; in fact, he suggests that both blacks and whites have adapted to this social order. One black man, for example, escapes from the prison to deliver a message to Big Man's wife and then returns the next morning before roll call.

It is the wife, Little Bit, who must make adjustments to the situation. Eighteen and a new bride, she must find a way to earn money. She gets what is considered an excellent job with the Morgan family, but she soon discovers that, in order to keep it, she must become the mistress of the oldest son, John, just returned from the First World War. Though she loves Big Man and has no desire to be involved in any way with any other man, she also understands that she must provide for herself. Out of this relationship comes a "red" child, a boy that Little Bit manages to send off with her sister to Chicago before the return of Big Man. What she does not get rid of is the large house that John Morgan builds for her in the center of the black neighborhood.

Here, Andrews is developing his own version of what Houston Baker has called the "economics of slavery" (*Blues, Ideology, and Afro-American Literature*, 23–31). Because of their status within a white-dominated society, blacks are economically dependent. The law, social practice, and supremacist ideology make up a discernible universe in which blacks are objectified as criminal and sexual slave. Fifty years after Emancipation, the black voice and black desire count for nothing in the social order. The black body can be violated in a variety of ways with impunity. The benefits that may derive from manipulation of the social circumstances in fact symbolize the state of dependence. Thus, Big Man calls Little Bit's house the White House, with both racial and political implications. When he cannot persuade his wife to move out of the house, Big Man begins fighting with her every day, beating her and being cut by her razor in return. This ritualized violence is the means of responding to the emasculating effects of living in the house built by John Morgan as payment (in the form of gift) for Little Bit's sexual favors. For her, the house represents compensation for the degradation she had to endure, degradation that, paradoxically, the black community sees as raising her status to the highest level. Material possession becomes the substitute for the recognition of her self that racist society will not permit. Thus, husband and wife are locked into fundamental conflict because of their subaltern condition. Those who control the social order remain untouched and, essentially, untouchable. Black-on-black violence is the only means of articulating frustration and humiliation.[2]

From early in the novel, Andrews is obviously interested in the connections among economics, psychology, and sexuality, then and now. The black body is an instrument of dominance by those who can control or buy it, and the implications are complex. Whether they are the bodies of women used as servants or sexual toys, those of black men used as laborers or lynched symbols of racial control, or those of athletes or entertainers, they find themselves at the mercy of those who control the power and the money. But Little Bit also suggests Andrews's take on the "welfare queen," a common representation of 1970s and 1980s political rhetoric: The black female body joins long-standing views of black promiscuity to manipulation of a social system designed to provide economic assistance.[3] In this reading, the novel suggests that the payment of assistance serves to perpetuate this stereotype rather than offering a means to escape dependency.

This social order remains in place well into the 1940s, including the killing of Big Man by the Nazi-like Sheriff Boots White. It begins to change with the appearance of Red, a stranger whose racial identity cannot be clearly determined. Having established the binary of black and white in the first part of the first novel, Andrews devotes the rest of the trilogy to undermining and complicating it. Physical difference in the form of skin color defines, in a race-oriented society, social status, political standing, economic condition, culture, and personal identity. In the trilogy, almost every character knows and places him/herself on the basis of race and is also so understood by others. Even the crossing of racial boundaries, as in the case of John Morgan and Little Bit Thompson, is defined by the rules of the social order. By emphasizing boundary-crossings, Andrews can articulate the dialectic by which the racial formation both sustains and destroys itself. But by repeatedly pointing to the confusion caused by such crossings and by characters of indeterminate race, such as Red, the author makes clear the extent to which race is a social construction necessary for the fulfillment of the basic desires of sex, power, and money.

The title character of the novel, Appalachee Red, is able to transgress the social order because he cannot be easily placed within it. Through him, Andrews can explore what has come to be called the "constructedness" of race. He is able to maintain an aura of mystery and power in large part because he does not fit the binary of black and white, a situation he manipulates to his advantage. Even Boots White is intimidated by him. Because Red is not clearly black, he cannot be treated as an inferior, subject to abuse; he might, after all, prove to be an influential white man. Because he is not clearly white, he ought to be subject to white authority; yet he does not behave as though White has any power over him. He is the true Other in a system that cannot name or position him; as such, he has freedom and power not available to others.

A closed society generally maintains itself by destroying or evicting aliens. Red avoids that fate by demonstrating an understanding of social needs and desires, especially the illicit ones. As transgressor himself, he enables the transgressions of others. He supplies gambling and illegal liquor, pays bribes to both public officials and ministers, while remaining largely invisible. He acquires a cafe through mysterious means that include the unexplained death of its owner. He even manages to liberate the sheriff's black sexual slave, Baby Sweet, without suffering any apparent consequences. Because his own motives and maneuvers are secret, a body of legend grows up around him. Blacks, who cannot imagine themselves able to do what he does and who cannot imagine a white man relating to them as he does, construct versions of his past that explain the anomaly. Their oral tradition is matched by that of whites who "know" that no black man is capable of such behavior yet cannot imagine any white man willing to share the lives of blacks. Together they seek to fit him into their discursive universe. This effort clearly suggests Andrews's underlying point that blacks and whites together generate and sustain the existing racial formation. It is not simply a matter of a dominant group imposing an ideology on subordinates. Thus, he would appear to make an essentially neoconservative point that blacks can and should move beyond race in order to achieve a better place in American society. But his perspective is not quite that straightforward.

What the readers understand that the other characters do not is that Red's efforts are motivated in part by his desire for recognition within the patriarchal structure. His first appearance in the novel takes place when he is dropped off by John Morgan Jr. at the bottom of Morgan Hill, the location of the family estate. What no one in the town knows, and what virtually none of them ever learn, is that he is the child of Little Bit and John Morgan Sr. He is, in fact, the oldest son of both. But since he is the product of miscegenation in a racist society, he cannot be granted his appropriate place within a traditional society. What could be a Faulknerian tragedy of obsession and frustration comparable to *Light in August* or *Go Down, Moses* becomes instead a dark comedy as Red gains his revenge by taking the black woman Baby Sweet away from the authority figure Boots White and by corrupting the town fathers through his gambling and bootlegging operations. He, in effect, constructs an alternative order within the society, one that grants status to blacks and makes whites dependent on him for those things—money, liquor, sex—that they desire even more than racial domination. In fact, this point is central to the meaning of his narrative: there are in reality desires that are much stronger than racial supremacy, and it is only necessary to recognize them in order to change reality.

Denied the identity to which he feels entitled, Red constructs a counterself that, with its emphasis on control and behind-the-scenes manipulation, replicates and subverts the invisible power of John Morgan. At the closing of the narrative, he completes his revenge by carrying off Morgan's young daughter, Roxanne, who has been presented throughout the book as fascinated and even sexually obsessed with him. But she is, of course, also his sister. Thus, incest is the natural outcome of a racist order that makes the white woman a sacred object and the (black) Other a sexualized one. Again, as an act of signifying on Faulkner, incest is the comically rather than suicidally embraced end of Southern history.

Andrews links this localized violation of taboo to larger national concerns. In addition to the key figures of Red and Sheriff Boots White, we have Blue, the child of Big Man and Little Bit, who becomes a civil rights activist and incorruptible opponent of his light-skinned brother. These three sons of legendary fathers emblematize not only the American South of the post–World War II era in their almost stereotypical roles of violent segregationist, civil rights worker, and materialist "Negro" but also the America of the 1970s, of Nixonian Southern strategies and political corruption, of the emergence of the new black bourgeoisie, and of attenuated efforts for social justice. They also represent the nation's past, present, and future: White as the old supremacist power, Red as the subversion of that power, and Blue as the new order. And in the author's view, it is not the nobility of the fight for justice but the recognition and manipulation of desire and power that moves history forward.

In Andrews's vision, this is not a smooth transition; it more closely resembles apocalypse. Red's killing of White and carrying away of Roxanne, with her eager cooperation, are not merely acts of personal revenge; they embody the great American racial fear that the black man will take away the white daughter and displace white power. By specifically dating this event, Andrews connects it to national disaster:

When word of the sheriff's killing went out into every crevice of Appalachee that night, the town's white populace—truly believing God to be dead on this maddening Friday, November 22, 1963—quickly got off the streets and took to their homes, where most of them barricaded themselves in with supplies of arms, ammunition, food, water, Band-Aids, television guides, and toilet paper. And on this particular night there blew a wind from north to south, bringing with it across the Great Divide of Morgan Drive noises that came from over behind the Great Wall [separating black and white communities] of Appalachee. These noises came to settle in the air over the still and darkened homes of the white community, where most of them sat imprisoned beneath their own roofs, listening silently and uncomfortably to the eerie sounds . . . sounds like the beating of tom-tom drums. The pendulum had swung. (282–83)

The swinging of the pendulum suggests a rhythm of history, not an end of it. The killing of Boots White, like the assassination of John Kennedy, does not mean the absolute end of one order and beginning of another. It means a shift in relationship and perception. Given Andrews's sympathy for the practical, entrepreneurial mode of Red, Rosiebelle Lee Wildcat Tennessee, Baby Sweet, and John Morgan Jr., it is not surprising that he presents history in this way. The revolution is made, not by destroying the white father, but by taking his daughter, or having his children, or using his means to accomplish one's own purposes. Blacks enter the realms of power using the methods available to them. This is not the way of ideal justice, as Blue would prefer, but it is the way of human nature. Neither Camelot nor a white supremacist utopia is part of human reality; the claimants to such places will be destroyed.

Such a conclusion to the first novel suggests its role as parody of the long-standing and fundamental fears of white society. Through his comic rendering, Andrews connects race, sexuality, politics, and economics. Whites oppress blacks, not because they believe in black inferiority, but because they believe their own mythology about black male potency and the potential for violence aimed at white privilege. The riots of the 1960s, the race-baiting rhetoric of the Wallace, Nixon, and Reagan campaigns, and the representations of black sexuality throughout the period imply an anxiety about what true equality and justice might involve. Red as hypermasculine, intelligent, shrewd, cold-blooded, and racially invisible serves as Andrews's commentary on those fears.

This sensibility does not make Andrews's narratives particularly cynical. All of his significant characters have good reasons for taking the approaches that they do. They experience injustice, cruelty, reification, and/or invisibility. Some become locked into that experience and lose themselves; the successful ones adapt without forgetting. Thus, Rosiebelle Lee, whose beauty led a jealous white man to beat her black lover nearly to death, begins a new life near Appalachee by mating with the richest white man in the area. Through her position, she acquires property and status in both the black and white communities. Her motive, as she makes clear late in her narrative, is to protect, to the extent she can, herself and black men: "I went right to the top myself 'n got the big white man hisself, Mist' Mac. When you got the big white man, ain' no other white man gonna mess wid you, lest he git hisself kilt. . . . No cullud man got kilt, or even whupped, heah in Plain View 'cause o' me. I'se right proud of that" (239).

No distinction is made here between ethical behavior and personal advantage. In a world in which love is dangerous and justice is defined by power, it is impossible to simply stand for what is good, true, and beautiful; these are inherently compromised terms. Acting on her understanding, Rosiebelle Lee constructs her own social order in which she uses her prestige to create a matriarchal order in which work and profit are secondary to nurture and relationships. The "economics of slavery" are replaced by barter and gift-giving. Whites are among the recipients of this system. This does not mean, however, that the outside world changes much. Unlike Alice Walker in *The Color Purple*, Raymond Andrews is not creating a utopian order.[4] The whites, including Mister Mac, remain racist in fundamental ways, and greed and possession remain the economic reality of the larger world.

Even the changes that do occur do not necessarily produce transformation. Louvenia, Rosie and Mac's first child, identifies entirely with her father and comes to visit only him while her mother is on her deathbed a few hundred feet away. She embodies a version of racial self-hatred that seeks identification with whiteness to the exclusion of a more hybrid reality. Their younger son, Speck, is an inverted case. He has long blond hair and light skin but wants nothing more than to be seen as black. His white appearance is a source of shame; he is never seen, even by his family, without a cap to hide his hair. His obsession is such that he can never be comfortable around members of the community because he assumes his "failed" blackness to be a fundamental flaw. He may be taken as a parody of many black nationalists of the late 1960s who desired a pure blackness that could displace their actual mixed heritage.[5] Through Louvenia and Speck, Andrews comments on the forms of false consciousness created by the American racial formation. Neither character can accept the actual self but must racialize it so as to give it a clear meaning within the social order.

If the stories of Appalachee Red and Rosiebelle Lee and her family represent black encounters with the white father, *Baby Sweet's* narrates the engagement of the white son and black daughter in paternal quests. As in the other stories, part of the motivation is revenge while another part is the search for a selfhood that can both embrace and transcend race. John Morgan Jr. can be read as an embodiment of Norman Mailer's "White Negro." From early in his life, he is fascinated by the "colored" world, even though he has only a vague, childish notion of it. He rejects the word "nigger" early on as inappropriate to the people and experience he associates with that world. He rejects the family tradition of serving in the military, choosing instead to study art at the University of Georgia during the last year of World War II. Art and blacks represent means of rebellion against the respectability of his name and fate; through them, he can express his rejection of Southern aristocracy. But, in fact, his choices are enactments of dominant cultural practices. Going to "Dark Town" to drink and have his first sexual experience is simply a variation on the practices of his father and generations of white masters. The black woman he truly desires, for example, an employee of his father's hotel, turns out to be the "property" of the chief of police. Black women and blackness generally have always represented for whites a release from the constraints of civilization. Thus, John Jr., in resisting his father, replicates him.

What is different in this narrative is that the son persists in his rebellion, in effect making it his life. Though the primary motivation remains oedipal, it is expressed through identification with the elements of Southern white male adolescence—sexuality, alcohol, self-expression—rather than those of adult respectability and social conformity. The mother that is desired is the black woman or her white equivalent (in the context of Southern racial discourse), the prostitute. John Jr. thus moves from being the young white gentleman to being the White Negro. He adopts the persona of the stereotypical black hipster in language, style, and behavior. By becoming the proprietor of Baby Sweet's, a brothel with black women that serves white men, he in effect becomes the antifather. When the business takes on an apparently white woman who insists on servicing only black men, he violates a fundamental taboo of the patriarchal order. When John Jr. finds out that Appalachee Red is in fact his older brother, he can finally break the hold of his father by confronting him on the parents' fortieth wedding anniversary. The revelation leads John Sr. to the brothel and to his death of a heart attack in Lea's bed. Thus, the king of respectability is overthrown and the king of chaos reigns.

If John Jr. represents the breakdown of the old order, Lea represents the emergence of a fundamentally different, though not necessarily new, South. She is the product of cross-racial, cross-class relationships. Her mother, Betty Jean, is the daughter of the poor-white family that lived across the road from Rosiebelle Lee. Her father is Sugar Boy, the oldest son of Rosiebelle and Mister Mac. Thus, she blends in herself all the elements of Southern society; in this case, however, the blending is not controlled by the white master. Symbolic of this difference is the naming of the child Lea, after Rosiebelle Lee. Betty Jean's story, as rendered by her daughter, is one in which white men play the role of villain. The white father ejects mother and child from his home, and Betty Jean is raped by a preacher on her journey to Atlanta. She repeatedly loses jobs when her employers discover that she has a "kinky haired" child, even though that child has light skin. She is finally forced to leave Lea at home and prostitute herself in order to get the singing jobs that will support both of them. The situation produces distance between mother and daughter, with Lea becoming embarrassed by her mother's behavior and appearance. Nonetheless, Betty Jean persists in seeing that her daughter has an education, including college. She dies on the bus ride home, having seen Lea graduate and having explained to her the circumstances of her life.

Lea takes as her mission revenge for the treatment of her mother. In a manner comparable to Rosiebelle Lee's, she manipulates white men so as to sexually embarrass them. Unlike her grandmother, however, she does not seek the security of a safe relationship, in part because she can successfully pass for white. Like John Morgan Jr., she exposes the weaknesses inherent in a white patriarchal order. When she learns of his brothel, she turns her attention to getting even with black men, in response to what she considers abandonment by her father, Sugar Boy. This effort lasts only a few hours, until she meets her Uncle Speck, who inspires in her a desire for family. He takes her to her grandfather Mister Mac and provides her with a way of contacting her father. In her case, affirmation of a patriarchal line, not the destruction of it, becomes the means of social integration and self-affirmation. If she is in fact the representation of the "newest" South, then Andrews is defining it in terms of hybridity, but not moral change. At the time of renewed emphasis in the nation and the region on racial difference in the form of rhetorics of black failure and irresponsibility and white backlash, he portrays a reality where race does not make a difference in terms of basic human nature. Lea is vengeful, angry, and manipulative, but she also is willing to accept, finally, all the ancestors that have shaped her being.

Raymond Andrews's complication of racial identity in his trilogy leads him away from any notion of a special people or special history as a characteristic of blackness. "Race" is, in his saga, a social construction that has very real historical effects. But he is more interested in the unexpected consequences of that construction than in portrayal of unmitigated suffering. His black characters are victims, but they are also manipulators, lovers, and avengers. Whites often display an arrogance of power, but some of them also suffer, love, and change. On both sides are acts of lust, greed, jealousy, and pride, as well as sacrifice and endurance. The Muskhogean trilogy suggests that race is one strand woven into the fabric of American society. It cannot be separated from individualism, community, desire, acquisitiveness, and power-hunger. Each character responds according to his or her nature to the conditions of Southern and national culture. Andrews's vision is ultimately satiric in that all the characters are flawed; his manipulation of folklore elements reinforces the limitations and often absurdities of their thinking and action.

His perspective may be said to be conservative in that the virtues he espouses are the traditional ones of family, community, and love. Red takes Baby Sweet away from Boots White, not merely as an act of countervailing power, but also as an act of mercy. And when he leaves her eighteen years later, it is Darling, the gay cook, who nurses her out of her depression. Rosiebelle Lee constructs a community around herself, and she devotes her life to nurturing it, often to the detriment of her individual family. She also remains loyal both to the black man who suffered for her love and to the white man who fathered her children. John Morgan Jr. rejects the isolation of Southern aristocracy in preference for a more vital existence among the marginalized—bohemians, rednecks, poor blacks. His personal oedipal quest produces a space that transcends the racial, sexual, and class divisions of society. Finally, Lea, in her own genetic makeup, represents that same transcendence; she is black and white, redneck and aristocracy, male and female. The death of John Morgan Sr. in her bed in the building made famous first by his son Red and then by his son John Jr. completes the circle of family and community.

What Andrews sees in America, then, is blindness to these connections. Separation, by whatever means and for whatever reason, falsifies human reality, which is based on some version of family. Everyone in his narratives is related, can "claim kin." It is the failure to recognize this truth that leads to suffering, self-hatred, and exploitation. The results can be disastrous, as the often apocalyptic language of the texts suggests. In the period of the 1970s and 1980s when these novels were published, the nation was proving once again, as it had repeatedly in the decades represented in the narratives, that human nature is deeply flawed and that the nation lacked both the will and the communal sensibility to improve that nature. In the post–civil rights era, moral principles offer little guidance; it is noteworthy that Blue, Red's activist younger brother, was seen by the time of *Baby Sweet's* as concerned with the segregation of the brothel. Principle had become a minor irritant by the text's 1966 time setting; moreover, principle was focused on corruption, not to end it, but to "integrate" it. Andrews writes history into the present in his trilogy, but it is a history that offers little hope for either social justice or individual change. Greed, lust, and power seem to be permanent human characteristics. What will mitigate their effects is not law or principle but recognition of relationships. If everyone is a brother or sister, then violence and exploitation become *somewhat* harder to practice. In Andrews's world, this "somewhat" is a major improvement.

Chapter Seven

POSTMODERN SLAVERY AND
THE TRANSCENDENCE OF DESIRE
The Novels of Charles Johnson

The neo–slave narratives of Charles Johnson must be understood in relationship to the culture of Ronald Reagan's America in which they
were produced. *Oxherding Tale* (1982) and *Middle Passage* (1990) are narrated by
characters caught up in slavery. Nonetheless, they represent their experience of
that institution in such a way as to suggest crucial concerns with American
society of the 1980s. Each text in some way considers the situation of the black
family, the status of the black woman and the black man, philosophies of race,
and the relationship of white intellectuals to black culture. At a time when the
president himself was declaring that racism no longer existed as anything other
than an individual aberration, Johnson constructed narratives that described
the holocaustlike experience of slavery and that implicated current social practices in that history. The 1980s discursive constellation of hyperindividualism,
greed, victim-blaming, and cultural exploitation was answered with stories not
simply of victimization but also of agency, self-transcendence, black self-
expression, and construction of interracial families and communities. In each
novel, the individual fails when she/he functions in isolation primarily for self-
aggrandizement or even through racial pride. Thus, these works do not follow
the pattern of *Roots* or even *Jubilee* in tracing the tale of the heroic black man or
woman.

But it is equally false to argue that these works fall into a black nationalist
narrative model. Though each work offers what might be considered an essentialist black image, those images are destroyed or transformed in the course of
the story and a much more hybrid reality remains at the end. Both race and
community are finally seen as necessarily constructed out of the experience of
suffering, and all who suffer are potentially members of this community.

If Sherley Anne Williams's *Dessa Rose* and Toni Morrison's *Beloved* can be seen as using the slave narrative formula to argue for the specialness of black experience, Charles Johnson can be said to be doing the very opposite. And in contrast to Raymond Andrews's trilogy, Johnson offers hope for meaningful transformation. In both *Oxherding Tale* and *Middle Passage*, he presents images of suffering that are even stronger than those in *Dessa Rose*. But as he creates graphic images of black pain, oppression, and exploitation, he refuses to accept them as the most important aspect of reality. Instead, he moves his narratives and their protagonists through suffering toward transcendence and unity. He makes the radical assertion that human beings, including African Americans, seek suffering and enslavement rather than resist it. This position is in sharp contrast to Williams and others who depict heroic struggles to attain freedom and selfhood. For Johnson, the crucial struggle is within the self, for the truth of Being.[1] His central characters, who are also the narrators, journey through a variety of situations that present them with a range of ways of being in the world. What they learn is the illusory nature of these ways. They are finally brought back to the essential truth of the self and, through this encounter, are able to authentically and freely engage others.

Like other contemporary African American writers, Johnson uses some of the techniques of postmodernism to achieve his purposes. But also like them, he ultimately rejects the postmodernist principle of indeterminacy. While he refuses to accept racial essentialism, he does insist, as do others in this study, on a fundamental moral order in the universe. And also like them, he uses the black experience of slavery as a holocaust experience to elucidate that moral order.

One device Johnson draws from postmodernism is his revision of genre. *Oxherding Tale* and *Middle Passage* both link the slave narrative tradition to the picaresque novel. The slave narrative generally follows a pattern where the protagonist struggles to achieve movement and change; he/she desires to escape the confinement of the slave plantation by moving north to freedom. The majority of narratives first established the evil nature of the fixed place and then described at length the movement to a new life. Motion here is always very purposeful. The picaresque tradition in some ways sees motion as the problem to be solved by recovering family and home. While the adventures along the way are often grand, they lack inherent purpose and value. What Johnson does with these patterns is suggest that human beings move constantly from one slavery to another, believing all the while that motion is freedom and that each new place is finally home.

He also signifies on the genres by offering protagonists who are not the initial innocents found in both slave narratives and picaresque novels. The literary convention and historical practice of enforced black illiteracy is inverted in *Oxherding Tale* and *Middle Passage*. Both Andrew Hawkins and Rutherford Calhoun are educated in their early lives in both Western and Eastern traditions. They are thus enabled to engage effectively in intellectual, philosophical, and moral debates on the complex nature of freedom and enslavement and the meaning of human existence. Unlike writers whose interest is primarily in portraying the historical wrong that was and continues to be done to African Americans, Johnson concerns himself with the ways in which historical reality intersects with human nature and illusion.

One way to see this difference is to compare *Dessa Rose* and *Oxherding Tale* in their treatments of excessive white female desire. In a brief episode in Williams's novel, Dessa Rose describes Nathan's experience with Miss Lorraine, who preferred slave lovers. Lorraine's reasoning is that a Southern white woman's intense sexual desire can only be satisfied by those whose silence can be required. Black men can be threatened and even punished with death to compel their silence. The level of white desire and the fact that the two-page episode includes two scenes of oral sex, seems intended to make an ideological point about the perversity of whites and the exploitation of blacks. Even Nathan's sense of his sexual interest in white women is essentially political: "It was the terror, he knew, that made it so sweet. If climax, as some men said, was like death, then a nigger died a double death in a white woman's arms. And he had survived it. He walked a little taller, aware of the power hanging secret and heavy between his legs" (171). Interestingly, his assertion here that it is the white woman who confirms his black masculinity is not contradicted within the narrative.

In contrast, Johnson devotes parts of several chapters to Andrew Hawkins's relationship with Flo Hatfield. Flo is even more demanding than Lorraine, and yet what Hawkins emphasizes is the narrow focus of her desire rather than its perversity and exploitative character. Its narrowness is what has led to its negative effects; thinking only in terms of the gratification of the senses, Flo has a distorted view of human experience, which leads to self-destruction, as well as destruction of others. But nonetheless, it is in fact a way, in the spiritual sense, to some truths: "The body (for Flo) was the touchable part of the spirit; the spirit the untouchable part of the body. Could thirst and hunger fit into American Transcendentalism? Could desire and the body be accepted, contrary to the texts I'd studied, as ways to celebrate man's incarnation?—we used them so those long fall evenings in Abbeville. For those interested in ways to improve their sexual performance, I suggest the following: 1. Extinguish the ego 2. Eat well 3. Exercise regularly" (64). Moreover, in sharp contrast to Williams's depiction of the white woman as evil exploiter, Johnson (through Reb) suggests that she is simply another victim: " 'She ain't free,' " he said. " 'Some women learn, like slaves, to study men. They learn to think like men. They knows what men want, how they look at women when they think nobody's watchin', they know what men are afraid of, what they *dream* about—just like I know Fitzhugh. They have to keep one step ahead. If you got no power,' said Reb, 'you have to think like people who *do* so you kin make y'self over into what they want. She's a slave like you'n me, freshmeat.' Reb's eyebrows speared in toward his nose. 'And you best be 'fraid of someone who's 'fraid of you.' " (62)

Those two points, the existence of multiple ways to truth and the universality of human suffering, constitute the essence of Johnson's moral vision. African American history generally, and slavery in particular, presents an important narrative resource for developing these ideas. One reason is that representations of that history have tended to be reductive. Either blacks had nothing that counted as history, as even Hegel (who is one source for Johnson) believed, or they did have a history that was a "holocaust," both in Africa and in the New World. The only question in this latter formulation is whether that history is pathetic or heroic. In either case, there are clearly delineated victims and villains. Johnson, in part because of training in Eastern spiritual traditions, takes a more complicated view. Everyone is caught in the web of suffering; even the most heinous villain is in some sense a victim. The author tests this idea by creating extreme instances of human evil. On the other hand, even the most victimized can find a Way within his texts. This does not mean acceptance of oppression; rather, it suggests a mode of living and dying with integrity, even under the most miserable of circumstances. Suffering, in fact, is only increased by our illusion that it can be escaped, through ideology, power, money, or religion. We add to our own suffering and, more malignantly, to that of others through our insistence on these false notions. Only by recognizing the universality of suffering and our complicity in it can we begin the process of healing. Johnson's fictions do not so much preach a Way as they explore a variety of Ways and intimate that what is essential is the need to search for our own Way, by recognizing the reality of suffering.

In *Middle Passage*, the image of corruption that approximates Flo is Ebenezer Falcon, the captain of the *Republic*, a slaving ship. When first presented, Falcon has just been sodomizing the cabin boy. Shortly after, he "enjoys" (to use the narrator's term) telling of an incident of cannibalism in which he participated. More significantly for the text, he is, in addition to slave trader, an imperialist and cultural plunderer of the first rank:

He was famous. In point of fact, infamous. That special breed of empire builder, explorer, and imperialist that sculptors love to elongate, El Greco–like, in city park statues until they achieved Brobdingnagian proportions. He carried, I read, portraits of Pizarro and Magellan on every expedition he made. Now . . . yes, now I remembered those stories well. Falcon, the papers said, knew seven African coastal dialects and, in fact, could learn any new tongue in two weeks' time. More, even, he'd proven it with Hottentot, and lived with their tribe for a month, plundering their most sacred religious shrines. (29–30)

Falcon also believes in the inherent inferiority of blacks; he readily accepts Calhoun's "darky" routine as reality. To pin down his evil character, Johnson has the captain expound upon the nefarious effects of a nineteenth-century version of affirmative action.

But having established Falcon's greed, arrogance, racism, and cruelty, Johnson then develops the intellectual, moral, and human grounds for the captain's "Way." He thereby undercuts any simplistic assignment of villainy. Falcon is modern man; he believes that conflict is inherent in human nature:

> "*Man* is the problem, Mr. Calhoun. Not just gents, but women as well, anythin' capable of *thought*. Now, why do I say such a curious thing? Study it for a spell. . . . For a self to act, it must have somethin' to act *on*. A nonself—some call this Nature—that resists, thwarts the will, and *vetoes* the actor. May I proceed? Well, suppose that nonself is another self? What then? As long as each sees a situation differently there will be slaughters and slavery and the subordination of one to another 'cause two notions of things never exist side by side as equals. . . . Conflict," says he, "*is* what it means to be conscious. Dualism is a bloody structure of the mind. . . . Mind was *made* for murder. Slavery, if you think this through, forcing yourself not to flinch, is the social correlate of a deeper, ontic wound." (96–98)

Falcon's rapacity is the logical extension of his worldview; if conflict is the central truth of human existence, then it is both natural and reasonable to conquer and pillage. Johnson is careful to position the captain's perspective as consistent with Western philosophy. Moreover, Ebenezer Falcon and his ship *Republic* are both made emblems of the United States. He is not an isolated sociopath or psychotic but rather the embodiment of Western culture. It is important to note, however, that he sees the source of his thinking and action as a "wound," not a virtue. In other words, he is a victim of the very culture and human nature he benefits from. This self-image is projected in his sensitivity to being a dwarf, his paranoia that his crews plan mutiny, and his dependence on the "money men" who finance his adventures and reap great financial rewards. After the Africans take over the ship, Falcon commits suicide rather than face those hard, greedy men. The "Way" of Western thought and American culture leads to self-destruction and general chaos.

Given the futility of the perspectives of Flo Hatfield and Ebenezer Falcon, critics of Johnson's work have, in good dualistic fashion, read the African Allmuseri as the desirable alternative.[2] Repeated references to them both in the author's long and short fiction and in interviews would tend to reinforce this view. The author has constructed a culture and worldview for this mythic group and, given the critique of Eurocentric culture in the narratives, the choice of a highly moral, unself-conscious, generous society is attractive. But Johnson is very careful to situate the Allmuseri outside history. When they enter it, they lose many of the qualities of their culture and, in fact, generally die. They represent not so much a way of being in the world as a standard against which societies, groups, and individuals can measure their own choices and beliefs. In *Oxherding Tale*, Johnson presents a single character, Reb, who is Allmuseri, while, in *Middle Passage*, he presents a group that has been enslaved and whose god has been placed below decks by Falcon.

Reb has achieved a state beyond desire that is also a place of wisdom. When Andrew Hawkins comes to Flo Hatfield's plantation, Reb is the one who explains the true nature of the situation. He, as indicated above, points out that Flo is a victim much like everyone else. Moreover, when Andrew displaces Reb's son Patrick as Flo's lover and Patrick then commits suicide, the father does not hold the new lover responsible: "I feared that Reb blamed me for Patrick's death. He did not. He seemed, in a way, to have known it was coming, was now unyoked from his son, and often said, 'I put his casket in the ground a month ago. You the one still carryin' it around, Freshmeat' " (61). This equanimity is based in the Allmuseri view that life is a unity: "He hated personal pronouns; the Allmuseri had no words for *I*, *you*, *mine*, *yours*. They had, consequently, no experience of these things, either, only proper names that were variations on the Absolute" (97). But it is also important to note that Reb's balanced state is a product of a personal history of suffering; he *learns* to forgo desire and attachment. He tells Andrew the story of his marriage and fatherhood. When his wife dies and his child becomes very ill, he tries begging for money, because the master will not pay for medical treatment. His efforts are unsuccessful until he is told by another beggar that he will fail as long as he truly *wants* anything. "His only strategy, the one option left, was surrender, accepting—said the Coffin-maker—the shock of annihilation" (76). At this moment, someone drops money in his lap; consistent with this narrative of sacrifice, his daughter has died by the time he finds and pays a doctor. "So often had food, property, and loved ones been snatched away that now he treated whatever he had as someone else's property, with the care and attention that another's property deserved. Reward he did not expect. Nor pleasure. Desire was painful. Duty was everything—the casket promised tomorrow, a carving for the blacksmith's daughter, the floorboards that needed fixing. This was his Way. It was, I thought, a Way of strength and spiritual heroism . . ." (76–77).

The Allmuseri of *Middle Passage* can be seen as presented in exactly the opposite way from Reb. In describing them, Rutherford Calhoun begins with their mythic purity, then shows their entry into the suffering of human history. Initially, they are the reverse of Ebenezer Falcon; conventional forms of knowledge, possession, and power, by which he defines himself, are foreign to their identity: "They saw us as savages. In their mythology Europeans had once been members of their tribe—rulers, even, for a time—but fell into what was for these people the blackest of sins. The failure to experience the unity of Being everywhere was the Allmuseri vision of Hell. And that was where we lived: purgatory. That was where we were taking them—into the madness of multiplicity—and the thought of it drove them wild" (65). Johnson develops here his own version of black nationalist mythohistory. The Allmuseri have a different and superior way of being in and perceiving the world. They exist within the unity of existence and therefore lack a sense of individual identity or even separate objects. Their language is relational and "natural": "When Ngonyama's tribe spoke it was not so much like talking as the tones the savannah made at night, siffilating through the plains of coarse grass, soughing as dry wind from tree to tree" (77). They lack science in the Western sense because it is premised on analysis, but they were able intuitively to grasp the meaning of the whole. Their moral order, in fact, made them desirable slaves: "Eating no meat, they were easy to feed. Disliking property, they were simple to clothe, able to heal themselves, they required no medication. They seldom fought. They could not steal. They fell *sick*, it was said, if they wronged anyone" (78).

While many nationalists and Afrocentrists might use such a representation to develop the glories of ancient Africa and the potential of its diasporan descendants, Johnson has other interests. Clearly, he sets up a contrast between Allmuseri spirituality and the dualistic evil done by "Christian" Western society. Through Falcon and others, he locates the flaws of modern society in its philosophical, ideological, and religious underpinnings. Hyperindividualism, Christian dualism, racism, capitalist/imperialist greed, and political oppression are the products of a defective value system and produce in turn human suffering on a global level. But Johnson seeks to go beyond this critique. The further question is what happens to spirituality when it enters this history created by the West. What happens, according to *Middle Passage*, is that even the pure become complicitous in suffering: "Stupidly, I had seen their lives and culture as a timeless product, as a finished thing, pure essence or Parmenidean meaning I envied and wanted to embrace, when the truth was that they were process and Heraclidean change, like any man, not fixed but evolving and as vulnerable to metamorphosis as the body of the boy we'd thrown overboard. Ngonyama and maybe all the Africans, I realized, were not wholly Allmuseri anymore. We had changed them. . . . No longer Africans, yet not Americans either" (124–25). The Allmuseri revolt and become capable of violence, including killing. They enter oppression, multiplicity, conflict—in other words, human history. It has not been their essence that has been different but their culture and circumstance. Disconnected from that culture and placed under different circumstances, they become like other people.

But Johnson goes further than depicting a fall from grace. The traditional culture of the Allmuseri was not an African golden age destroyed by Western greed. One of the men is said to be one-handed because the tribal punishment for theft is the cutting off of the right hand. This missing hand is clear evidence, not simply of Allmuseri virtue, but also of their awareness of human flaws and thus the need for law and punishment. Moreover, in *Oxherding Tale*, Reb tells the story of an Allmuseri king who converted to Islam, stole land from Reb's great-grandfather, and then hated him for practicing the old religion. In revenge, the ancestor brought a rain that caused insanity in all the people, including himself. The king, having been warned, had preserved uncontaminated water. " 'His subjects, in their lunacy, were all the same—they took the fantastic world of their madness to be real, understood each other, and he, the king, could not speak a word to them that made sense. For weeks he wandered among them, hugging his jug of fresh water, shouting, "I'm *sane*, you're *not*," and everyone laughed, especially Rakhal, and pointed significantly at their temples as he passed, for the Real, if it was anything at all to the Allmuseri, was a matter of consent, a shared hallucination' " (49). The story reveals the common human qualities of power-hunger, greed, revenge, and sectarianism to be a part of the Allmuseri history. In addition, the observation that for them the Real might be "a shared hallucination" makes this a cautionary tale about assuming the essential purity of their culture.

In place of some inherent racial virtue to be identified and practiced, the Allmuseri represent a way of defamiliarizing and identifying American (and Western generally) values and practices. It is the stories of the protagonists,

Andrew Hawkins and Rutherford Calhoun, that are central to Johnson's vision. These are young black men who have been inculcated with the principles of Western philosophy, religion, and social order, including racial beliefs. While they resist racist assumptions, they do so primarily in Western terms, as becomes evident when they have difficulty in debates with those who have mastered the philosophical underpinnings of racism. Contact with the Allmuseri provides not so much a wholly different way of being as a different way of seeing the world. Each protagonist is presented with different Ways, some of which have been presented above. But all of the paths of others, including the Allmuseri, are wrong for these young men. Each, according to Johnson, must find his own Way, based on his own personality, circumstance, and history. This individual Way, however, does not lead in the direction of individualism or value-free self-expression. Instead, it leads to cross-racial marriage and extended multicultural family. The "truth" each Way leads to is love, healing, and justice.

In the case of Andrew Hawkins, he escapes slavery and the "concentration camp" experience of Flo Hatfield's mining operations by passing for white and by marrying the white daughter of a doctor. In doing so, he believes he has outwitted the Soul-catcher, a mysterious figure who recaptures slaves by entering their thinking and waiting for them to reveal their desire to return to slavery. The runaway's intense desire to be "normal" and thus invisible reflects his/her belief that "slave" is the true identity. Andrew deludes himself into believing that he is "normal" and thus can escape his history. He maintains his surface identity until he comes across a slave auction in which his first lover is on the block. She is, in Freudian terms, the return of the repressed, that part of himself that Andrew must deny in order to survive. But he does not deny her; instead, he buys her, even though she is seriously ill with pellagra, and takes her home to his white wife. He then must reveal his true history, thus making himself (and Minty, the slave) vulnerable to white attitudes and actions. But Peggy, out of love for him and sympathy for Minty, accepts the truth. Pregnant herself, she, along with Andrew, begins to nurse Minty, who refuses pity and insists on working despite the effects of her disease, which are shown to be the direct consequence of mistreatment under slavery. Johnson presents her deterioration in graphic detail, so as to force readers into the experience of human suffering. The point is not an ideological attack on racism nor the arousal of pity for victims, but rather the inescapability of suffering. Not coincidentally, at the time of Minty's death, Andrew is freed from the threat of the Soul-catcher, who has quit his work because he failed to capture Reb, the one man he ever sought who desired nothing and therefore feared nothing. But, more deeply,

Andrew is free because he has chosen love, mercy, and justice over self. His Way is not Reb's Way, which is one of solitude and self-sacrifice. Rather, it is one that crosses race, gender, and cultural boundaries in order to embrace humanity.

Rutherford Calhoun also finds his truth by returning to his past, but his path is more convoluted. While Hawkins can be seen as an innocent abroad, Calhoun is more in the tradition of rascals and vagabonds. He leaves home because his brother, foolishly in his eyes, keeps for them virtually none of the estate left by their master. Instead, he distributes it among all the slaves. So Rutherford goes to New Orleans and becomes a successful thief. He meets and is courted by Isadora Bailey, an educated Bostonian working as a governess. She wants to make him respectable, as a moral project. He, however, feels such an impulse to be confining. When she goes so far as to make a deal with Phillipe Zeringue, the black community's crime boss, to engage Calhoun's debts for a marriage vow, he decides to flee. This he does by stealing the papers of a sailor on the *Republic*, a slave ship. Thus, his character is established early as self-centered, irresponsible, and dishonest. Two aspects of this character are important to the story. The first is that Calhoun associates his criminality with his racial experience. His life as a slave, though it provided him with moral and intellectual training, left him economically deprived and psychologically dependent. When times were bad, for example, food he received was food his brother gave up. Moreover, he was a possession who literally wore the discarded possessions of whites. Thus, his status meant that he was not permitted to have anything, including himself. Any possession by a slave was a criminal act: "The Reverend's prophecy that I would grow up to be a picklock was wiser than he knew, for was I not, as a Negro in the New World, *born* to be a thief?" (47). He places the responsibility for his being outside himself, in a world he cannot control and can only react to.

But the second aspect of his character conflicts with the first in that it emphasizes control and "transcendence":

Slipping away from my watch and into his [Falcon's] room, easing his door shut with my fingertips, I felt the change come over me, a familiar, sensual tingle that came whenever I broke into someone's home, as if I were slipping inside another's soul. Everything must be done slowly, deliberately, first the breath coming deep from the belly, easily, as if the room itself were breathing, limbs light like hollow reeds, free of tension, all parts of me flowing as a single piece, for I had learned in Louisiana that in balletlike movements there could be no error of the body, no elbows cracking into chair arms in a stranger's space to give me away. Theft, if the truth be told, was the closest thing I knew to transcendence. (46)

This might be called the Zen of burglary. It follows the techniques of meditation with the same goal of being totally attuned to the present moment. This present-mindedness contrasts with the effort to blame the past for his current activities. Here, he does what is necessary to control the situation. Moreover, it is also a moment of physicality, where one is aware of his body and surroundings but is not thinking about them so much as being them. The experience both foreshadows Calhoun's development into a person capable of responsible action and connects that development to something inherent in him. Transcendence and self-mastery are already goals and achievements for him; the question is to what greater purpose he pursues them. More than a sea adventure or a diatribe against human oppression and cruelty, though also these things, *Middle Passage* traces the movement of the self from victimization to self-actualization. The title in this sense has multiple meaning. It refers, of course, to the historic transportation of Africans to the New World; it also suggests what happens to those Africans as they enter Western cultural hegemony; and, finally, it is the transition for the protagonist from thief to angel of mercy and justice.

The path of transformation is self-awareness, but that awareness must be forced on him. Like many students of Eastern spirituality, Johnson believes that the self is often content in its way of being, though that way produces unhappiness. Virtually all of his characters may be seen as illustrating this point. Through his encounters with Falcon and the Allmuseri, Calhoun is presented with extreme versions of being. On the one hand is total absorption in the self, its possessions, and its power; on the other is the negation of self and of multiplicity. Each compels the protagonist to confront his own being, the one by intellectualizing greed and dominion to its logical end and the other by insistence on a transcendence that eliminates all difference. At various moments in the narrative, Calhoun identifies with the representatives of both positions.

Finally, however, he is forced to face himself when he encounters the Allmuseri god. The god had been taken by Falcon as a precious object to be sold in America. But it had not yet lost its powers. It was said to drive men mad, but it did so by serving as a mirror to the soul. What Calhoun sees is the image of his father, Riley, who ran away when his son was only four. He was large, handsome, and musical. He was also promiscuous, but he blamed this flaw on slavery: "You couldn't rightly blame a colored man for acting like a child, could you—stealing and sloughing off work when people like Peleg Chandler took the profits, and on top of that so much of their dignity he couldn't look his wife Ruby in the face when they made love without seeing how much she hated him for being powerless, even with their own children, who had no respect for a man they had seen whipped more than once by an overseer and knew in this world his word was no better than theirs" (170). In these conditions, Riley responds not by attacking his oppressor but by fighting family and other fellow sufferers. If manhood is defined by domination, then violence and sexuality were the means available to him. Thus, the vision reveals to Rutherford the source of his own attitude and self-justification.

But it also does something else. The pictures continue through the father's attempted escape, which is foiled when he loses his way and is murdered by the patrol. The absent father who was the source of trouble and the object of hatred now becomes present in his suffering and dying; he becomes the victim, not of abstract insults to his race, but of concrete history, of actual racial hatred. Ironically, in becoming "Eternal Object," he finally becomes to his son a human subject. This image of the father transforms the son:

> A thousand soft undervoices that jumped my jangling senses from his last, weakly syllabled wind to a mosaic of voices within voices, each one imma- nent in the other, none his but all strangely his, the result being that as the loathsome creature, this deity from the dim beginnings of the black past, folded my father back into the broader, shifting field—as waves vanish into water—his breathing blurred in a dissolution of sounds and I could only feel that identity was imagined; I had to listen harder to isolate him from the We that swelled each particle and pore of him, as if the (black) self was the greatest of all fictions; and then I could not find him at all. He seemed everywhere, his presence, and that of countless others, in me as well as the chamber, which had subtly changed. Suddenly I knew the god's name: Rutherford. (171)

This moment of mystical experience could be read as Johnson's embrace of spiritual blackness, the return of the father to his rightful place among the ancestors and, through him, the son's recovery of his own connection to racial essence. Certainly this is a theme that has been expressed often in African American writing. It is evident in the Harlem Renaissance, including Marcus Garvey's back-to-Africa movement, in black Muslim theology, in the black arts movement of the 1960s and 1970s, in contemporary writers as different as Alice Walker and Ishmael Reed, and in Afrocentric thinking. As has been seen earlier, it shapes the conclusion of *Dessa Rose*. But it is important to be careful in Johnson's case. After all, one of Rutherford's insights is that "the (black) self was the greatest of all fictions." What creates that "fiction" in this novel about a slave ship was the holocaust experience of the slave trade. Those with African ancestry are connected primarily by a history of human degradation based on skin color. As Andrew Hawkins points out in *Oxherding Tale*, "the wretchedness of being colonized was not that slavery created feelings of guilt and indebtedness, though I did feel guilt and debt; nor that it created a long, lurid dream of multiplicity and separateness, which it did indeed create, but the fact that men had epidermalized Being" (52). Skin color determines self. To construct an identity based on blackness as a positive rather than negative essence simply replicates and reinforces "multiplicity and separateness." To do so may at some level reduce the "wretchedness," since it appears to grant agency to those who have been denied their subjectivity, but it also enslaves in that it fosters a fiction that prevents transcendence into the unity of Being.

The test of Calhoun's vision is in his actions in the last few pages of the novel. This thief, who tried to play all the sides in the conflicts aboard ship, who was willing to serve on a slave ship in order to avoid the "imprisonment" of marriage, who used his past to justify his irresponsibility, works to save the lives of the white cook and an Allmuseri child when the ship is destroyed. He then finds Isadora, who has resigned herself to having to marry Phillipe Zeringue, who turns out to be one of the financiers of the *Republic's* slave cargo. Calhoun saves her by telling Zeringue's assistant Santos, an Allmuseri, of his boss's racial treachery. But even in these classically heroic actions protecting honor and justice, he reflects on his change: "The voyage had irreversibly changed my seeing, made of me a cultural mongrel, and transformed the world into a floating shadow play I felt no need to possess or dominate, only appreciate in the ever extended present" (187). He confronts Zeringue with the logbook proving his complicity, a truth that frees Santos to demand and inflict punishment for the crime of slaving and betrayal. Calhoun does not manipulate this situation, but allows it to emerge. In other words, he uses his power not to dominate but to obtain justice and security.

He then turns to Isadore, who represents the other term of the algebra of desire. If dealing with Zeringue represents the overcome temptation of greed and masculine control, the encounter with Isadore represents the temptation of resolution through sexuality. After she tells her Penelope-like story of resisting Zeringue's advances as long as possible, they both assume that they must have sex. But what Calhoun realizes during their awkward attempts at intercourse is that establishing their lives together in terms of desire merely perpetuates separation into male and female. After their experiences of suffering, something else is required: "Accordingly, she lowered her head to my shoulder, as a sister might. Her warm fingers, busy as mouths a moment before, were quiet on my chest. Mine, on her hair as the events of the last half year overtook us. Isadore drifted toward rest, nestled snugly beside me, where she would remain all night while we, forgetful of ourselves, gently crossed the Flood, and countless seas of suffering" (209). Abstention here is not a moral principle but a moment of stillness in the present. It is a means of connecting not merely in private but as part of a larger human history. After all, the seas over which they travel, as Robert Hayden pointed out in his poem "Middle Passage," are filled with the bones of slaves who died on that passage. Calhoun then constructs a family of sufferers—Isadore, Squibb, Baleka, even perhaps Santos (who may be Baleka's distant cousin). But he builds this "culturally mongrel" group, not because of their suffering, but because of their shared humanity.

In creating these historical narratives, Johnson speaks to and through contemporary social issues. He neither denies the harshness of the nation's racial history nor sees it as the determining fact of black life. He thus resists the black conservative position that individual responsibility is the only concern and the Afrocentric position that a racial essence links black people throughout time and space. The denial of the economic, political, social, and psychological impact of slavery and racism is as false to history as the claim that any sort of behavior can be justified by oppression and victimization. For example, while the fathers of the novels' protagonists certainly felt the frustration and emasculating effects of slavery, the narratives clearly condemn their claims that promiscuity is permissible because of their condition. Johnson, in a variety of ways, addresses the situation of black men in society: his characterizations and episodes speak to violence, to self-hatred, to sexism, to material success, to education, and to image. But he does so in ways that avoid entrapping him in current discourses. He does this by offering representations of personality rather than analyses or clearly parallel situations. What interests him is the mental slavery that racism has produced and the multiple forms that can take. The work is done by figuration, not allegory.

Moreover, the solution(s) offered cannot directly translate into policy categories. He is not, by implication, advocating a Million Man March or affirmative action or any other program. Rather, he insists on a spiritual quest, a search for a Way. That Way is through the self, but, unlike many New Age solutions, it does not stop there. The self must be examined and transformed in experience and in the world, so as to change the world. In this connection, Johnson moves beyond much Buddhist practice that shapes his thinking. The Allmuseri could not survive their encounter with history. They entered the world of multiplicity. But Johnson's point is not that that change was tragic or fortunate but rather that it was inevitable. To be human is to live in suffering; this is a given of the author of these novels. The question is what happens next, and this is what Johnson explores. All suffer, including those we consider despicable. Some suffering is caused by such people, but the point is not to define the self either by accusation or by denial. Rather, it is necessary to accept the fact of suffering as real and then to find ways to deal with it. Many ways exist, but most are illusory in that they only perpetuate the troubles. What Johnson seems to be saying is that we must accept responsibility for the search for self, not to advance individualism, but to enable the healing of ourselves and others. Given the conditions of American culture and racial history, such a task is Herculean. But, then, that is what makes for good stories.

PART THREE *Family*

Chapter Eight

FAMILY SECRETS

Reinventions of History in
The Chaneysville Incident

The black family has been one of the most hotly debated subjects of the past forty years in both history and the social sciences. Since at least the Moynihan Report of 1964, contentions over its structure, its character, its effects, and its relationship to crime, poverty, welfare, and morality have been recurrent in both scholarship and public policy. Moynihan's initial characterization of the family as "pathological" has reappeared in many of the commentaries by neoconservatives. It has also been seen historically, especially by blacks, as a crucial institution in a nation that, for much of its existence, did not permit African American participation in the public sphere. Not surprisingly, then, family has been one of the key themes in black literature. Whether as saga in *Roots* or as dysfunctional patriarchy in Alice Walker and Gloria Naylor or as source of black identity and story in John Wideman, family has been central to contemporary narrative. In this and the following chapters, this theme is connected to the patterns of history, as family becomes the means of understanding the self's relationship to the past. In Wideman, David Bradley, and Leon Forrest, the complexities of blood are traced as family members are lost and found, as their stories are repressed and recovered, and as the authors and narrators attempt to construct a usable history out of the convolutions of a personal, familial, and national experience.

In *The Chaneysville Incident* (1981), David Bradley creates a professional writer as narrator in order to tell stories of the past. Through historian John Washington he can raise issues about contemporary intellectual activity while demonstrating the archaeological process of uncovering the hidden, suppressed, and forgotten material of African American history. In *Divine Days* (1992), Leon Forrest uses a fledgling playwright who collects the stories of local people as possible material for his writing. In the process, he discovers a much more complex, generally unspoken story he needs to reveal. What joins these two purposes and thus brings together these very different texts is the extent to which such opening up is essential for the narrators as much as it is for their materials. Both novels argue for the importance, ultimately, of the personal in the quest for historical reality. Only through an acceptance of individual responsibility, not only in the intellectual effort but also in personal life, can something like the truth of the past be ascertained.

Both of these substantial novels focus on the narrators' attempts to bring coherence out of a mass of materials; both Bradley's John Washington and Forrest's Joubert Jones comment repeatedly on the processes they use to bring order out of chaos. Part of the point being made is that there is in fact a wealth of information to be gleaned about those who historians and novelists have traditionally ignored: the exploited, the oppressed, those nonwhite and nonmale. Thus, Bradley and Forrest reinforce the endeavors of emergent social historians and minority writers of the 1970s and later to demonstrate that history and experience need to be understood from the bottom up.

At the same time, however, they offer resistance to newer approaches and ideologies while questioning "official" versions of the black past. Even as they present what Forrest calls the "nightmare of history" and Bradley the "history of atrocity," they refuse any simple victimization narrative. In fact, Joubert Jones explicitly repudiates any notion of blacks as a chosen people comparable to Jews. African Americans are consistently granted agency, choice, and moral responsibility, even if it is within rather narrow boundaries. In other words, there is an insistence by both writers that anything like subaltern status (to use the language of postcolonial studies) must always be interrogated. Thus, representations of the past that read blacks as passive and those that see them as ciphers in the large pattern of history are challenged. At the same time, Bradley and Forrest reject straightforward heroic narratives, which they also understand to be a simplification of black experience.

In order to tell complex, personalized stories, the authors construct polyvocal texts in which the strongly held views of the narrators about their projects are disputed and questioned by other voices, past and present. In both novels, these voices are of personal significance to the narrators and thus have subjective authority beyond their status as witnesses to history. But this subjectivity itself complicates the possibility of coherence because it leads to contradiction and concealment by its very nature. Family and community have secrets to keep even as they have stories to tell. In addition, both narrators face the irretrievability of the past in trying to understand it and its meaning for the present. Crucial elements are lost in time or are so layered with legend and deception that claims of objective knowledge must be discarded. At the same time, the linkage of self and present to history makes it imperative for both narrators to attempt to locate the truth.

Given the epistemological and ontological problems the writers have set for themselves, their texts exemplify black postmodernism. As in the work of John Edgar Wideman, so with Bradley and Forrest, notions of self, race, and history must be constantly problematized without being understood as simply arbitrary, as tends to be the case with white postmodernist writers. Self, race, and history are constructions, but they are constructions that have a direct impact on human beings. The key question, then, is how they are and have been constructed. Each narrator seeks to work through the narratives, rituals, ideologies, and self-projections that are presented to him in order to generate for himself and others a version of reality that makes sense of black experience. Both Washington and Jones ultimately understand that their construction is an act of the imagination that approaches truth not through its direct correspondence to fact but through its usefulness in the present.

The Chaneysville Incident may be said to be a fictional reply to the historiographical practices of the 1960s and 1970s. Beginning with Kenneth Stampp's 1956 *The Peculiar Institution*, historians began a major revision of the story of slavery. In contrast to the claims of earlier professional generations that slavery was a relatively mild system that had generally positive benefits for whites and blacks, Stampp argued that it was cruel though profitable exploitation of human beings. Stanley Elkins, in *Slavery* (1959), applied the language of the Nazi concentration camps in describing the dehumanization and victimization of slaves. The early 1970s saw the renaissance of slavery studies as pressure from emergent Black Studies programs and the development of the methods of social history allowed the perspective of slaves to shape historical understanding. John Blassingame in 1972 suggested a theory of slave personality in *The Slave Community*, while Eugene Genovese in *Roll, Jordan, Roll* (1974) reinterpreted slavery as a dynamic institution in which, to some extent, slaves were able to negotiate the conditions of their servitude. The most controversial work of the time was *Time on the Cross* (1974), in which Robert Fogel and Stanley Engerman used the most advanced methods of statistical analysis to show that slavery, in material terms, was not nearly as harsh as earlier studies had suggested. In sum, in the decade before the publication of *Chaneysville*, historians were involved in constructing, on what they saw as increasingly objective grounds, a sophisticated portrait of the central experience of black history. Works of local and specialized (folk, family) history were filling in the details of this big picture. In conjunction with popular and middlebrow fiction (*Roots, Jubilee, The Autobiography of Miss Jane Pittman*, and *Song of Solomon*), the widespread recognition of Black History Month and the more clearly ideologically driven efforts of the Black Studies movement, black history and especially slavery had become crucial to the understanding of race in America by the end of the 1970s.

In *The Chaneysville Incident*, David Bradley challenges the dominant discourse on slavery and black history generally. That discourse assumes that African American history can be known from the outside and can be known through the application of traditional Western methods of historical research. The only necessity is to find an effective, rational tool to draw the appropriate conclusions from the available evidence. The subject position of the historian, including his (or her) ideology and personal values, is excludable from the process, as are the subjectivities of those being studied. Thus, whether the approach is Fogel and Engerman's econometric model or Genovese's Marxist dialectic, the scholar remains outside the material and not subject to the history being described; those observed remain ciphers, responding to the forces determining their experience. These positions are in fact central to the meaning of modern historiography.

At the same time, Bradley also resists the impulse of the Black Studies movement to assume a priori the meaning of the past. This trend, which Clarence Walker has called the "romanticizing of the slave community" (xi–xxvi), reads the central narrative as one of heroic resistance, cultural autonomy, and moral superiority, all grounded in racial essence. Racist structures and evil individuals used any means necessary to maintain white supremacy.[1] Thus, black history is the story of struggle, victimization, and noble action that can serve as models for constructing contemporary black identity and carrying on the struggle.

In one sense, John Washington can be understood as initially acting on both of these agendas. The chapter titles are a string of numbers that represent his method of research. They list, as precisely as possible, the year, date, and time of an event. Used on index cards, they help to establish a sequence of events that might help determine cause and effect. Events at various levels—local, regional, national, international—and in different areas—economics, culture, politics—can be integrated into the system to identify possible patterns that would not otherwise be apparent. Historical study becomes the search for coherence in the apparent randomness of information. To divide his narrative in such a way implies Washington's attempt to understand his own story in the same terms.

Moreover, his preferred mode of conversation is the minilecture, in which he presents a brief exposition on whatever topic happens to occur. For example, in the opening chapter, he responds to his lover's implied question about a phone call that woke them both up with a discourse on the invention and technological development of the telephone. This pattern seems most common as a means of avoiding any emotional expression. He is, then, very much a product of a rationalistic system of training who has incorporated that mode into his sense of himself and his relationships.

At the same time, he repeatedly refers to history as a study of atrocity, including slavery. He sees his professional role (and personal one as well) as revealer and debunker of the pretensions and myths of the past (and present). He sees the world filled with inequalities, conflicts, and efforts at concealment: "Societal institutions act as fig leaves for each other's nakedness—the Church justifies the actions of the State, the State the teachings of the School, the School the principles of the Economy, the Economy the pronouncements of the Church. . . . America is a classed society, regardless of the naive beliefs of deluded egalitarians, the frenzied efforts of misguided liberals, the grand pronouncements of brain-damaged politicians" (6). He might even be labeled a radical social historian in that he insists that "the key to the understanding of any society lies in the observation and analysis of the insignificant and the mundane" (6). For example, the claim about social class above is demonstrated by reference to the restroom facilities in the nation's main modes of public transportation: the lower the status of consumers, the worse the facilities.

While he is engaged in the use of objectivist methods that serve a critical, radical perspective, it is also clear from the first page of the novel that it is impossible to separate John's personality from his professional commitments. The phone call referred to above comes from his mother and concerns an old friend of his who is dying. In both his response to his mother and his explanation to Judith, he reveals an edge of anger and sarcasm. His conversations consistently reveal precision of language and desire for control that maintain a distance similar to his academic method. He is a man who recurrently comments that he lacks imagination and can only speak what he knows. In a variety of ways, then, including the fact that Judith is white, he appears to be a portrait of the deracinated black intellectual so frequently commented on, both positively and negatively, during this time. A crucial part of the debate over Black Studies in the university, for example, was the extent to which its scholars should follow the methodological traditions of the social sciences and humanities or develop new methods, often promoting an identifiable liberationist agenda.[2] John Washington, even with his critical impulse, both personally and intellectually follows the traditional model.

What prevents *Chaneysville* from falling into a narrative that simply critiques or affirms this position is the presence of ghosts haunting John. These do not constitute presences in the sense of *Beloved*'s embodiment of the child, or *Mama Day*'s George, or Brother in *Sent for You Yesterday*; rather, they are embedded memories of those who have shaped John's life and relationships. The life and death in Vietnam of his brother Bill defines his relationship with his mother. His personality and vocation seem to be determined by a father whom he hated in many ways. His notion of history as atrocity reflects the tales he heard in childhood of the people on the other side of the Hill who died of smallpox in significant numbers because everyone else was afraid to cross over to help them; moreover, even in his own life, people want nothing to do with the Other Side. Only Jack is willing to live there, and he was always rejected by respectable members of the black community.

But beyond these specifics, which can be rationalized, a more general aura of hauntedness fills the text. It is apparent, again, from the first page:

> Sometimes you can hear the wire, hear it reaching out across the miles; whining with its own weight, crying from the cold, panting at the distance, humming with the phantom sounds of someone else's conversation. You cannot always hear it—only sometimes; when the night is deep and the room is dark and the sound of the phone's ringing has come slicing through uneasy sleep; when you are lying there, shivering, with the cold plastic of the receiver pressed tight against your ear. Then, as the rasping of your breathing fades and the hammering of your heartbeat slows, you can hear the wire: whining, crying, panting, humming, moaning like a living thing. (1)

It is significant that these words, which open the text, are not the product of the message delivered nor of any dream that is interrupted by the call. They reflect something inherent in the process of communication itself, a process highly technological that John shortly afterward comments on in very rationalistic terms. Unlike the notion of "white noise," which deadens communication, or "noise" generally, which interferes with it, the sounds of the wire enhance and reinforce the sounds passed along it. Moreover, the language used suggests that the ghostliness is objectively "there," not subjectively imposed by the listener.

This passage, and others like it throughout the text, imply that reality is haunted, even in its most advanced elements. To Western reason, Bradley adds a version of African spirituality in the sense that all being contains spirit and that the dead continue to exist in the world. But the fact that these are haunting presences indicates a refusal of the black nationalist view that the figures of the past are necessarily nurturing and helpful. They can be "whining," "crying," "humming," "panting," or "moaning." John Washington's project in the text can be said to be to identify and, where necessary, to exorcise those ghosts; the message of the novel would seem to be that they are everywhere and inescapable. John's vocation of writing the history of atrocity is ultimately doomed, not because of the nonreality of atrocity, but rather because his method cannot ever get at its authentic being. For him, every act of communication in both means and method is a conversation with ghosts; only by recognizing this pervasiveness can he begin to learn how to live with the spirits rather than drive them out.

His relationship with Jack begins with the death of his father, Moses. Prior to that death, John had thought of his father primarily as a distant, rather disagreeable figure whom he disliked. Jack himself was a disreputable person who Yvette Washington prohibited from entering her house, even though he had helped to build it as a wedding gift for her. When a drunken Jack bursts into the funeral reception to try to talk to John and even take him away, it only adds to the scandalous reputation of Moses that Yvette has had to endure. When John ventures to the Other Side to find Jack, he learns that his father had left instructions for his son's training in skills and knowledge of survival in nature. In the process of that training, Jack also communicates the legends associated with Moses.

As the text shifts between the present time of John's return to take care of a dying Jack, the past of John's childhood, and the deeper past of the adventures of Moses, Jack, and Josh White, it becomes apparent that the survival training is primarily a metaphor for intellectual skills of careful observation and interpretation. Moses, through the illiterate Jack, is teaching his son how to read signs, especially those whose meaning is not apparent or is suppressed. John is constantly interpreting bodies, conversations, patterns of behavior, stories, and lives, as well as the ground, the sky, and natural forces.

He also is alert to misreadings by himself or others. For example, he is initially puzzled by his mother's preparation for him of a meal she knows he dislikes. Finally, he realizes, as she does, that she has slipped in time and prepared the favorite food of his dead brother Bill. This error is intensified in the sense that John holds his mother responsible for Bill's death, in that she virtually forced him into military service in Vietnam after John had persuaded him to evade the draft. For both mother and son, this moment of error conjures forth Bill's presence/absence, though the meaning of his ghost is different for each of them. In fact, it is John's effort to read the moment that opens the wound of the past that he and his mother usually manage to deny.

Here again we see the coming together of the personal and the professional; the social skill of observation and interpretation is the same as John's intellectual skills as a historian. Moreover, the purpose also seems much the same: he tries to remove the layers of denial, social nicety, hypocrisy, and rationalization so as to expose the uncomfortable truth. He gains power and control, in nature, in personal relationships, and in his profession by knowing more than others and by being quicker at analyzing new information. It also encourages an arrogance and coldness that several people comment make him much like his father.

This doubling seems to be by Moses's design. He wanted his son to become self-reliant and highly skilled because he had a task of historical investigation that he himself could not complete and so left it for John. He chose this son in part because John was thought by many people to think too much like whites, but what the father needed was precisely that ability. So he encouraged John's education while also creating puzzles and difficulties that would make him distrustful of anyone but himself.

The novel is more about this process than it is about the historical puzzle itself, in part because the puzzle could not be solved solely on intellectual grounds. This was the error of both father and son. Moses believed that everything and everyone could be understood and manipulated rationally. He was willing to sacrifice emotional relationships to gain his ends. But what he searched for was as much moral truth as historical information. He needed to know what had happened to his ancestors, who seemed to have been caught up in the racial struggles of antebellum America. Having been, in effect, captured by these ghosts, he sought to reconstruct their narratives by replicating their lives. He then produces a son in his own image who will complete the quest.

John comments several times in the text about the relationship between story and death: "And then I began to think about what a man's dying really means: his story is lost. Bits and pieces of it remain, but they are all secondhand tales and hearsay, or cold official records that preserve the facts and spoil the truth; the sum is like a writer's complete works with crucial numbers missing. . . . But the gaps in the stories of the unknown are never filled, never can be filled, for they are larger than data, larger than deduction, larger than induction" (48–49). Death creates "gaps" that cannot be filled by the processes of reasoning, in part because they are the life itself, not the information. But those spaces are not merely empty; they are haunted by that life now gone. Only by accepting the reality of hauntedness is it possible to recreate some version of the story. John must learn to use his imagination, based on his knowledge, both personal and professional, in order to complete the task of historical research started by his father.

Bradley, then, challenges the practices of both old and new historians and, more generally, the abuses of history (as reality and interpretation) apparent in American society. The story of black experience cannot be made meaningful by increasingly sophisticated methods of historical analysis. These methods must always miss the "story" by pursuing the "facts." Moreover, such a method dehumanizes those it describes by turning them into ciphers and thus reinforces the dominant culture's denial of black subjectivity. Even if this approach does not recapitulate the racist assumptions of earlier historians, it does the more subtle work of reducing black agency and selfhood to insignificance by emphasizing social forces and statistical models.

At the same time, a commitment to reason is a necessary part of the historical project of understanding the black experience. What John learns from what his father has left him is not only legends and folk wisdom but also a documentary trail that can link stories to information in such a way that valid conclusions can be drawn about the past. The point is not to reject reason or imagination but to recognize the limits of each and to bring them together in a coherent reconstruction that tells the human story in all its complexity.

What John discovers in the narrative he creates is a love story, an adventure tale, a slave narrative, and a family legend that links him to the black struggle for freedom. He uncovers an ancestor who lived on the margins of society, engaging in criminal activities in part to aid the cause of escaping slaves. This figure is repeated in his father, whose mysterious behavior and attitudes are thus explained, at least partially. He discovers a woman who sacrifices her own security for the sake of love and freedom. He identifies a white slave catcher–intellectual, much like those seen in other novels in this study. But he also locates a white man who cares enough for this band of blacks to bury them with dignity. And he learns of the self-willed deaths of the black man, the woman, and the slaves they led; this group suicide explains the song at John's father's funeral: "Before I'll be a slave/I'll be buried in my grave." It also explains the death of the father, who, it becomes clear, killed himself at the site of the deaths of the ancestors in order to follow them into the spirit realm.

John learns something different from his father: love, not death, is the point of the story. It is not only the love of C. K. and Harriet, in all of its moral vision, intensity, and dignity, that has meaning for John and Judith as they seek a way to commitment through the obstacles of racial and personality difference. It is also the deep concern of the white man Iames, involved in the Underground Railroad, who makes the effort to bury the bodies with respect for the relationships of the people. This discovery challenges the racial biases held by John, Jack, and Moses that whites are never to be trusted and impossible to love.

Through this narrative of black history, then, Bradley speaks to his own time, though he risks being absorbed in the dominant discourse in the process. He addresses the issue of interracial relationships but problematizes it by requiring both John and Judith to change their perspective in order to achieve success. Her devotion to the relationship is never at issue; in fact, one question is why she would want to sustain the connection given John's coldness, arrogance, and cynicism. With these negative traits, the explanation would almost seem to be located in an assumption of the white woman's fascination for the black man's sexual prowess or else her own racial guilt and the corollary of the black man's enthrallment with the white woman. Bradley's reticence on motivations for the relationship opens up the interjection of racialized readings in a narrative that appears designed to contradict them. Certainly requiring the two contemporary characters to "work" toward each other through the vehicle of a historical love story suggests the author's resistance to such readings. Once both learn the traumatic nature of black experience and the transcendent power of love, they can find a basis for their own relationship. Judith must give up the privilege of her white skin and her related assumptions of an American history defined by justice, fairness, and freedom, while John must surrender his notion that atrocity, even if it is the major pattern of history, is the only part of the story to be told.

Through these characters and their respective educations, rather than through the history they recover, Bradley addresses the present. Whites must let go of the belief that the past is a story of unceasing progress toward democracy, justice, equality, and individual success. This includes rejecting the fantasies of works such as *Roots*, which present blacks as pure and their struggle as a simple desire to be conventionally American. C. K.'s marginality, criminality, and ambivalence subvert such views. Understanding can come only by seeing history as trauma, as great, undeserved suffering that cannot be mitigated or disguised. Moreover, the novel asserts that this understanding cannot be merely intellectual or sentimental; each way of understanding allows the perpetuation of otherness and attendant white privilege. Rather, the comprehension must become personal, so that it becomes necessary for whites to take responsibility for the nation and all its citizens. Judith comes to recognize her connection not only to the sympathetic Iames and the self-sacrificing Harriet but also to the brilliant but terrifying slave catcher, who uses his reason and knowledge to determine what the runaways will do in order to capture or kill them. Judith, a psychiatrist, may be said to be engaged in a similar process with John. She wants to bring him within the conventions, to get him to give up all his secrets in order to satisfy her needs for an appropriate mate. Like the white historians, sociologists, and political commentators of the 1970s, she believes she knows better than he does what his life means and how it can be made better. By accepting the trauma of the past as her story as well, she provides a model of a different kind of relationship.

The parallel for John is to get beyond survivor guilt and anger; through him, Bradley is questioning the nationalist impulse among African Americans. The truth is complex and cannot be reduced to heroism and villainy, to black and white, in any sense. Moses Washington, in his quest for the past, sacrifices his family. His obsession leads him to make his son hate him so that John will carry on the quest. He even commits suicide to follow the trail, thus depriving his family of a father and husband. The importance of this action may be seen in what happens to Bill, an athlete passed along without a real education until his eligibility runs out; at that point, he is failed. One result is that he is drafted and dies in Vietnam. While John blames this sequence of events on community whites and on his mother, it is also an effect of the death of Moses, who knew enough to see through such manipulations and had the power to prevent it. In effect, the father searches for death and not only finds it but produces it in the present. Because he refuses to speak the experience directly, preferring to leave a trail for his son to follow to the site of memory and loss, John must try to recover the suppressed and unspeakable on his own.

Likewise, his companion Jack, who is John's guide to history, literally lives in the world of ghosts in his cabin on the Far Side. He has no trust in either women or whites and repeatedly castigates John if he believes him to be associated with either. He also rejects any form of modern ("white") knowledge. While he can teach his student much about the realm of nature and about the legends of the region, including the stories about Moses, he cannot prepare him for the education necessary to carry out the research his father wanted done, which required books and method. Jack can provide the personal, human quality by telling the stories and passing along the folk wisdom, but his is only part of the task.

It is not enough to have only the lore of the past, as valuable as that is; fixed in the past, it cannot effectively adjust to changing circumstances. Implicit in this contention is Bradley's rejection of a romanticized black past, either in the sense of a purity of wisdom and virtue or in the sense of victimization. To live in that world, the text declares, is to die in it. Jack literally dies as John carries him to the inhabited side of the Hill, to the modern world. Likewise, John cannot move beyond his anger, obsessions, and separateness until he accepts all the world, past and present, in which blacks live. Life in a world defined only by race is a dead end, a haunted house. An ideologically driven black history that assumes its meaning before undertaking the exploration cannot provide adequate resources for a living present. It is only through boundary-crossings, transgression of suppression, and openness to both multiplicity and horror that a useful history can be constructed.

Finally, then, David Bradley argues for a version of Du Boisian double-consciousness in the sense of a respect for both the recognition of the horrors of the past and an awareness of the tools to change the present. Some of these tools have traditionally belonged to the master, but they are nonetheless essential if the ghosts are to be properly appreciated and properly used for the benefit of the living. The point, then, is not to be haunted but to be nourished for the tasks of the present.

Chapter Nine

FAMILY TROUBLES

History as Subversion in Two Wings to
Veil My Face *and* Divine Days

In his novels, Leon Forrest consistently concerns himself with
what Ralph Ellison called "the complex fate" of being black and American.
For Forrest, the condition requires an emphasis on the process of storytelling,
involving many voices and discursive practices.[1] It includes layers of meaning
that constantly shift and re-form. Narrating such experience necessitates recognition of the history embedded in the everyday life of the present, as well as
in the tales told or untold by his characters. Each work has as its central
character a young black man who is compelled to try to make sense of the past,
usually because he has lost significant members of his family; the problem in
each case is the wealth rather than dearth of materials and possible interpretations that are available to him. At the same time, the history revealed has
implications for the seeker's sense of identity and place in the world, in part
because it incorporates family experiences that might aid him in understanding
his own situation as an orphan and a black man in the contemporary world.
Forrest argues that the recovery of family history, which can serve as metaphor
or metonymy of group history, is the most effective means of understanding
and working through contemporary problems. Without an appreciation of the
past and its impact, present concerns will seem insurmountable. Thus, Forrest
reworks the holocaust motif so as to both acknowledge and move beyond it. In
creating a thematics of troubled families and orphans, he figures African Americans as special, but only in the sense of being the most fully American of the
nation's people.

In constructing his version of the past, Forrest implicitly challenges virtually
all of the standard readings of black experience circulating in the 1970s and
1980s. Both heroic and pathological readings that suggest that African American history can be reduced to a simple cause for the present are rejected; neither

Afrocentrists nor neoconservatives engage the full complexity of the group history. A crucial theme for him is the interested nature of telling history; those who construct the past have an investment in their version of events. One reason for the multivoiced character of his narratives is a belief that some kind of truth only can emerge from a profusion of speakers, each with his/her own master narrative. Thus, at a time when black history was claiming a significant place both in the academy and in popular culture, he was warning against any tendency toward narrow ideological interpretations.

His choice of family history at this time is also significant, since that story is for him the means of understanding African American experience. Under slavery, families were often destroyed through violence or commerce: children were sold away, husbands and wives (who had no legal relationship) were separated, and those who sought to escape were often killed. Moreover, social rules permitted white men to have intercourse with their slaves, whether for pleasure or profit. Thus, family was valued precisely because its status was so fragile. After Emancipation, the rules changed to some extent, but Jim Crow laws, racial violence, and economic dependency created an unstable environment. More recently, the black family, especially in its one-parent form, has been blamed for many of the ills of post–civil rights America.[2] To challenge this version of black history, Forrest develops narratives of the complex structures and emotional power of African American relationships. His families cover many generations and cross racial, class, religious, and regional lines. And the effects of family are always powerful, both positively and negatively. His, then, is a counterhistory designed to subvert the dominant discourse on the subject.

Forrest's first two novels, *A Tree More Ancient than Eden* (1973) and *The Bloodworth Orphans* (1977), have as their central figure Nathaniel Witherspoon, but they use him primarily as a vehicle for presenting the black community, both in the immediate and geographical sense and in the larger historical sense.[3] *Two Wings to Veil My Face* (1983), the third of the Forest County works, focuses more directly on Nathaniel's personal and familial concerns. As in the earlier books, his consciousness is the means by which Forrest explores the complexity of the African American experience; in this novel, however, that is done through the stories of the Witherspoon and Reed families. Moreover, storytelling itself becomes a central issue in the narrative. Readers are asked to consider the relationship of the teller to the truth of the tale, the possibility of truth itself when both speaker and listener have important interests at stake, and the relationship of gender to the narrative of family history.

In a sense, *Two Wings to Veil My Face* is a traditional patriarchal narrative. It is a quest for fathers, with an underlying assumption that the identification and understanding of fathers provides the key to the identities of the children.[4] Thus, Sweetie Reed, the principal narrator, tells Nathaniel the stories of her husband and Nathaniel's grandfather, Jericho Witherspoon; her father, I. V. Reed; and her grandfather, the slaveholder Rollins Reed. The story becomes Nathaniel's patrimony, told to him after he turns twenty-one and intended to explain his spiritual and material heritage. In this sense, Forrest, though from Chicago, follows in the Southern tradition of William Faulkner and Robert Penn Warren both in tracing Southern patriarchy and in creating a complex pattern of storytelling that problematizes history even as it records it. The past is not a finished product of agreed-upon data but a struggle for coherence in a field of competing voices, of myths, of conflicting facts, of divergent interests, of lacunae and silences, of distortion and lies, and of prejudices, needs, and desires that constantly shape and reshape the story. The novel takes the form of stories embedded within other stories, such that, for the reader, the narrative voice is constantly changing. Moreover, this shift means that the novel changes time frames often and employs repetition, contradictions, and silences. Each voice is self-critical and also challenged by other voices about its veracity and interests in the narrating process; in this way, storytelling itself is foregrounded as a device. The text in addition incorporates songs, newspaper articles, and letters as alternative means of access to the past. To this modernist narrative process, Forrest adds the complicating factors of race and gender, not merely as themes, but as perspectives to be accommodated within the telling.

Thus, the story that Sweetie tells Nathaniel goes far beyond her declared purpose. She claims to want to explain to him why, fourteen years before, she had refused to attend the funeral of her estranged husband. At the time of the telling, Sweetie is in her nineties and apparently near death. She rejects Nathaniel's offer to tape-record it, demanding instead that he actively participate by recording it in longhand.

Sweetie tells of a much earlier time when she returned to the deathbed of her father to hear *his* explanation of *his* behavior, both before and after her birth. Roughly half of the novel is taken up with I. V.'s story of slavery and the immediate postbellum period. Only near the end and after considerable prodding from Nathaniel does she explain that her separation from Jericho was not only because of his lack of religious faith but also because her son Arthur (Nathaniel's father) was in fact the product of a liaison between Jericho and another woman. Thus, the completion of the quest deconstructs the very patriarchal order that motivated it. The story of the father is the story of the violation of law and morality. The characterization of Jericho as heroic by both

Arthur and Nathaniel throughout the novel only strengthens the ironic force of the revelation.

The conclusion also serves, on the surface at least, to validate the lengthy telling of I. V. Reed's story. If the tale of Jericho Witherspoon is the narrative of a flawed hero, that of Reed is one of a cringing antihero. Sweetie describes her father as one "whose body had been touched to *the wishbone of the master; a tongue flapped backwards and pressed to the sole of a footless shoe*" (6; ital. in original). He slept under Rollins Reed's bed, even after the emancipation, so that he would always be available to meet the white man's needs, and he was generally despised by the other slaves because of his obsequious nature. I. V. Reed seemingly serves as the counterpoint to Jericho Witherspoon in a fictional version of the dichotomies so often found in black history: house/field slave; Booker T. Washington/W. E. B. Du Bois; Martin Luther King/Malcolm X; Ralph Ellison and James Baldwin/LeRoi Jones. Such a pairing suggests that Forrest is voicing his variation on a black "master narrative."

But I. V.'s own life story subverts such a narrative in both detail and structure. As he confesses on his deathbed: "Auntie Foisty told me before she passed, slaves would see me as a bloodhound all my days yet they would never tell on me—but would whisper my name in their heart of hearts and never trust me. The sole way I could ever hope for salvation was to tell the whole story out loud before I died to each of my children and each of their children's children unto my last dying gasp. . . . Me personal, not through any hired third hand, but by my very own lapping tongue" (139). Confession becomes the means of salvation, though not through a priest or other religious authority but through family history. The narrative, then, is sanctioned, not by law and patriarchal order, but by responsibility to the personal and familial past and future. Significantly, the authorizing figure is Aunt Foisty, who, as shall be seen, acts as the representative of God and the black experience simultaneously.

I. V. speaks to save himself; whether he in fact speaks the truth is constantly being brought into doubt by Sweetie, both as audience for his tale and as teller of her own. She sarcastically refers to him as "honest Ivy," the name given him by the plantation owners. A key question, given her skepticism, is why she is so obsessed with his story. She has little interest in his salvation, since she seems to consider him doomed from the beginning. She does, however, need recognition from him: "I had not seen him since I left that plantation, twenty-four years before. Maybe I wanted to hear him say just simply *I tried to love you, Sweetie;* . . . to give me a portion of recognition as his child, that never sprang from his tongue while I was there" (45).

In effect, she seeks from a man of lies the truth of herself. Such desperate effort is necessary because her life has been one of negation. The defining experience of Sweetie's childhood was the kidnapping of her and her mother, Angelina, by white men determined to enslave them even though the war had been over for several years. Rollins Reed and I. V. arrange a ransom payment, but only Sweetie is returned; Angelina had already been raped and murdered. Thereafter, I. V. merely watches her; he offers no parental comfort. Sweetie's emphasis is on what I. V. should do as father; because he fails to meet this standard, she is negated as his child and must define herself in part through her hatred of him. Sweetie's perspective makes I. V. the patriarchal villain of the narrative of *her* suffering and of the victimization of black women.

But I. V.'s apparent disregard opens up family history in a way that questions the message of Sweetie's tale. I. V. is as much a figure of suffering in that scene as his daughter if we see him in human rather than demonic terms. Sweetie is not only the returned loved one but even more deeply the emblem of what I. V. has lost. She is a constant reminder of the loss of Angelina and a constant stimulus of the intolerable pain of that loss. What he seeks to scratch out is not the child but the pain; unfortunately for Sweetie, the two are inseparable for her father. Forrest seems to be suggesting here a reading of black fatherhood that understands it not as a simple set of negative personal behaviors, as often seemed to be the social scientific explanation since the 1964 Moynihan Report. Rather, he makes a case for a psychologically complex black masculinity that cannot allow itself to become emotionally engaged because it always loses that which is most valued.

That I. V. resists speaking of this pain on his deathbed is the whole story as far as Sweetie is concerned. In this refusal, he foreshadows her own narrative to Nathaniel years later. Both stories have an absence at their centers; in fact, the narratives exist precisely as the avoidance on the part of the teller of the key element for the audience. They insist on telling the truth "slant," in the mode of indirection so often found in African American narrative traditions. What I. V. puts in the place of direct representation of that experience is the story of his own destiny; in the process, he forces a reconsideration of the thesis of female victimization.

The central tale he tells seems only tangentially related to Sweetie's life. Involving people she never knew, it occurs before she was born, and it takes the form of a morality play in which an apparently minor act of spite is shown to have vast consequences. At the age of thirteen, I. V. becomes angry at Reece Shank Haywood, the plantation's black driver, because Haywood has taken I. V.'s girlfriend. In retaliation, the boy tells the driver one night that Rollins is in the cabin of Jubell, another woman Haywood desires for himself. In anger,

Haywood tries to kill the master. While I. V. has no love for Rollins, he had intended only conflict, not murder; to stop the killing, he slings a stone that strikes Haywood on the temple. When Haywood then drops Rollins and runs away, I. V. resuscitates the master somewhat and seeks help from Aunt Foisty, the plantation conjure woman and healer.

The ambiguous meaning of this drama is revealed in the two directions the story now takes. On the one hand, Haywood is captured and punished and then dies. But if Haywood is doomed by I. V.'s act, Rollins is saved by it—literally and figuratively—for the master is profoundly changed by the ministrations of the conjure woman. This part of the narrative follows the form of the Pygmalian story, with, as shall be seen, important gender and racial implications.

The Rollins Reed who is carried into the shack is the archetype of the evil master:

> My remembrance is back to when Master Reed was an unleashed bloodhound to his niggers. I recollect when he'd whip them soon up in the morning till nightfall can't stand moonlight's shadow; he'd shake down hot red peppers into their wound lashes; other times drop hot wax from candles into their bleeding sores and scabs, left there from the master's earlier lashes. . . . Love to go cutting after slave women. . . . —From the soles of his feet to the temple of his crown Rollins Reed was baptized in pure meanness and cruelty. (86)

Foisty works to save this moral monster, not because she is a version of the stereotypical mammy who feels compelled to aid white folks, but precisely because the situation gives her the opportunity to change the nature of power on the plantation. She brings him back from the verge of death and cleanses him of his evil nature.

In this process, she claims divine authority for herself and inverts the traditional plantation hierarchy. Normally the master creates the slave—designating a role, naming, holding the power of life and death—in part on the basis of religious authority. The slave woman here invokes the divine patriarch in order to subvert Rollins's patriarchal position and, in doing so, raises herself to the position of author and creator.

But her authority as a maker of men is not merely self-proclaimed. Foisty is in fact both the embodiment and the keeper of black history. She came over on a slave ship and, according to I. V., was midwife to half the slaves on the plantation, as well as wet nurse for both Rollins and his father. Moreover, she is the true memory of all their experiences, black and white, and her power is human history. Foisty's memory supersedes the white written word. She recalls not what is most important to the master—the monetary side of the ledger—but the human side, which the numbers effectively erase. She knows *how* slaves died rather than just *when*. She knows the story *whole*, instead of merely its economic significance. Thus, when Foisty tells Rollins that he has brought "woe" to the slaves, there is no denying her.

One crucial twist to the narrative is Foisty's demand that I. V. become Rollins's personal servant and sleep beneath his bed. While she intends this as I. V.'s punishment for what happened, she also wishes to provide Rollins a constant reminder of the experience he has been through. Thus, she who defines the past also shapes the future. Further, she pushes her influence into later generations by compelling I. V. to pass his story down to his children and grandchildren. This command also guarantees that he himself will be read by Sweetie and, in the present time of the narrative, by Nathaniel, as the villain of the Reed-Witherspoon saga. But I. V. seeks to counter this interpretation and thus disrupt the simple text that Sweetie wishes to create. He reminds Sweetie repeatedly that he is her father and Rollins her grandfather and that her own faith requires a degree of respect for him; moreover, such paternity means that part of what she is came from them. She is the trace of his being beyond his mortal life, but he is her connection with the past, with that sense of family she so deeply desires.

Such insight does not keep Sweetie from reading I. V. Reed as demonic, and she persists in despising his character and actions. She stops only when he comes to her part in the narrative. She had always assumed that Witherspoon and her father and grandfather (Rollins) had arranged her marriage. What I. V. explains is that it was Jericho who paid her ransom, though he thought he was purchasing Angelina's freedom. When he learns that Angelina was murdered, Sweetie is offered to him, though she is forty years younger. Thus, Sweetie is doubly negated; she was freed with money intended for Angelina, and she is married as her surrogate. The three men against whom she has defined her life—Rollins, I. V., Jericho—acted out of love rather than hate or disdain, but it was not love of her. Her father's narrative reshapes the meaning of her existence: she is a lack rather than a fullness. The history she learns is of her own insignificance except as a signifier of her mother's absence. In place of the morality play she had constructed, which placed her heroically in the center against male antagonists, she now has a human tragedy, in which she was merely a minor figure. Being the sign of loss rather than desire, Sweetie becomes, in effect, one of the orphans so common to Forrest's fiction.

In offering this narrative, Forrest rewrites the story of black female victimization current when his novel came out. *Two Wings* was published a year after *The Color Purple* and during the period when Gloria Naylor, ntozake shange, Gayl Jones, and, to some extent, Toni Morrison were building reputations on tales of female suffering, usually at the hands of black men. Forrest's response was not necessarily to show a different kind of man but rather to complicate the gender dynamics. Foisty is as powerful and nurturing a woman as found in any novel, but she uses that power for the good of the whole community, both black and white. Moreover, Sweetie's problem is not so much deliberate victimization as a misreading of the workings of love.

The story that Nathaniel has been waiting for ultimately brings the notion of orphanhood full circle. Just as Sweetie is deprived of her place in family history by I. V.'s narrative, so Nathaniel has his taken by Sweetie. One function of the shifting narrative voices and time frames that structure the text now becomes clear. Sweetie's narration of her father's story and her own alternates with Nathaniel's memories of his childhood, including his grandfather's death and funeral and his father's responses to both Sweetie and Jericho. Just as she demonizes I. V. in her voicing of his experience, so Nathaniel, through his own and his father's memories, monumentalizes Jericho as a king. The effect of Sweetie's tale, however, like that of I. V.'s, is to demystify those made extrahuman by their descendants.

The secret of the text goes to the heart of patriarchal power. Sweetie reveals to Nathaniel that his father, Arthur, was illegitimate. Because Jericho requires an heir in order to perpetuate himself and because Sweetie cannot produce one, he goes outside the marriage to find a woman who can meet this need and then brings the infant to Sweetie to raise as his son. She is torn between desire to protect a motherless child and shame and anger at her husband's behavior. Jericho exercises the patriarchal prerogative of imposing a role and burden on her while he evades confrontation with her moral indignation. The acquisition of an heir transcends moral boundaries; the man who carries the literal brand of slavery on his back, who risked his life for freedom, and who purchased hers has expanded his freedom from the right to control his own life to controlling those of others. Jericho, in this instance, seems to fall in that line going back to Rollins and I. V. that makes orphans of children.

But if the patriarchs paradoxically generate orphanhood in their pursuit of family lines, then it is up to the women and children to nurture and embrace each other. Sweetie and her friend Lovelady set up a kitchen to feed the needy of the community, but they also ask that recipients give whatever they can, in order to maintain their dignity. Unlike Jericho, who demands something specific (a baby) from his wife in exchange for her life, Lovelady and Sweetie accept whatever can be offered and thus can give the "lost soul" a measure of freedom, as well as dignity.

So Sweetie offers Nathaniel his inheritance: in her safe, he finds a tintype of Lucasta Jones, his biological grandmother, and, hidden in I. V.'s shoes, diamonds that belonged to Sylvia Reed, Rollins's wife. The sign of patriarchal order—inheritance—is embodied here by emblems of illegitimacy, slavery, and orphanhood. Nathaniel is the doubly illegitimate heir to the diamonds: they come through Rollins's illegitimate daughter Angelina to Jericho's bastard's son.

It is an inheritance fraught with ambiguity. The diamonds were originally bought with wealth obtained from brutal slave labor, but they now financially liberate one of the families originally enslaved. Nathaniel sees in the tintype not only his biological grandmother but also the image of the saintly Angelina and finally that of his own dead mother. His reading of the visual text disrupts not only his notions of good and evil but also those of Sweetie. She persists in hating Lucasta even as she compels Nathaniel to accept her. She had told her story in part to get from him sympathy for her years of emotional suffering, but instead he performs for her the troubling function she saw as her own: "I do love the truth of Justice, no matter where the beacon's taper light falls, Mother Sweetie Witherspoon Reed. . . . But can you recognize Lucasta from Angelina? Oh, you never lied, most sacred liar prophetess. I do. I do love within my / our loathsome inheritance. . . . But do I only love the enlightened cause of Justice? Oh no way out but to burn out the alabaster blight of this blindness; oh, light of the body is luminously of the eye. . . . No two wings to hide the riddles features upon my fated American face" (294; ellipses in original).

The end is not resolution but the tension and conflict that love generates. The polyglossic tale that is black history is not necessarily harmonious, but neither is it neatly dichotomous. To insist on either is to descend into sentimentality and self-righteousness. Lucasta, Angelina, I. V., Foisty, and others have their part in the story, and they cannot be reduced to each other or tidily divided into absolutes. Each has a voice, irreducible and articulate. Sweetie Reed's telling of their tales does not turn them into a monologue. All the voices demand to be heard; she and then Nathaniel resist their speaking but cannot finally silence it. The truth is not in resolution but in the multiplicity of voices. All the orphans produced by all the different fathers (who are themselves motherless) have gifts to bring and stories to tell. Nathaniel's true inheritance (and that of Forrest's readers), then, is not some tidy patrimony but all the voices in the wind of all the mothers and fathers. And his gift to them is the recording of their words; he creates, in effect, their testament. They made him an orphan; he gives them a family history.

Two Wings to Veil My Face *and* Divine Days 145

In the construction of this deeply ambiguous history, Forrest problematizes virtually all aspects of the African American experience but simultaneously implies new possibilities. He suggests ways to move past the contentions of gender, by acknowledging the complex motives and desires of contending forces. Women who seek power and equality must recognize the struggles of black men who find their masculinity threatened within a racialized and sexualized America. And men must acknowledge the powers that women are capable of exercising and encourage their development. Moreover, all must recognize the shared humanity of all the ancestors and the common experience of suffering, even among presumed enemies. And, finally, it is essential to understand that all are orphans and perhaps bastards, that this is the American condition, and that family must be created, not by the tracing of bloodlines, but by the recording of all the ancestral voices and the embracing of all the other "lost-found." Thus, in a post–civil rights era of culture wars, gender conflicts, and Reaganomics, Forrest implicitly called for recognition of an American past of great complexity that had in fact given birth to a present that was deeper and richer than ideologues from all sides acknowledged. It was also a past that produced a shared present and a common destiny, whether we like it or not.

In *Divine Days*, Forrest creates, in effect, a model for contemporary African American writing at the very time (1992) that that literature was reaching a new plateau of success: in that year, works by Terry McMillan, Toni Morrison, Gloria Naylor, and Alice Walker all appeared on the *New York Times* bestseller list; within a year, Morrison was awarded the Nobel Prize; and Pulitzer, National Book Award, and PEN prizes were regularly being given to African American writers. So the issue in 1992 was not, as it had so often been in the past, the lack of attention being paid to black culture and specifically black literature. For Forrest, at least, the question was the place of that literature in the larger context of American and world literary traditions. He and many of his contemporaries were still being read as "special cases," artists to be judged within a fairly narrow frame of reference, such as black literature, black women writers, black magical realists, or black postmodernists. In other words, the writing was always racialized (and in many cases gendered as well). Movements such as Afrocentrism continued to read this difference as affirmation, while, to some extent, writers themselves encouraged such readings in the ways they described their own careers, sources, and theories of artistic production.[5]

In *Divine Days*, Forrest breaks this frame by claiming all of American and world culture as the context for his fictional creation. His narrator's speech and thought, like that of other characters, is filled with acknowledged and unacknowledged literary and cultural references. Homer, Greek dramatists and philosophers, Shakespeare, Milton, Melville, Emerson, Russian novelists, Joyce, Faulkner, Ellison, Baldwin, and Alice Walker, among others, are alluded to through quotation or parody. The references are often foregrounded as a display of knowledge. This self-conscious literariness affirms the author's claim to a Western patrimony, not one confined within racial boundaries. Moreover, the structure of the novel as a *kuntslerroman* set in a narrow time frame invites comparison to the work of canonical modernists, including Joyce and Faulkner. Forrest has asserted that he wants to be understood as writing one of the world's great novels, not simply an important African American or even American novel.[6]

The basis of his project, as indicated repeatedly in the text, is the exploding of W. E. B. Du Bois's notion of double-consciousness, at the very time that Du Bois's notion reemerges as a paradigm.[7] Black identity is to be understood not in terms of a racial dichotomy but as a plenitude and multiplicity. Region, class, gender, religion, personal and family history, skin tone, and personality type are as important as race in determining individual identity, in Forrest's view. While all people whom society designates "black" experience racial oppression, other factors shape how one understands, reacts to, and uses that experience. Since these factors have affected all people throughout time, the insights of all artists may be of some value in defining a specific life or experience. Forrest accepts, as certainly the cultural nationalists of the 1960s and many of the Afrocentrists of the 1980s and 1990s have not, the centrality of the individual in understanding and representing human nature. He has stated that a major reason for the length of *Divine Days* (1,135 pages) is that he wanted to play out the possibilities of a wide range of characters (Byerman, "Angularity," 440). They are not types but individuals whose meanings are to be seen in complex, perhaps finally mysterious ways. Thus, any ideological frame that negates individuality necessarily misunderstands how race actually functions in the world. This point is repeatedly made in the novel.

Forrest's use of Western traditions of literary production does not, however, lead to a deracialized text or to the conclusion that the author, to paraphrase Countee Cullen, wants to be known as a novelist first and a black second. Making such distinctions, which is common to the dominant discourse, is precisely the false practice Forrest seeks to expose and repudiate. It is the function of the artist to violate categories, to insist on re-visioning the world in terms that subvert conventional wisdom and one-dimensional thinking. One piece of that wisdom and one that is at the core of the contemporary racial formation is that "black" is a transparent signifier. This view is held by virtually all members of American society and is fundamental to the existing order. While the meaning of blackness may be taken as positive or negative, may be defended or attacked, essentialized or constructed, it is, to a large extent, fixed.[8] This consensus on its transparency is crucial to maintaining social affiliations and distances, to creating public policy, to perpetuating the economic system, and to comprehending cultural and even personal expression. "Black" is different and other, but in definable ways.

Joubert Jones, the narrator, seeks to be a writer, not by shaping experience on the basis of racial identity or nonidentity, but rather by making some sense of the voices, stories, encounters, texts, and memories that constitute his world. "Making sense" does not mean creating categories into which characters and events can be neatly placed but rather identifying relationships, probing mysteries, and uncovering secrets and repressed knowledge. One implicit argument of the text is that American racial oppression is in part the result of suppression and repression of kinship. The novel is filled with partial truths, incomplete gossip, trickster behavior, denial of family, incestuous desires and acts, miscegenation, lies, verbal games, and interrupted narratives, all of which imply hidden reality and the need for manipulative control. But they also suggest a plenitude of experience that may be beyond control, especially when it comes to black experience. To delve into the secrets threatens order, including the order of the constructed self. Joubert, making himself into a writer, finds that his assumptions about his world and about himself are constantly being undercut by what he discovers. He hopes to exploit others for source material but finds his own image being assaulted and fragmented by his efforts.

The narrative is set over an eight-day period in February of 1966. It is thus positioned in the middle of Black History Month and between the assassinations of Malcolm X and Martin Luther King. One way to understand the structure of the novel is by seeing the first half as a study not so much of Malcolm as of the mythic frame in which he operated and the second half as the frame of history and love in which King operated. Forrest creates the figure of W. A. D. Ford, a trickster who is an obvious reference to W. A. D. Fard, the semimythic founding figure of the Nation of Islam. Ford appears and disappears, generates a theology that has himself at the center, and gathers true believers around him in various organizations. Like Forrest, who served for a time on the editorial staff of *Muhammad Speaks*, Joubert Jones has a journalistic interest in this black-oriented faith. Much of what is included in this part is a parody of Black Muslim belief and practice, including Ford's sexual activities, a reference to the allegations against Elijah Muhammad that led to Malcolm's break with the group. In contrast, Sugar Groove represents love, struggle, and sacrifice for others, though some of this only becomes apparent as Joubert digs out and remembers the story. Sugar Groove, in an echo of King, dies on a mountaintop gazing, if not at the promised land, at some notion of truth about human experience.

It is important not to overemphasize the parallels between actual persons and events and fictional creations since Forrest is not espousing a great-man theory of history or offering an allegory of the 1960s. Rather, he is interested in how that time period reverberates in our own and how it poses issues and suggests truths that transcend time. The key question for the text would seem to be how one makes sense of history and reality; this is especially necessary for Joubert, who wants to work in the relatively disciplined form of drama. He is filled with voices and stories that he has heard or experienced and must find a way to structure them. His problem might be said to be one of mapping, that is, configuring all the material into something coherent enough to be presented in the time-space of the theater.

The process he uses is archaeological; by moving back through layers of story, he can identify patterns and draw conclusions that tie together different moments in the past and the present. The consistent link is family or at least close personal relationship. At the same time, through constant literary allusion, the narrator can make reference to similar findings and conclusions across literary history, thus suggesting larger meanings for private experiences. The danger of the method is that conclusions will be drawn or assumptions made about what will be found before the evidence is in. Joubert is constantly forced to rethink his positions when a new story or new twist on a story is told. Moreover, this questioning involves not only information for professional use but also issues of his own selfhood and moral responsibility. The chief lesson appears to be that there are always more layers, stories, and voices to challenge conclusions and self-image. An experientially driven art, then, can never be finished, can never be more than a "play," a fictive gesture in the direction of truth.

Nonetheless, there are patterns discernable in the apparent chaos, and, moreover, there seems to be one master story, with infinite variations. That is a story of almost universal suffering, often undeserved and seldom in any rational relationship to any act committed by the victim. The exception of "almost universal" is Ford, who operates as a force rather than a person. He is the principle of chaos, deceit, and manipulation that causes much of the evil and pain. But even he has positive uses, since, among other things, he forces believers to choose masks that reveal their true characters. He is a reminder of human weakness and the capacity for self-delusion. He also is never truly conquered, while those who live in history must ultimately lose, to death and their own limitations. Ford disappears into nowhere at the end of the novel, just as he came from nowhere at the beginning, but his apparent absence only means that he has transformed himself in the present. He is the source and ever-active agent that is the nightmare of history.

Within this cosmological pattern are the more specific narratives of history that, in this work, are of particular interest in understanding the African American past and present. Forrest takes on education, black identity, feminism, Afrocentrism and other forms of nationalism, interracial relationships, commodification of culture, and violence, among other topics. In effect, he is trying to indicate how such material can be brought into the literary realm without sacrificing the literariness of the work. In this sense, he is in some ways a traditionalist, as his list of sources—Shakespeare, Dostoevsky, Melville, Joyce, Faulkner, Ellison—implies. He seeks to become part of the canon, not to destroy or displace it. But, as T. S. Eliot has stated and Forrest clearly understands, one becomes part of the canon by changing it, by revising what has gone before and by adding what is truly modern, in this case a sense of the African American place in culture and history.

His method, appropriately, is implicit in a line he repeatedly cites from *Othello*: "Speak of me as I am, nothing extenuate, nor set down in mean-hearted malice" (V, ii). Forrest, through his narrator, is interested in flaws, deformities, sins, contradictions, and ambiguities, but even more, in how these interact with ideals, talents, virtues, beauty, eloquence, and power. He seeks to make every story and character, no matter how minor, polysemic and mysterious. Because he is doing this within the context of African American experience, he subverts the reductiveness of representations of blacks within the dominant discourse. Young and old black men, light- and dark-skinned people, Southern white masters, single mothers, alcoholics, police officers, the black bourgeoisie, religious believers and leaders, and artists are all presented as complex beings who suffer and who act. Two examples will show how Forrest develops the dialectic of the Othello allusion in refusing both extenuation and malice in constructing narratives that link past and present, private and public, racial and universal dimensions.

De Loretto, who calls herself Imani to signify her African sensibility, is a young woman trying to come to terms with the responsibilities of black artists. She is also a social worker and Joubert's girlfriend (she refuses to become his lover). She is caught up in the expressive modes of the time, doing portraits of Malcolm X and of local gang leaders. She also buys bad imitations of African masks, which later are found to conceal heroin, from a con artist who has recently renamed himself Sambi!. What she does not paint are the people and experiences associated with her social work. Those people are symbolized by the child who calls herself Cinderella and who is apparently the victim of incest. While Imani becomes very involved in such cases on the job, her art remains separate from such experience, even though it is the true narrative of the black suffering she says is the center of her art. Further complicating her situation is the support she receives from a wealthy white patron, who seems to prefer her images of aggressive black men to the harsh reality of community life.

In creating such a character, who is often aware of the contradictions of her life and work and in fact agonizes over them, wondering if she is truly "black" enough, yet criticizing Joubert for a too-easy acceptance of middle-class life, Forrest critiques the Black Power and cultural nationalist movements of the 1960s and early 1970s. But more generally, he is attacking those forces that push the artist toward ideological expression rather than deeply felt creation. For African American artists, these forces can be both whites who presume to know what black art should be and are willing to pay for that and only that, and blacks who have their own agendas and use racial politics to enforce them. The artists who surrender to these pressures and temptations have, in Forrest's view, compromised their art. Despite some pointed barbs at Alice Walker and, by implication (through the white patron), at her literary heroine Zora Neale Hurston, he is more troubled than angry at the artists involved. They become victims of their own ambitions and insecurities.[9]

Imani goes to a retreat on black consciousness but ends up being the target of vicious attacks on her identity and her art. Those who assault her claim to be her friends but are unrelenting in questioning the quality of her blackness and the nature of her success. The result is so devastating that she commits suicide. In reading her journal shortly after her death, Joubert begins to understand the depth of her conflicts and confusions. He struggles to get her right. As an artist himself, he begins his reading with the possibility of using the journal for a play, but that exploitative motive becomes less important as he seeks to understand the life he reads in all its complexity. It becomes a story of loss, not only of a physical life, but of the talent and caring that could have truly helped others. It is a loss generated by a too narrow focus on a single dimension, in this case race.

The site of reading here becomes a site of memory and of mourning that is simultaneously a site of social critique. Joubert watches on television the alliance of white patron and gangs, and Sambi! comes to retrieve his drug-laden masks. In addition, by reading the journal, Joubert can assign responsibility for what happened to Imani, who, among other efforts, seemed obsessed with locating "lost" siblings, though she had little but so-called spiritual evidence for claiming the relationships. He can see how her need for deep connections made her vulnerable to the exploitation and insult she suffered. At the same time, her desire for origins and purity was her great weakness and, by implication, the failing of all those who seek to make race foundational to identity. What is truly postmodern in Forrest's narrative is the understanding that hybridity is the basis of African American experience. Any other perception about it is the result of ignorance or deceit, and since much of recent black culture has focused on such one-dimensionality (what Theodor Adorno calls "positive identity" [146–51]), those cultural expressions must be distortions of reality. The story of Imani suggests that the distortions are truly harmful.

Joubert finds in the apartment, among Imani's other work, a series of portraits of Sugar Groove. Their presence suggests both the connectedness of life that is basic to Forrest's philosophy and a principle and practice of art superior to Imani's other work. The narrator finds in the journal reference to these paintings and the circumstances of their creation, as well as correspondence between them. Sugar Groove was a legendary figure in the community; even his name was frequently interpreted and modified to suggest his larger-than-life qualities, especially his sexual prowess. He was also a mysterious figure, appearing and disappearing in ways that lent him some of the aura of the shape-shifter/trickster associated with Ford. But Sugar Groove is also linked to worthy causes and to personal suffering. He had involved himself in the early days of the civil rights movement. He is the parallel figure to Ford in that he represents a quest for good and truth rather than evil and deceit. Imani's efforts to paint him thus signify, not the easy expression of ideological values evident in her other work, but rather the tragic and ambiguous meaning of human desire and struggle. He cannot easily be reduced to one of Imani's (or Joubert's) heroic images, and thus the ability to capture him on canvas or paper is a greater achievement.

Joubert learns the story of Sugar Groove's early life from the man himself one night in the barbershop where Joubert works shining shoes. Typically for Forrest's narrative method, his story comes out of a question the boy asks about a story in his own family; rather than answer directly, Sugar Groove begins his own family saga. He was the son of a white plantation owner and a beautiful black woman; his mother died in childbirth. When the boy became older, he was sent regularly to the Big House to receive money, which the black servants understood to be the son's inheritance, one that would have been denied if it had been included in a will. One evening while awaiting the father, Wilfred Bloodworth, the boy finds suggestive pictures of his mother in the father's

Bible. A classic oedipal scene develops as the father and son struggle over the photographs.

The fight is in essence a struggle for control of representation of the black woman: Is she to be the pure maternal figure of the black son's imagined memory or the sensual woman of the white father's experience? In posing the question, Forrest is confronting one of the central, though usually unspoken, issues of the American racial formation. As Forrest and others have pointed out, sexual desire has been one of the forbidden subjects of African American cultural expression.[10] The underlying issue has been the fear of validating white stereotypes of black lust. But Forrest problematizes desire by clearly suggesting that the lover/mother appears to enjoy the photographic experience and is not overtly coerced by the master's gaze. The picture is torn in the fight, and Bloodworth nearly kills his son. He is stopped by the voice of the dead mother, which both of them hear: "How can you destroy what we created?" (336). The question becomes a prohibition; the father cannot kill the son, now or later. And as understood by the son, the voice grants him the acknowledgment of paternity he had really been seeking.[11]

By association, the story also airs another anxiety of African American culture as Forrest sees it: the quest for legitimacy. Given the high proportion of African Americans who have white ancestry and the resistance of white fathers to acknowledge such children, genealogy becomes a central, if not fully spoken, issue within the culture. Descent, in the framework of America's racial history, is highly problematic. The white father, who disdains acknowledging his offspring, must himself be suppressed by those children. A perpetual state of illegitimacy is created by this denial on both sides. If the white father existed, then black identity cannot be pure, just as white supremacy cannot be sustained. Questions also must be raised, as Forrest does in this novel, about the character and behavior of the ancestral black mother. If she is not pure victim of rape, but was a desiring being and occasionally willing agent, then the narrative of black holocaust is disrupted. The primal scene becomes a site of shared humanity, not horrendous crime. The point of creating the narrative of Sarah Belle and Wilfred Bloodworth is not to deny the reality of sexual exploitation but rather to challenge its status as the sole narrative. One effect of this narrative subversion is to construct an alternative view of black identity as hybrid, multivalent, and always already in process. It also constructs American history as relational, regardless of the actions and beliefs of parents and children. It also reinscribes black experience in America as orphanhood. To be black is to be "lost-found," an expression Forrest borrows from the Nation of Islam but changes to mean those who share a condition of lost, suppressed, denied parentage. Identity is thus constructed out of absence, not presence, out of history, not essence.

What Forrest does in *Divine Days* is in part an anatomy of the widely varying responses to this condition. One response is that of Ford: manipulate the fluidity of identity to personal advantage and power. Another is that of Imani: obsessively seek out origins and family, naively believing in total recovery. The two options Forrest approves are those of Sugar Groove and Joubert. The older man's is heroic: face the truth of illegitimacy and fluidity of self but turn that into action that nurtures community as something made, not found, and made through confrontation with truth. Life itself becomes an endless quest for the truth, not just about the father, but about the nature of existence. To the mother's question, How can you destroy what we created?, is added the son's (and daughter's), Why was I born?

The mother's query is of course larger than the Sugar Groove narrative; it is, for Forrest, the great American question. Between the descendants of Europe and of Africa have been created not only a new group—African Americans— but also the complex possibilities of the New World. This "racial group" is the form of modernity, laden with history, but deprived of its meanings, an orphan forced to create a new self. And because the conditions of illegitimacy, in many senses of that term, continue to operate through racism, self-hatred, and confusion of identity, that creation must happen anew each generation. The mother's question must be asked repeatedly because of the high risk inherent in being black in America, but it is a question equally for the white father (and mother) and the black mother (and father). To the son's question, the appropriate response can never be a simple claim of origins, whether Eurocentric or Afrocentric, because neither is true in itself. The answer must be made, not found.

In this sense, Forrest is arguing for a spiritual meaning to history and to black life, but it is not found in religion or in the ideological exuberance of cultural nationalism or Afrocentrism. Rather, it is something close to the Buddhist perspective Charles Johnson describes; a recognition of the reality of suffering but also of the insights possible in seeing through the suffering.[12] Part of the "seeing through" is awareness of suffering as common to humanity and thus not a special quality of a particular race or other group. But this insight does not lead to the passivity of victimhood; rather, it leads to a sense of responsibility to relieve suffering wherever possible. It also leads to an assignment of responsibility for unnecessary suffering. Individuals who cause pain for others must be called out; societies that perpetuate systems of oppression must be held accountable; ideas that justify abuse must be challenged and discredited. The story of Sugar Groove points a way to join the personal quest to the social task.

The role of Joubert, as he discovers in this week of "divine days," is different. As artist, he becomes a spiritual journalist. He is the one who hears the voices and collects the stories and puts them into a narrative for others. Initially, he seeks out the mundane and the eccentric. He has managed to write a drama about Ford, but it has been rejected for reasons that never become clear. What fascinates him about Ford is his demonic qualities—his corruption, manipulation, sexuality—and he never succeeds in humanizing him. Similarly, he is attracted to life in the Night Light Lounge, his aunt's tavern where he works as a bartender; he finds the people there to be odd enough to be good characters for his plays. He adopts a superior attitude toward most of them that prevents his understanding of the complications of their lives.

His turn to the story of Sugar Groove is a major reason for his increasing human sympathy. While he sought initially to do a work comparable to that on Ford, he soon discovers that his research leads him onto a different level of creative possibilities. The facts, as conventionally gathered and put together, simply will not serve the purpose. Instead of fearing and evading the voices in his head, he begins to listen to them. By waiting, listening, and remembering, he finds the drama implicit in life, not one imposed by his ideas. He comes to see the material of his work as subject and not object, and he also comes to appreciate the subjectivities of the various tellers of tales. That which has been suppressed, denied, or erased still exists, but it cannot be uncovered by conventional methods that allow the investigator to remain distant from the story. Joubert must express that which he has repressed through all the novel, his own complicity in suffering and his own orphanhood. He must face his own hesitation to help another and his own bastardy. The refusal to "extenuate," as in *Othello*, must apply to the artist as well. He has to tell the truth of and to himself and thereby be empowered to tell the larger, human truth.

Joubert calls what Sugar Groove does "reinvention":

What saves them from the dead was that some remnant, some streak was still there of Negro, not African, and not European, but Negro—with that fabulous impulse to reinvent, to make a way out of noway. The Negro-American's will to transform, reinvent, and stylize until Hell freezes over. Hell Elijah had reinvented Islam over here, where the checks are cashed. . . . Reinvention was what King and his spirit of Freedom Movement followers had attempted to do with Christianity, which we got from the white man, and re-made into something else that might even renew them. Then they transformed it (King and his spirit of Freedom Movement) into a political instrumentality, even as the whites were always talking about a separation of church and state. . . . Why couldn't we see that Douglass was really remaking the July 4th celebration—all the while talking about how we couldn't participate in it. (1128)

The task of the artist is to reinvent as he/she speaks for the voices that have been suppressed and tells the tales that have been denied. The point is not to identify something purely black, because no such thing exists. It is rather to take all of the experience, regardless of its beauty or ugliness, and shape it into a narrative: "Speak of me as I am, nothing extenuate, not set down in mean-hearted malice." The task of the contemporary African American artist is not to tell a highly selected part of the story determined by ideology or by market considerations but rather to recognize how black experience is synechdoche for the American experience and the human experience. Through reinvention, taking whatever is available, from whatever sources it might come, it becomes possible for the artist to offer a model of survival in a time when African American life in particular and American life in general are being simultaneously degraded, homogenized, and falsely celebrated.

In his novels, Leon Forrest insists that the way to the future is through the past and that the haunting voices can provide guidance. Moreover, unlike some of his colleagues, he believes that that way is one of recognition of all the ancestors and all the relatives, of whatever race. Being black, for him, is deeply and complexly intertwined with being American. The only true writing about that experience, then, in whatever field, must come to terms with this hybridity.

Chapter Ten

LOST GENERATIONS

John Edgar Wideman's Homewood Narratives

In *Fatheralong* (1994), his "meditation on fathers and sons, race and society," John Edgar Wideman argues that a crucial feature of black life in contemporary America is the inability of black fathers to serve as models of masculinity for their sons. Each generation, he says, must construct its own version of manhood and thus must always fail. He places the blame squarely on a racist society that consistently subverts the development of strong, responsible, positive self- and group images. Through academic and media representations, as well as public policy, black men are infantilized, criminalized, and bestialized, as they have been throughout American history. The result is that male children feel compelled to father themselves if they are to be men.

While Wideman's expository statement of this view has come only recently, his fiction has been dramatizing the problematics of patrimony virtually from the beginning. The theme becomes especially clear when he turns to family history in his Homewood narratives. The raison d'être of this postmodern saga[1] may be said to be the quest for the Black Father who can serve as model and, by extension, for the Law of the Father that can provide the principles of black manhood.

The issue is more complex than simply constructing an appropriate image of fatherhood and showing its relevance. Wideman is intensely aware of the ironies and ambiguities of history and its snarled connections to the present. He moves between the potentially useful stories of the past and the difference between past and present, a difference that raises doubt about such usefulness. He also operates in the matrix of family, with suggestions about the value of matrilineal structures. Working back through the mothers reveals a tradition of endurance, but it also problematizes the role of fathers. Wideman shapes his fiction within a classic master narrative: his male figures engage the world, often aggressively and dangerously, and either succeed or fail, while his women feel the pain of the struggles of their fathers, husbands, brothers, and sons. And it is the women who keep and pass on the narratives that create the family history and thus the meaning of family. The women perform the traditional role of keepers of the culture.

The role of the collector of these narratives is a significant one in defining male possibilities. Wideman blurs the boundaries between fiction and autobiography in the telling; he names his often-used participant-narrator John, and the family tree provided essentially matches the writer's. While in interviews he has made conventional distinctions between "real life" and the materials of his craft, the blending serves effectively to suggest a way of being in the world. In his role as listener to and preserver of the family history, he enacts the function of women; but in the separation from the family that enabled him to become the artist-intellectual, who then must return to collect the stories from women, he plays the male role. Moreover, his writing of the material removes it from the oral tradition and presents it to the larger world. In the public sphere, he fathers the narrative of fathers and mothers. His individual fictions alternate between the sexes, but he consistently incorporates the struggles of sons who are lost.

He also clearly establishes the racial terms of his narrative. In "The Beginning of Homewood," the last piece in *Damballah* (1981), Wideman offers the story of Sybela Owens, the founding mother of his fictional family. She is a powerful figure who escaped from slavery with her two children and endured the harshness of life in a racist North. Significantly, however, her husband, Charlie Bell, is relegated to a minor role in the story, despite the fact that he is the one who instigated the escape and who confronted hostile whites in Pittsburgh. His secondary status is the result of his whiteness. He stole Sybela and their children from his own father and brought them all to freedom. He fathered all her children and thus was the patriarch of the family. He was also in some sense the founder of Homewood, the black community whose history Wideman re-creates. But he is not granted this status. In fact, the twenty children that they had together are nonexistent in the family narrative. The author requires some removal from white identity in order to tell the family story.

Having moved toward a stronger identity with black culture in the years before publication of the Homewood trilogy—*Damballah*, *Hiding Place* (also 1981), and *Sent for You Yesterday* (1983)—Wideman sought to construct an African American narrative;[2] placing a strong white man at the foundational moment of his saga would have created a variety of difficulties, not the least of which would be its impact on his desire for a black audience. In addition, he was writing and publishing the trilogy at the time of the *Roots* phenomenon. Alex Haley had created a noble African ancestry, with its survival in the New World. Black genealogy became one of the commodities of the moment. The black father, whether real or fictional, was crucial to the discourse. Moreover, this was also the time of Republican resurgence, which included Ronald Reagan's claim that racism no longer existed. Because black literature is always in some sense political in that the writers are assumed to be speaking for "the race," whether or not that is part of their purpose, creating the white father can be taken as staking out an accommodationist position.

The logical question is why Wideman portrays Charlie Bell at all. His absence would in some ways be less problematic than his presence. One reason would be the author's understanding of the relationship of fiction and history. History is filled with discontinuities, lacunae, and contradictions, so a fiction that presents itself as speaking out of and to history would have similar traits. Wideman has made clear in a variety of comments that he concerns himself primarily with the past.[3] For him this has meant, among other things, faithfulness to those who have told the stories of the family and the community. Charlie Bell is an inconvenient "fact" of the history he has heard and now tells. His saga carries an aura of authenticity if it faces such "facts" despite their ideological inappropriateness.

This particular white presence, moreover, serves to subvert the dominant discourse in two ways. First, it challenges notions of black racial purity implicit in the *Roots* narrative. There is no Kunta Kinte as the racial origin of African Americans; they are always already in Wideman's narrative a hybrid people. Fatherhood is always problematic under the historical reality of slavery and racial domination. But the story also rejects the claim that such domination is the whole story. Charlie Bell makes himself a fugitive by "stealing" his family and leading them to freedom. He consciously chooses to give up his socially approved position as master-rapist in order to have a life as a family. And when the white community they move to indicates their dislike for mixed marriages, he moves his family to the place that becomes Homewood. In the process, Sybela places a curse on the original land that, according to the storytellers, remains in effect. Thus, this white man, at the beginning of the saga, identifies himself with black life and enters history.

But in addition to questioning a simplified black history, Wideman through Charlie Bell challenges the white narrative of American history. In his story, this white man is not central. Black memory is not focused on him in either a positive or negative way. The attention is on Sybela and certain of her descendants, for those are the tales relevant to present-day black life. Bell is quite properly in the margins, because this cannot possibly be his story. He might be a worthwhile model for white behavior, but the characters in these stories need their own usable past, and he is not really part of it. Precisely because of continuing racial domination, his actions and choices are not available to his black sons. In effect, Wideman is saying that history has been racialized in the sense that whites put themselves at the center of it and blacks operating in the context of that discourse respond by generating an equally distorted past. The truth is somewhere else.

Wideman's alternative father appears in "Damballah," the first story of the collection. On the surface, Wideman would appear to be replicating *Roots* in presenting a resistant, heroic African. He sets up this patriarch in a prefatory note that defines his title. He cites Maya Deren's study of Haitian voudon on Damballah: " 'Damballah Wedo is the ancient, the venerable father; so ancient, so venerable, as of a world before the troubles began; and his children would keep him so; image of the benevolent, paternal innocence, the great father of whom one asks nothing save his blessing' " (7). He is the embodiment of a golden age. He provides a useful myth for African Americans in that he is a New World figure untainted by white influence. He is powerful yet innocent and "benevolent." Deren also notes that he is sometimes asked to "gather up the family."

Wideman's use of this citation is in some ways ironic. His stories are about "the troubles," not about some peaceful time; and they do not suggest access to Damballah's power. The image is clearly a mythic one; whatever strength African Americans display comes in and through history. In this context, it is important that Wideman juxtaposes the Damballah myth to the dedication of the book to his imprisoned brother.

But this textual arrangement also suggests another level of meaning. The author is "gathering up the family" through the stories that make up the Homewood narrative. He thus claims for himself in this sense the role of Damballah, the one who generates and holds together. He goes about his gathering in a way that is consistent with the character of the mythic father. He does his work by listening and recording, not by imposing his reading on the storytelling process. He emphasizes the voices of narrating characters, either through their storytelling or through interior monologues. This gives him a version of the detachment associated with Damballah. This essentially artistic process, his own kind of negative capability, is a model of tranquillity and wisdom. He engages and embraces the stories and the tellers while maintaining a "benevolent" perspective.

Such perspective is essential because the entry into history is involvement in "troubles." The title story of the collection challenges the impulse, represented by *Roots*, to elide history and myth. Orion, like Kunta Kinte, is a strong-willed African who refuses to learn the language of the master. He also insists on maintaining African customs. But unlike Haley's hero, Orion is neither progenitor of a great family nor revered in the African American slave community. The only one who respects him is the young boy through whose consciousness the story is told. For others, he is a "crazy nigger" whose talk was "heathen." Despite their status, they see themselves as American and raise the boy to be the same.

The child identifies with Orion's strength and resistance, but what is emphasized is the difference within this identification. This would-be spiritual son already is part of a different world. When he observes the rituals, their strangeness is the primary quality: "Orion drew a cross in the dust. Damballah. When Orion passed his hands over the cross the air seemed to shimmer like it does above a flame or like it does when the sun so hot you can see waves of heat rising off the fields. Orion talked to the emptiness he shaped with his long black fingers. His eyes were closed. Orion wasn't speaking but sounds came from inside him the boy had never heard before, strange words, clicks, whistles and grunts. A singsong moan that rose and fell and floated like the old man's hands above the cross" (21). The ritual has power but it does not communicate a meaning.

This is evident later when the boy enacts his own ritual after Orion is killed because of his recalcitrance. He carries the severed head of the man to the river and then waits: "Damballah said it be a long way a ghost be going and Jordan chilly and wide and a new ghost take his time getting his wings together. Long way to go so you can sit and listen till the ghost ready to go on home" (25). The boy's discourse blends Christian and traditional African references in a hybridizing process that allows him to pay tribute to Orion but not to become him. He is at this moment truly African American. The passage goes on to note that he listened to Orion tell the old stories, but there is no indication that he can himself pass them on. Orion is the end of something, and the boy is the beginning of something new and different. This new person is the true father in his recognition of the need to live in the present while respecting the past. But he does not confuse the two. The realities of history require that the son must father himself.

While the family tree Wideman creates for this saga follows the female line, from Sybela through Maggie, Gertrude, Freeda, and Lizabeth to the present generation of John and Tommy, it is the men, both fathers and sons, who receive the most attention. The chief of these is John French, Freeda's husband and Lizabeth's father. He is a strong figure within both the family and the community, but his power is limited to these spheres. He is physically large and able to impose his will on others. But these very qualities are sources of concern, as "Lizabeth: The Caterpillar Story" suggests. The story is told as a series of interrelated narratives involving French, Freeda, and Lizabeth. The core tale is about Lizabeth biting a caterpillar, which frightens her mother, who fears that her child will die. French insists on knowing how much she had eaten and then swallows the rest, declaring that if such a large section does not kill him, then the small bite she took will not harm Lizabeth. This is a story that the girl wants her mother to tell again and again as an example of her father's love.

One day when the two of them are engaged in this ritual, Freeda sees a man come up behind her husband as he approaches the house. This man pulls a gun and aims it at French. Freeda rams her fist through the window to warn him and thus saves his life. Sometime later, she finds a gun hidden in the house that she recognizes as one that someone else used in a killing. She demands that French get rid of it. Later on, when someone begins dumping ashes on a lot her father intends to use for a garden, Lizabeth stays awake at nights because she knows that her father is waiting to shoot the perpetrator. She plans to warn the trespasser, because she does not want her father to kill someone and then disappear, as happened with the owner of the hidden weapon.

The linking together of all these elements has the effect of turning a sentimental story into a cautionary tale. The lives of black men, even the powerful and respected, are filled with danger and trouble. The impulse to demonstrate one's masculinity through forceful action is threatening even within the community. Even the caterpillar incident is seen as problematic by French's wife, just as Lizabeth wants to read it as loving:

> The very one you nibbled a little corner off.
> Then he ate the rest.
> The whole hairy-legged, fuzzy, orange and yellow striped, nasty rest.
> Because he thought I might die.
> As if my babygirl dead wouldn't be enough. Huh uh. He swallowed all the rest of that nasty bug so if you died, he'd die too and then there I'd be with both you gone. (48)

His action endangers the family without doing anything effective for his daughter. It is an act of bravado that demonstrates his lack of concern for his own life.

A similar attitude leads him to treat losing fellow gamblers in such a way that they want to kill him, to conceal the gun of Albert Wilkes, accused of killing a police officer, and to take the law into his own hands over the dumped ashes. As Freeda tells her daughter, "I hear you talking and think about John French and know there ain't no way he could have lived long as he did unless a whole lotta people working real hard at saving that crazy man. He needed at least as many trying to save him as were trying to kill him" (47). The very meaning of black manhood is tied up in risk. And while John French represents a strong personality, he can only function successfully within a community, primarily of women, who care more for his life than he does.

Two other narratives suggest the limits of such a life. In "Daddy Garbage," French and his friend Strayhorn find and have to deal with the body of an abandoned baby on a cold winter day. The reason that French is available for this unfortunate task is that the white man who was supposed to employ him never came, so he spent the day in the Bucket of Blood, drinking gin. While the story's central concern is to reveal the communal principle of shared responsibility for all members of the community, it also clarifies economic realities. French, said to be the best wallpaper hanger in town, cannot get regular work because of his race. He must take whatever work he can get, at whatever pay whites choose to give him. The situation is both humiliating and enraging. The measure of French's character is not his income or his work ethic but rather his persistence in seeking work and his skill in performing it when available. He has no belief in an American Dream of hard work and success, because such belief would be foolish under the circumstances.

What Wideman suggests by placing French in this situation is the historical conditions faced by black men. The restricted capacity to provide for the family means that the African American community has never had the conventional American option of the single-earner household dominated by a man because of his income. Thus, part of the dominant culture's definition of manhood cannot apply to even so strong a personality as John French. All of the hand-wringing by policy makers and scholars in the 1960s and 1970s about black male irresponsibility and the matriarchal family was, Wideman implies, a distortion of old news in the black community.

Part of the alternative represented by French also reveals a difference from the generations of sons who will come later. He does persist, in the face of frustration; he continues, in the terms of the folk expression, "to make a way of no way." This persistence grows out of an ethic of survival, not achievement. This moral rule requires an enlarged notion of family. After Strayhorn's dog, Daddy Garbage, finds the dead baby, French knows that they must take responsibility for it. As always, one element of this is racism; they cannot simply turn the body over to the authorities because that opens opportunities for questions and perhaps even abuse. French firmly believes that the legal system will use any chance to attack black men. At the same time, he has no faith that the church can be trusted to do right by the dead child since its parentage and even race are unknown. So it is up to the two of them to carry out the appropriate rituals. This they do despite physical and emotional discomfort, which is alleviated in part by their drinking. Through this narrative, Wideman challenges assumptions about morality, responsibility, and manhood. Within his historical moment, John French does what is possible and what he understands to be the good. His way, Wideman suggests, is the one denigrated by the larger society and not followed by later generations.

But French's own choices are problematic in the first part of *Sent for You Yesterday*. Some of the information and stories about him are carried over from *Damballah*, including a central relationship, that with Albert Wilkes, only briefly mentioned in "Lizabeth." In the novel, this character is much more fully developed as a version of the "Bad Nigger" of African American folklore. Reckless, fearless, and promiscuous, Wilkes is in the tradition of Stagolee as an emblem of black male rejection of the values of the dominant culture.[4] He sleeps with a married white woman, kills a white policeman, and expects to die violently for his actions. Most important for this analysis, he is the friend of John French, whom he immediately seeks out on returning from seven years in hiding. Wilkes serves as the embodiment of what French would have become had he not married and had a family. He stands for all the danger associated with outlaw figures and specifically for black men who attempt to live by their own rules. For these reasons, he is also legendary in Homewood. Important for this text is the additional fact that he is an artist, in this case a blues musician.

Freeda, French's wife, understands Wilkes's nature and, for the sake of her family, wants her husband to stay away from him. Their argument late in the first section of the novel indicates contrasting notions of manhood:

> I'm sorry for Albert Wilkes and sorry for everybody else but now I just need to sit here awhile and be sorry for me.
> He'll stay at the Tates' tonight. He'll be all right over there.
> And where will you stay?
> Be right here with you.
> How long? Till he come scratching and whistling? [As he had done the night before.]
> How you gon be a friend you don't help when there's trouble?
> There's all kind of trouble, man. Didn't you hear what I said to you? Ain't

I been in the deepest trouble there is today? . . . You think I care whether Albert Wilkes at the Tates' or burning in hell? I have these babies to face, these babies to feed. And a man act like he ain't got wife nor child the first. That's real trouble. Youall just playing games. And Albert Wilkes the worst. He looks for trouble. He made all the trouble he ever had. He don't belong nowhere. Don't answer to nobody. He needs trouble. Couldn't find enough wherever he was those seven years so he's back here again. Back to stir up trouble and you just itching to be out there in it with him.

The man needs to come home.

Man like that don't have a home. His home is trouble. He tears up homes. Never heard a good thing about him. Except he could play the piano. And what's he do with that piano but cause more trouble? Playing nasty music and driving a bunch of drunk niggers crazier than they already are.

He's a man like I am. Breath and britches. Walks on two legs. He ain't got no horns sprouting out his head. Ain't got no tail. He's a man like me, and I been knowing him ever since I been in Homewood. Seems like we go back further than that. Seems like I always been knowing Albert, and if he's in trouble I got to do what I can.

You have to be with him all hours of the night and day so when the police come to kill him they'll kill you too? Is that what you mean? Is that why you've been gone since dawn and why you'll go running again when he comes scratching tonight? (82–83)

For John French, manhood means, among other things, loyalty and risk, when that loyalty requires it. It counts the most when there is trouble, and it does not matter whether, as Freeda points out, Albert Wilkes is himself the main source of the trouble. For her, this is a crucial factor; by her rules, one's relationship to difficulties is a moral issue. Wilkes "needs" trouble the way junkies need heroin; because he has chosen his life, he cannot be a good man. She then reads everything else about him, including his art, in these terms.

A crucial point is the contrasting definitions of "home." For her, the word implies a set of relationships and responsibilities. It is a moral structure; a man without these connections and commitments is homeless, regardless of where he goes or how long he stays. In contrast, for French, Wilkes's home is the place where he has ties, primarily male, and where he is accepted for who and what he is. Albert's "home" is the place where he has known John French and where people listen to and understand the nature of his music. His responsibility is to himself; through that primary commitment, he gains the loyalty of his friends and expresses the truth of his art. In this homocentric world, women and children can be important but they are not central.

French himself must live between these positions and does so often uncomfortably. He endangers himself and sometimes others because risk is part of the meaning of black male existence. He suffers the frustration of working for condescending whites because he must support his family. He maintains loyalties to both Albert and Freeda, but that means that he may be home, but he is never quite "at home" in his world. His death, told twice in the Homewood narrative, symbolizes his position. He dies trapped between the toilet and the bathtub in the room he built primarily for his daughters but that was not large enough for him. The story, part of family tradition, undermines his heroic status through its absurdity but at the same time grants him a larger-than-life quality. One implication is that he was a man who belonged in a different world, one more like that of Orion from "Damballah." Despite his sense of style and authority, as a black man he was reduced to cheap wine, frustrating work, and a ridiculous death. In the circumstances, he had to construct a self that was respected and self-respecting. The ideal was perhaps Orion and Albert Wilkes, but those models did not produce progeny. To do so meant uncomfortable but necessary compromise in the meaning of manhood.

The issue is brought into the more recent past through the story of "John's" father. Even if John French did not quite fit his home, he was still the center of it. By the time we get to Edgar, the black man has been marginalized even in this most intimate of spaces. In "Across the Wide Missouri," Edgar works at a regular job to support his family, but, for reasons not explained in the narrative, he must stay on his family's margins quite literally. His bedroom is a cell-like space outside the main rooms of the apartment. He is not shown exerting any authority within the home. Since employment, whether regular or not, is presented in Wideman as marginal for black men, Edgar's status within the family and community is the measure of his manhood. In this instance, a rule of respect is in place, but it appears to have little significance.

For his son, Edgar is a distant figure. It is this distance between father and son that drives the story. The narrative is given retrospectively, and the speaker opens in some confusion. He notes that he keeps thinking of Clark Gable when he tries to recall his childhood. In fact, he says, "The white man in the movie is my father" (*Damballah*, 134). This image is one of elegance, sophistication, and command: "One is Clark Gable brushing his teeth with Scotch, smiling in the mirror because he knows he's doing something cute, grinning because he knows fifty million fans are watching him and also a beautiful lady in whose bathroom and bedroom the plot has him awakening is watching over his shoulder. He is loud and brisk and perfectly at ease cleaning his teeth before such an audience" (133).

This is in sharp contrast to his actual father, who sleeps on a cot in an unheated closet and who works as a waiter in a department store restaurant. The son's description of the waiters at work suggests the difference from Gable: "I stare at all the black faces. They won't stay still. Bobbing and bowing into the white faces or gliding toward the far swinging doors, the closely cropped heads poised and impenetrable above mandarin collars. [Jean] Toomer called the white faces petals of dusk and I think now of the waiters insinuating themselves like birds into clusters of petals, dipping silently, silently depositing pollen or whatever makes flowers grow and white people be nice to black people. And tips bloom" (136). Black men serve whites and engage in rituals that gain for them some pittance in this ceremony of racial control.

The son's discomfort in this white world, a world in which he fears that he will be exposed as an interloper at any moment, is little alleviated by the father's presence. Certainly the father offers little in the way of guidance for the son in negotiating this hostile terrain. Nonetheless, the presence of the father supersedes all other considerations. Significantly, filial respect is demonstrated through the silencing of the child. The powerful presence, which in the telling is devotion, effectively erases the son's self. He cannot speak his anxieties, his love, or his desires, even in so simple a matter as the choice of movie to see. The movie the father chooses is "Across the Wide Missouri," with Clark Gable. As the adult remembering this moment, the narrator recalls turning Gable into his father and "seeing him for the whole ninety minutes doing good and being brave and handsome and thundering like a god across the screen" (140). This transformation is necessary because the father himself must live the restricted life given to black men, and the son cannot help but know these limitations. Possibilities exist only in fantasies and specifically those acted out by white men.

An important aspect of this story, and of the Homewood narrative generally, is the ambivalences emphasized in the storytelling process itself. The narrator informs us that this is not the first time that he has told this personal experience. He repeatedly comments on the changes he is making in this version, as well as the forgetting he has done. He claims that the earlier rendering was more conventional in that it was a son's quest for the father, whereas the "reality" was the mother's effort to bring father and son together. In this telling, the son is an innocent and dependent child. The narrator also points to his own forgetfulness: he cannot remember the words of the theme song of the movie or how many times he and his father went out together.

As in Toni Morrison's *Beloved* and several other contemporary fictions, forgetting seems as important as remembering and in fact seems to serve a crucial narrative function. The erasure of experience implies the unspeakability of history in the very process of constructing it. About the song, and by implication his experience, the narrator says: "The last time I heard the song my son called it *Shenandoah*. Maybe that's what it should be called. Again I don't know. It's something a very strong instinct has told me to leave alone. To take what comes but don't try to make anything more out of it than is there. In the fragments. The bits and pieces" (139). In the very denial of special importance is evidence of it. The song must be suppressed precisely because it has the power to call forth the troubled nature of the relationship and, by extension, the whole history of black men in America whose relationships with their sons are troubled.

Forgetting also reveals the passing on of such troubles. The narrator recalls having failed to attend his son's concert, where the song was performed, because he thought it more important to advance his career. It is not surprising that the story ends with comments on this son's forgetfulness. He cannot even remember his grandfather until he is reminded. The last paragraph reinforces the aura of ambiguity: "But he forgets lots of things. He's the kind of kid who forgets lots of things but who remembers everything. He has the gift of feeling. Things don't touch him, they imprint. You can see it sometimes. And it hurts. He already knows he will suffer for whatever he knows. Maybe that's why he forgets so much" (141).

This is a son who cannot be innocent. He has foreknowledge of his own pain, a pain that is the product of history, experience, and knowledge. The only way to escape is through forgetting. This young man is in this sense his father's and grandfather's heir. The inheritance is a lack, not a plenitude. In order to save the sons, the fathers must be silent, for the truth of history is that black manhood is not permitted in American society. Not even the "successful" narrator, with his artistic and intellectual life, can guarantee to his son society's recognition of his identity.

In effect, these narratives of fathers are Wideman's re-visioning of the nation's obsession with the absent African American father. That absence is not so much physical as spiritual, and it is not by choice so much as necessity. The man who cannot offer his son a model for adulthood because the society does not grant him that status saves himself and his son by creating distance and thus compelling some alternative development. Consistently, the adult males in these stories are outlaws and marginalized men who, whatever their virtues, cannot demonstrate to their sons their authority and authorship of the world around them. If narrative and history are the quest for the father, then the stories by which the sons construct their being are filled with gaps and silences because the fathers cannot afford to remember.

The narrative equation is completed through the stories of various sons, whose tales show the effects of paternal absence. Carl French, John and Freeda's son, says of what Homewood has become: "What am I supposed to do? I'm just Carl French. Never had nothing. Never will. Won't be long I'll be selling pencils and rattling my tin cup. Then one day I'll get my name in *The Black Dispatch* when somebody finds my ashes. Nothing I can do about any of it. How my supposed to change what's been happening all these years? Mize well try and feed the starving babies in Africa and China as change the way things always been in Homewood" (*Sent*, 197). The hopelessness expressed here led him and his friends Brother and Lucy Tate into drug addiction and virtually lifelong unemployment. One explanation for this situation is that while John French was useful as legend, he could not provide his son with a model for adulthood in the modern world. In the post–World War II period, the future was in education, fostered in part by Freeda's ambitions for her family. But those very ambitions require greater contact with the world outside Homewood, a world still largely committed to notions of white supremacy. So when Carl seeks to develop his artistic skills, he makes himself vulnerable to the racist attitudes of white instructors. He has few resources to draw on to defend himself; John French, who was himself always economically dependent, could offer little guidance in how to function effectively in that other world. His manhood was defined within the boundaries of Homewood, not beyond them. Given the shifting economic, social, and cultural realities of the new era, the community could no longer provide sustenance for self-realization.

This difference raises important questions about the value of the narratives that are collected here. Lucy's response to Carl's despairing comment about himself suggests the limits of history:

Looked for something different in your eyes. Looked for the old folks in there. And you just listen another minute, Carl French. Tell me if you could ever look through your daddy and the rest of them. Tell me if you could see through them or if they were solid. . . . They made Homewood. Walking around, doing the things they had to do. Homewood wasn't bricks and boards. Homewood was them singing and loving and getting where they needed to get. They made these streets. That's why Homewood was real once. Cause they were real. And we gave it all up. Us middle people. You and me, Carl. We got scared and gave up too easy and now it's gone. Just sad songs left. And whimpering. Nothing left to give the ones we supposed to be saving Homewood for. Nothing but empty hands and sad stories. (*Sent*, 198)

The stories have come to be a way of measuring failure in the present rather than a means of determining practical behaviors or ethical standards. For those no longer capable of heroic or even responsible action, the "sad" tales serve as nostalgia or validations of self-hatred. History becomes a narrative of decline rather than progress. Part of the forgetting, then, is the need to evade the guilt of failing the ancestors.

Wideman struggles to overcome this implication in the stories associated with the most important of the Homewood sons, Tommy. He is one of the central characters in *Hiding Place* and the focus of two of the stories of *Damballah* and the title story of *All Stories Are True* (1993). Since he is based on the experiences of Wideman's brother Robby, he may be said to also inhabit *Brother and Keeper*, a 1984 autobiographical narrative. Moreover, *Damballah* is dedicated to Robby and he is referred to in the conclusion of the collection's last narrative. Thus the story of the imprisoned son/brother is even more prominent than the legend of John French in the Homewood saga.

Tommy represents the author's effort to subvert the dominant discourse that criminalizes the black male. He does this by refusing any of the traditional representational choices. Tommy is neither a simple victim of circumstance or environment nor a socially generated beast (as in *Native Son*) nor the "bad nigger" antihero of black nationalist rhetoric or gangsta rap. Instead, he is a figure who recognizes the wasteland that Homewood has become and who understands that he is in effect a waste product of contemporary society. There is no socially useful role for him to play; he cannot be a meaningful father or husband because he cannot provide financial support for a family. Even the often demeaning jobs held by his father and grandfather are no longer available. The neighborhood itself is drug-ridden, impoverished, and dangerous, and there is nothing he can do about it. Under these circumstances, his sense of manhood must be created in terms of the culture of the street. This means sexual promiscuity, drugs, and petty criminality. He repeatedly refers to himself as "fucked up" for living the way he does, but the texts suggest that he has few options. Wideman's point ultimately is that the lack of choice is a judgment on the society, not on the individual.

Tommy is placed in a variety of situations that reveal his condition. The point of different narratives is to subvert one-dimensional representations of such figures, exemplified by a detective's comment: " 'These are a couple of mean ones. Spades from back East. Bad dudes. Wanted in Pennsylvania for Murder One' " ("The Beginning of Homewood," 199). By showing the character from several perspectives and in several roles, the author challenges his audience in much the same way that Harriet Jacobs, in her slave narrative, insisted that her white Northern female readership could not judge her since they had not endured her suffering. By showing Tommy as father and husband (*Hiding Place*), as his mother's son ("Solitary"), as brother ("All Stories Are True"), as member of an extended family (*Hiding Place*), and as criminal and fugitive ("Tommy" and *Hiding Place*) in stories told by himself, his brother, his mother, and his great-aunt, Wideman makes it much more difficult for his primarily white audience to categorize and reify the character. The point is not to excuse or justify criminal behavior but rather to explore the humanity of the one who has been labeled criminal.

One means by which this is achieved is through the doubling of the narrative of murder. "Tommy" (in *Damballah*) and *Hiding Place*, published in the same year, tell virtually identical versions of the crime in which Tommy is involved. This repetition compels readers to rethink the experience. By using the same words, with some adjustment for context, Wideman forces his audience to consider perspective while encouraging a ritualization of the narrative. Just as the family, through retelling of the caterpillar story and the death of John French, gives concrete meaning to the nature of love and death while shaping the meaning of their own family history, so the author constructs a litany of Tommy's experience through which he seeks to define contemporary black manhood and to ponder its fate.

This central narrative is structured as a physical and spiritual journey through a wasteland to a fated end of murder and doomed escape. The two versions of "Tommy" present a world without fathers and thus without any meaningful authority. They describe the wasteland that Homewood has become by the 1970s. This harsh environment becomes the context for narrating the crime itself. The street expression "Nothing to it" runs like a refrain through the tale, suggesting that everything is easy but also connoting existential despair. There is "nothing" to Homewood, to Tommy's life or those of his companions, or to the future. Thus, in such circumstances, criminal acts to get money are easy to conceive—"Nothing to it."

The first half of the story is structured as a journey through the contemporary wasteland. Seen through Tommy's consciousness, it is a place of ruin, decay, and silence. Unlike classical quests or pilgrimages, the protagonist here has no guide or high moral purpose. Unlike other narratives in *Damballah*, but consistent with other segments of *Hiding Place* and most of *Sent for You Yester-*

day, this one offers no hope or meaning. It begins with Tommy looking for his Uncle Carl, who would buy him a drink. When he cannot be found in the bar, where there is "just the jukebox and beer smell and the stink from the men's room door always hanging open" (389), Tommy knows that his uncle is at the clinic getting his methadone. This opening reveals the failure of male elders to provide direction for younger men. They have their own troubles and dependencies and so cannot be a model for others. The heroic ancestors and somewhat marginalized fathers found elsewhere become the embodiment of failure here. In place of the voices of the past, there is only "nigger music and nigger talk" (389), terms used in a highly derogatory manner.

Outside, the heart of Homewood has become nothing but abandoned buildings, empty lots, and broken parking meters. They are measures of the loss of vitality and community. But in this narrative, the past was not golden or even particularly pleasant. Consistently, Tommy's memories of places are highly ambivalent. He recalls a childhood in which he made money by carrying groceries for neighborhood women. The boys competed for white customers, who tipped generously. The black women, who were matrons of the church and surrogate mothers, made them work much harder for far less money. In addition, youthful sexual exploits are associated less with sensuality or intimacy than with missing the last trolley and thus a long walk home.

The present offers so little that Tommy has a momentary apocalyptic vision: "Somebody should make a deep ditch out of Homewood Avenue and just go on and push the row houses and boarded storefronts into the hole. Bury it all, like in a movie he had seen a dam burst and the flood waters ripping through the dry bed of a river till the roaring water overflowed the banks and swept away trees and houses, uprooting everything in its path like a cleansing wind" (*Hiding Place*, 56). The imagery of destruction piles on here. Burial, flood, and "cleansing" wind are brought together in the effort to represent the obliteration of Homewood. Only this combination is adequate to the task of complete annihilation. Tommy wishes for the place not to be, in part because the ruins not only symbolize present frustration but also measure the steep decline from even an imperfect past. Only by wiping it all out can anything new be started. Moreover, the very rhetoric of destruction reveals the effects of time. While some of the language is biblical in character, Tommy pulls the image from a Hollywood movie and not from church or family. The choice suggests his alienation from the past and his absorption of the discourse of the dominant culture.

The people, like the places, are ruins. Anonymous voices in the pool halls try to borrow a quarter, with insincere promises to repay. Young men, with no respect or fear, will kill even the elders for a little money. They also lack even basic skills: "Niggers write all over everything don't even know how to spell. Drawing power fists that look like a loaf of bread" (*Hiding Place*, 58). People park in the middle of the street and ignore those trying to get by. All are incompetent, self-centered, aimless, and verbally if not physically violent. Even the basketball players, elsewhere in Wideman's writing an emblem of energy and creativity, work harder for the games than they ever did on jobs. Tommy brings together place and people in another of his conceits: "Thinking this whole Avenue is like somebody's mouth they let some jive dentist fuck with. All these old houses nothing but rotten teeth and these raggedy pits is where some been dug out or knocked out and ain't nothing left but stumps and snaggleteeth just waiting to go. Thinking, that's right. That's just what it is. Why it stinks around here and why ain't nothing but filth and germs and rot. And what that make me? What it make all these niggers? Thinking yes, yes, that's all it is" (58).

Violence, neglect, and corruption have created a condition not merely of decay but of irreparable rot. The blame for this is diffuse: after all, the "somebody" allowed the "jive dentist" to do his work. And the people are part of the rot. Self-hatred has become central to their identity and to Tommy's. His use of the word "nigger" in this context indicates a return to a derogatory, insulting connotation, in contrast to the efforts in (primarily) male African American communities to redefine it as an affirmative, affiliative term. In Tommy's usage, it comes close to its original white racist meaning.

Thus, the frustration that led John French to spend much of the day drinking "Red Dago" and that led Carl to addiction and resignation has become in Tommy self-hatred and despair. While in some ways he appears the most insightful of the (male) family members in his larger view of the community, his ability to construct metaphors of its condition, and even his relative self-awareness, he nonetheless is also the most self-hating and self-destructive. Something or someone was always present to pull earlier generations back from the edge. Even though Tommy (like presumably the others he describes) lives in a world of family and history, these are no longer sufficient to save him. Whatever he thinks of his mother, father, brother, wife, and son is secondary to the seductive power of "Nothing to it." He lives in a world not of jobs but of pool-hall hustles and criminal scams. The rules of his life are defined by drug-addicted friends and by popular culture-induced images of easy money. Black manhood is disconnected from responsibility and family; it is linked only to the problematic aspects of early figures such as John French and Albert Wilkes: danger, anger, and self-assertion.

What saves Tommy from reification as the black "Monster" of much recent public discourse is the range of situations and perspectives through which Wideman represents him.[5] In *Hiding Place*, he is shown seeking shelter from his great aunt Bess; the narrative shifts between them, allowing readers to see each in distinct ways. In this circumstance, Tommy tries to negotiate between his sheer desperation as a fugitive and his role as a family member taught to respect elders. In this relationship and the one with his wife, he comes to see the limits of his ability to "get over" through verbal skills. Neither woman cares about his rhetoric; they are concerned with his failure to be responsible.

In "Solitary," his mother must deal with his imprisonment and the burdens it places on her: the travel to the prison, the strategies by which prison personnel criminalize visitors, and the hostility that he primarily directs at her, because she is the only one who will take it. Yet she continues to make the journey, even though it increasingly is costing her her religious faith; a good God could not endure such a cruel world.

The *Damballah* version of "Tommy" takes him to his brother's home in Wyoming. There, while his fellow fugitive plays cowboys and Indians with the children, thus suggesting his immaturity, the brothers talk seriously about the situation. Near the end, the words are all spoken: Tommy "feels his brother squeeze then relax the grip on his shoulder. He has seen his brother cry once before. Doesn't want to see it again. Too many faces in his brother's face. Starting with their mother and going back and going sideways and all of Homewood there if he looked long long enough. Not just faces but streets and stories and rooms and songs" (174). Even if Tommy resists his brother's sorrow, the reason itself signifies the possibility of hope and perhaps even redemption. His brother's face is the image of history, of all the mothers and fathers who have endured frustration and mistreatment in the past. This is not merely the Homewood of the present, a wasteland, but also that Homewood created by the family. Such a history, in the face of racism, economic oppression, and self-hatred, signifies a heritage of strength that is available even to the weakest members of the family. The prodigal son is never truly lost as long as the past is available as a narrative.

The saving of the history, through the efforts of the storytellers and narrator, thus becomes not simply a nostalgic gesture or a heroic tale of strong men and supportive women, but rather a demonstration of how sons can be saved, despite the horrors of racism and the frequent descent into self-destructive behavior. But even this limited hopefulness must be contextualized, not only by the core argument of *Fatheralong*, but also by the "troubles" experienced by Wideman's own family, a narrative incorporated in various ways in his work.

The theme of the 1994 book, as suggested earlier, is the difficulty of connection between fathers and sons. He uses the story of his adult relationship with his father as an example of the problem. They have never really managed to resolve the conflicts associated with the father's marginal status in the family. What is intriguing about this perspective is that Wideman presents himself as son, as he does in the Homewood books, but never as father. The absence is significant because it challenges his argument about black male marginality and its relevance to current issues in the African American community. Despite his own literary and professional success and commitment to family, his son Jake committed a murder and is imprisoned for life without parole, the same punishment meted out to Robby. Although he has included so much else of his life in his fiction, Wideman remains silent on this circumstance. It is, in a sense, a personal trauma that cannot be narrated, in part because it would compel a revision of the narrative that has made sense of the trauma that has been family history.

That narrative, through the Homewood saga, refuses to reduce the difficulties faced by the African American community to a simply represented individual or social evil while also insisting that the story can in fact be told. It spells out the psychological and social consequences of an America that has derided the efforts of black men, but it also suggests the resources available through memory, not merely of what happened, but of what could have been possible.

PART FOUR *The End(s)*

Chapter Eleven

APOCALYPTIC VISIONS
AND FALSE PROPHETS

*The End(s) of History in Wideman,
Johnson, and Morrison*

In 1903, W. E. B. Du Bois argued that "the problem of the
twentieth century [was] the problem of the color-line" (*Souls of Black Folk*, 3).
At the end of the century, and of the millennium, three novels dramatize the
apocalyptic effects of the century's failure to find a solution. In *Paradise*, *Cattle
Killing*, and *Dreamer*, Toni Morrison, John Wideman, and Charles Johnson,
respectively, dramatize moments of history's explosion into violence, chaos,
and death. In this sense, they are linked not only to contemporary obsessions
with technological and political disorder and religious and media images of
Armageddon but also with historical recurrences of such concerns at end
moments of centuries.

But consistent with other works in this study, these novels do not engage
directly in the immediate (in this case millennialist) discourse. Instead, they
present crisis moments in (real or fictive) history and reconstruct those in ways
that signify on the present. By exploring the sources of the crises and the
meaning of transformative moments, the writers imply the truth of our moment. In this sense, the "end of time" becomes an opportunity to consider the
ends of history. In each case, the end that concerns them is race. Does its
persistence into our fin de siècle imply that it is an end rather than a means in
history? How is it that a problem of 1790s Philadelphia, the civil rights era, and
an all-black town in midcentury America can look so much like the problem of
the multicultural, postmodern United States? And why should this be the
concern of highly respected, well-placed, successful writers? Why should their
texts, through portrayals of murder, disease, and riot, reflect despair much more
than hope and disintegration much more than healing? In effect, their works

echo the prophecy of Du Bois by serving as jeremiads that confirm his vision and proclaim the nation's failure to respond.

By considering the works in the chronological order of their historical settings, it is possible to construct a fictive "archaeology" of the resultant cultural despair. The underlying issue here, as it is in current discussions of the European Holocaust, is whether a life-affirming meaning can be found in events of unspeakable violence. In this context, does narrative itself construct a false sense of meaning? A key character in Johnson's *Dreamer* comments: " 'All narratives are lies, man, an illusion. Don't you know that? As soon as you squeeze experience into a sentence—or a story—it's suspect. A lot sweeter, or uglier than things actually were. Words are just webs. Memory is mostly imagination. If you want to be free, you best go beyond all that' " (92).

The struggle to "go beyond" characterizes the narrative patterns of these texts, as will be seen. The problem is how to offer witness to acts of inhumanity without descending into sentimentality, closed ideological rhetoric, simplistic allegory, or postmodern relativism that subverts the quest for truth. In general, the answer of these texts is to multiply narrative positions, but in such a way that they reveal common patterns of experience. Those patterns suggest that the Other is always a threat to the self and its community, that reductive readings of history produce damaging falsehoods, that history itself is recursive, that witness is dialectically related to silence, and that social, cultural, and personal healing can only happen if wounds and nightmares are revealed. But healing is not guaranteed; exposure may only produce horror and denial. Each of these narratives ends in ambiguity; the voices that close them seem to speak of hope but do so in the context of uncertainty and disorder.

The Cattle Killing is set in the 1790s in Philadelphia and rural Pennsylvania. At one point, the principal narrator notes that it is October, which would make it the tricentennial of the arrival of Columbus in the New World. The dating also implicitly looks forward to the end of the twentieth century; Wideman reinforces this connection by situating the opening and closing passages in the present and by references to Ramona Africa and Nelson Mandela.[1] The significance of the book's title is established immediately in a prologue to Part I. As the author-narrator walks to his father's apartment to read to him from his new book, he reflects on his own youth in the neighborhood. This eventually leads him to the news of the previous night: black boys of fifteen and fourteen had been shot while attending the same kind of party he had years before. Then the connection: "Shoot. Chute. Black boys shoot each other. Murder themselves. Shoot. Chute. Panicked cattle funneled down the killing chute, nose pressed in the drippy ass of the one ahead. Shitting and pissing all over themselves because finally, too late, they understand. Understand whose skull is split by the ax at the end of the tunnel" (7). This passage is followed by the legend of the Xhosa people, who believe a prophecy that the only way to rid themselves of white invaders is to slaughter their own cattle. Since the cattle are the basis of life, killing them is killing the people. This principle of self-sacrifice becomes Wideman's explanation for America's racial experience.

Several issues must be addressed to make this claim into believable narrative. Who are the scapegoats in this process? To what ends are they sacrificed? Who benefits from such practices? Who owns the slaughterhouse? To what extent are the victims complicitous in their suffering? After all, in the opening example, the black boys are killing each other. Finally, how can this pattern be shown to be continuing in the nation's history and not simply an aberration?

Of course, such questions cannot be addressed directly, in part because the narrative would then be subsumed within current "conversations on race" and reduced to allegory. But more important even than that, Wideman is concerned with representing experience, not with constructing argument. In this sense, the facts of history and contemporary society are less important than the felt reality of black life. How is it possible to explain what would appear beyond the explanations of sociology, political rhetorics, and historical analyses: the feeling that African Americans seem to always be victims, even when some become successful and others engage in self-destructive behavior? Why, after the eras of civil rights, black pride, and affirmative action, after the inclusion of black history and culture in the national life, are black boys still killing each other? For Wideman, the answer must be sought in the nation's cultural and not just political history. Cornel West has described what he calls "black nihilism" as a spiritual crisis (*Race Matters*, 11–20). For Wideman, that crisis is a chronic national condition based on a fundamental inhumanity.

The specific historical moment that he uses to dramatize his "diagnosis" is the yellow fever epidemic that struck Philadelphia in the 1790s. He previously used this moment in his short story "Fever" (1989), which focuses on the life of Richard Allen, who founded the African Methodist Episcopal Church as a response to the segregation practices of mainstream churches and who tirelessly aided others during the epidemic despite their frequent racism. In the novel, Wideman expands his narrative world to include medical practices in England and the United States, rural life, aesthetic theory, racial politics, and the treatment of black women and children, as well as the African culture that produces the key legend.

The principal narrator is an African man who serves as an itinerant preacher in the Pennsylvania countryside and eventually travels to the city to help fever victims. Through this narrative device, Wideman is able to bring together a wide range of stories and to suggest the expanse of the national disorder. It is also important that, though a slave who together with his brother purchased their own and their mother's freedom, the unnamed narrator does not express bitterness toward whites or even toward the system that held them. His religion seems to free him from such a response; in fact, slavery plays very little part in the shaping of the narrative. Much of his early religious work is among rural whites, with mixed success. In place of this more general historical target, Wideman focuses on local and personal experiences that cumulatively demonstrate that it is ongoing and pervasive racism rather than a time-bound institution that is the central issue. He also constantly shifts perspective, not only from one character to another, but also from third to second to first person in relation to the same character. While such changes are in one sense disorienting, they also affirm the point that the reality is the same from almost any point of view.

Thus, we first see the principal narrator from a limited-omniscient perspective as he approaches an isolated farm and seeks food for work. Here he finds an old dying white man and the body of his wife. Though it is obvious from the desolation that there will be no food, he chops wood and offers to lay a fire. Instead of gratitude, he sees fear and hostility in the man's eyes and is asked if he is a black devil. Even in a moment of greatest desperation, the white man cannot overcome his racial hostility. He would rather die than be helped by such a person. By changing to first person at this point, Wideman enables readers to see how the narrator comes to terms with the experience and how it is linked to other events in his mind. In addition, it also identifies him as a witness offering testimony, since he tells the story to an unidentified woman who he is trying to assist by telling stories. His role is to hear the stories of others and add to them his own witness; he is the survivor who must contain and pass on a history that otherwise would not exist.

If this first story registers the situation of blacks as victims of almost pure, self-destructive hatred, the others consistently complicate this notion. The narrator speaks of meeting a city woman on the road who carries an obviously dead child. Since the baby is white and she is black, he assumes that she is its mother. She asks him to lead her to a nearby lake. When he does so, she quietly walks into the water carrying the child; he can only watch as she disappears. He later learns that a child of a wealthy Philadelphia family was cast out by its own parents when it was discovered to have the fever. The nurse, who was healthy, insisted on taking it rather than allowing it to be dumped like garbage.

In the telling of this story, the narrator has to engage his listener's criticism for his inaction during the woman's death. What he struggles to explain is that he was waiting for her, not watching her die. He claims that his real fault was not in observing but in failing to wait long enough: "I lost faith. Deserted her. She trusted me, asked me to help, but I didn't wait long enough" (48). He (and the author) in this passage distinguishes himself from indifferent observers, whose gaze is a means of objectifying those they watch, and from those who presume to help without troubling to discover what would in fact constitute help. The significance of calling himself and the woman African also becomes clear in that crossing the water is the spirit's way back to the African homeland. He believes that she returned after she was certain that the baby "was safely on its way home" (48). That a white child can be included in this ritual suggests that Wideman rejects racial exclusiveness in matters of suffering. The child has become Other through its infection; therefore, it is acceptable to treat it as potentially harmful waste. In this sense, it has been marked as "black."[2] Its true mother, then, is the servant woman, and its spiritual home is with those who have been treated in the same manner. Through this narrative, the text enlarges the problem of inhumanity to include the nation as a whole. Victims are not defined by their race but by their status in the eyes of those who have power over human life.

Those who use difference, including suffering itself, as a means to deny the humanity of others lose all capacity for human sympathy. But the text also indicates a belief in justice: members of the family that eject the baby and close themselves off completely in order to fend off the fever are nonetheless infected and die horrible deaths. And because they have locked themselves in, no one can come to their aid. This version of the narrative can easily be read as a parable of the exclusionary practices of elements of American society, especially when contemporary discourse makes use of the language of pathology to describe problems of homelessness, poverty, and inner-city life.

Another aspect of this particular narrative is its spiritual component. In order to justify his action, the narrator must understand the experience as one that transcends conventional understandings of life and death. He must believe that there is a possibility to move between the realms of the seen and the unseen that would allow her to come back and not simply drown. Wideman proposes such a condition in a brief passage that precedes the historical narrative: "Certain passionate African spirits . . . are so strong and willful they refuse to die. They are not gods but achieve a kind of immortality through serial inhabitation of mortal bodies, passing from one to another, using them up, discarding them, finding a new host. Occasionally, as one of these powerful spirits roams the earth, bodiless, seeking a new home, an unlucky soul will encounter the spirit, fall in love with it, follow the spirit forever, finding it, losing it in the dance of the spirit's trail through other people's lives" (15). The narrator would seem to be such an "unlucky soul," as he repeatedly encounters women or the stories of women whom he cannot save and yet cannot ignore. Thus, the repetitions of the text in terms of his experiences and those of others carry spiritual weight. They are neither coincidences nor accidents but part of a cycle of love and death that shapes history. The narrator cannot escape such encounters; he is haunted by them. And because black women in a white world must always suffer, spiritual reality becomes racial reality as well.

But, again, Wideman does not limit his cultural critique so narrowly. The middle third of the novel is devoted to the story of Liam and Mrs. Stubbs. This is a story of suppression and silence, as well as one of overt racism. It is about how victims respond, as well as about what is done to them. Liam and his wife are from England, but their marriage must be hidden since he is black and she is white. Thus, she must pretend to be the widow of Mr. Stubbs, with Liam as her slave. From the perspective of the wife, the effects of social denial have been devastating to their marriage. Though they came to the New World in part to be free, their isolation has gradually turned the once-eloquent Liam almost totally silent. The situation has had similar effects on their intimate life; though old, the wife still is a sensual being who must now suppress her desires. Moreover, Liam's effort to be an artist has been frustrated by his cautiousness about any self-expression in this environment.

The presence of the narrator creates a different environment, one in which Liam's voice can be recovered. What he speaks is an otherwise lost counterhistory to the dominant Anglocentric narrative. He tells of being one of many children taken from their Ebo home as children to England to be trained by the church. Since more of these children survived their poor treatment than was expected, several of them were indentured to merchants, "a matter of our repaying to the church the expenses incurred in transporting us from Africa" (104). He begins what is supposed to be a lifetime servitude to the elder Mr. Stubbs. Thus, the church is implicated in the commodification of African bodies, and all pretense of moral and civilizing efforts are exposed as fraudulent, as part of what Liam calls the madness of racism.

Moreover, Mrs. Stubbs's story expands the madness to include others in subordinate positions. As a servant girl with no family, she is forced to submit to the sexual abuse of gentlemen: "After pleasuring themselves upon me, they'd mark me with teeth, fists, feet, a riding crop. Tithes I must pay, as if I'd sought the men out, as if I'd stolen something precious from them" (102). The subaltern is not only victimized but made responsible for that victimization. By implication, the discourse of domination, wherever and whenever it occurs, operates by "marking" the subordinate so as to erase the responsibility of the powerful. Part of what is erased, what the young woman "steals" from English gentlemen, is the element of desire, whether sexual or material. As civilized beings, products of the enlightenment, they cannot acknowledge any loss of rational control implicit in greed or unregulated sex.

Other parts of Liam's story clearly establish this connection. He moves from work in the slaughterhouse (which ties this story to the opening observations about young black men) to work as the personal servant of Stubbs's son George, who is an artist. This role leads Liam deeper into examination of the "madness." George develops his skills by dissecting bodies, both animal and human, and by observation of medical practices. He (and his servant) are observers at childbirths, an occasion closed to men at the time but possible nonetheless under conditions of disguise. Such subterfuge is considered necessary for the advance of science; the disguises and other concerns for the modesty of women are considered nuisances. The welfare of mother or child is not considered of importance compared to the development of scientific knowledge. This practice is carried to its logical end when one of the "resurrectionists" auctions the recently deceased body of a pregnant black woman to the highest bidder for research purposes. The woman, who is another version of the figure who haunts the narrator, is reduced to an object of racist commentary by the doctors, though Liam identifies with her as son, brother, father. Through these experiences, Liam comes to an understanding of the relationship of science and art to racism. Processes of investigation, whether scientific or aesthetic, involve the stripping away of layers to uncover what lies beneath. But this requires a willingness to sacrifice the life of that which is flayed, to turn it into an object for one's own use.

Such an understanding of Western culture necessarily sees slavery and racism not as aberrations within that culture but as part of its structure and logic. This is the deepest level of Wideman's critique: the achievements of the Enlightenment are inextricably linked to its "madness." Art, science, commerce, religion, and individualism necessarily require not only the recognition of the Other (whether animal, female, or "colored") but also the exploitation and destruction of that Other for the benefit (intellectual, economic, artistic, spiritual) of the Self. But because achievement is linked to such abuse, it may well be impossible to end the "madness." In that sense, the New World will remain, as Liam says, "a graveyard for African people" (127).

Liam attempts a way out, but it is doomed. After years of self-suppression and silence required by the need to hide from the madness, he is able to recover his voice in the presence of his African American visitor, the narrator. He is also able to regain some connection to his earlier being; he and his wife return to passionate lovemaking, and he begins painting her. But his painting is something different from that of Stubbs; it appears not to strip away and control life but to transform and liberate it: "If there is a woman on Liam's canvas, she is beset by a storm of paint. A forest of paint. . . . Somewhere in the holler of it, the woman's figure surely was forming, surely as patches of familiar melody formed the quilt of Liam's tune. When he looks at her again, beyond the canvas through it, she's changed. . . . Not what Liam imagined or he imagined or she imagined, but what would come next. After this time. Next and next. Always unknown. Always free" (181–82).

Wideman proposes here an alternative art, one that engages its subject in call and response, rather than destroys and controls it. Art in this case represents its subject in a particular moment, a moment that is transforming for both. It is art in time, in the process of change. By being the subject of the art, the woman is enabled to become the next version of herself, and the art has a new subject. Art and life are endlessly entangled and creative. But life is not reduced to art's object; it is not "killed" by the artist's gaze. Such a notion, of course, validates Wideman's own art as intensely engaged with time and with the issues of life. Liam's artistic process is also modernist in its expressive rather than coldly mimetic form. This, too, can be seen as the author's justification for his simultaneous experimentation and critical engagement.

But the hopefulness of the aesthetic idea is subverted by the fact that at the time the narrator is recalling this scene, Liam and his wife have been murdered by their white neighbors, as had been virtually all of the blacks of the community of Radnor. Liam had not succeeded in hiding; he and his wife, like others, are eventually caught in the madness he sought to understand. Art, truth, and love are not guarantees of protection from the underlying hatred in society.

When the narrator escapes to Philadelphia, he moves to another level of the social insanity. Here he encounters not physical violence but the more insidious moral dishonesty of a so-called tolerant world. In the place of murdering neighbors, we have the arrogant and condescending Dr. Thrush (Benjamin Rush) and his both morally and physically blind wife. In them, Wideman depicts American liberalism, which prides itself on its beneficence and enlightened attitudes in matters of race but which in fact operates in a closed realm of self-interest. Thrush will, for example, help finance the building of a small, all-black church, but he does not question the racist practices that force its construction. He will not publicly repudiate the calumny that blacks brought the epidemic to the city and that they are immune to it; engaging in the debate would not be good for his reputation at that moment, though his black "friends" are endangered by it.

Similarly, the wife keeps a journal, which is physically written by her maid, in which she notes the virtues of her husband and her friendship with the maid, at the very time that Thrush is nightly sexually assaulting Kate, that same maid. Kate herself is silent in all this, except for italicized comments that offer her counterversion of reality. The wife finds usefulness in working in an orphanage for black children who lost their parents in the plague. Her "work" is primarily telling them that God is good and that the fever is somehow a blessing. Meanwhile, the children are being starved and imprisoned in a cellar at night. Eventually a fire kills them all.

The narrator is given the journal by Kate, who thereby can reveal to him her experiences. Thus, he is enabled to gather all the stories, from all perspectives. But his efforts to speak them, the burden of telling, has produced a stutter: "Losing my facility in this language that's cost me far too much to learn" (205). Moreover, it is not clear that the telling serves any purpose: "Time to give it up. This speaking in a strange tongue, this stranger's voice I struggle to assume to keep you alive. The stories are not working. I talk, maybe you listen, but you're not better, nor stronger. I'll lose you any minute. You cannot live in this fallen place. Love can't live here. Time to go. Give it up" (205).

Without a clear shift in voice, the text moves from this moment in 1790s Philadelphia to the present and connects the African legend not only to that world but also to ours: "I must warn you there are always machines hovering in the air, giant insects with the power to swoop down spattering death, clean out the square in a matter of instants. . . . And warn you there are prophecies in the air, prophecies deadlier than machines. If you deny yourselves, transform yourselves, destroy yourselves, the prophets say, a better world will be born" (207).

The narrative voice here offers its own prophecy of the dangers of sacrifice of both individuals and cultures. It attacks external forces that produce high levels of black imprisonment and executions and accusations of black corruption, drug use, promiscuity, ignorance, and laziness that can only be cured through increased police vigilance and reduced assistance. It also attacks internal black conservative arguments that self-restraint and acceptance of a color-blind bootstraps philosophy will automatically produce entry into the American dream. The vision addresses as well those who believe that only violence within the community will gain them the respect they deserve and cannot otherwise gain. If African Americans (and other minorities) will only give up any semblance of a distinct cultural identity that might value anything other than individualism and self-aggrandizement, then the world would be a wonderful place. And for those who refuse, there are the machines in the air, like the mosquitoes who carried the fever in Philadelphia.

The only hope is that someone will listen to the stories and learn from them. The image of stripping away the skin, used throughout the novel, echoes the treatment of Jews and others in the death camps, even as it reflects Du Bois's concern for the inhumanity of a society defined by skin color. It ties two horrors together and suggests the logic of the view that some people are necessarily better than others. In such a world, it becomes possible to believe that human sacrifice can create a better society.

If Wideman challenges the present from the perspective of two hundred years ago, Charles Johnson does so from the point of the recent past. Although he sets his narrative in the late 1960s, he creates an environment similar to that of Wideman. Though *Dreamer* is concerned with the meaning of the life of Martin Luther King Jr., it focuses on the last two years of that life, which are presented as the most difficult phase of the civil rights movement and perhaps even its death throes. Johnson sets his story primarily in the North, and especially in Chicago, as opposed to the South. One purpose for this strategy is to raise questions about the implications of the movement for the nation as a whole. Does the passage of laws, such as the Civil Rights Act of 1964 and the Voting Rights Act of 1965, mean that the country is truly committed to racial justice? Does it mean, in the essentially spiritual terms that most interest Johnson, that it is possible for brotherhood to supplant the view that difference means a despised Otherness? Or is this moment at a historical crossroads another point at which the nation fails to live up to its lofty rhetoric? And what is the implication of repeated failure? For Johnson, it is spiritual death.

The key mechanism by which he constructs his vision is the imagining of a double for King, a man who has a strong physical resemblance but whose life experiences are profoundly different. This character allows the author to consider both King's philosophy and his national values from a variety of perspectives. It permits consideration of the linkages of an ethics of love to class, education, personality, and other social conditions. It can be viewed in relationship to a *choice* of suffering rather than a necessity of it. It also becomes possible to explore the truly radical nature of such a philosophy.

Throughout the novel, the story of Cain and Abel serves as an intertext. It is first introduced by King, who in a troubled meditation, defines the Cains of the world as outcasts who are the true revolutionaries since they defy what seems to them arbitrary authority. This train of thought is associated with the first meeting with the double, Chaym Smith, who by implication is the Cain of the pairing. He is poor, violent, apparently uneducated, and cynical, a man who feels that the world has mistreated him. His motives for involving himself with King are never quite made clear: he needs income, he is already mistaken for the black leader and sometimes abused for that error, he may be working in some subversive capacity for the government. The one time he is actually used as a substitute, the results are disastrous.

But Johnson rejects any neat dichotomy of Smith/Cain and King/Abel that would turn the novel into another paean for the civil rights leader. Sections of the narrative told from King's point of view reflect self-doubt, spiritual quest, and the problems of celebrity. These sections also reveal the possibility of strategic errors, such as the campaign in Chicago. Finally, they reveal a nation and a movement in chaos: not the "creative tension" King had defined as essential to social progress but riots, inter- and intraracial violence, and a loss of direction as younger people challenge the goals and methods of the movement. *Dreamer* is the story of a historical end, an end in which we are perhaps still living.

The principal narrator is Matthew Bishop, who, as a minor figure in the movement, serves as an observer of the action rather than creator or central actor in it. He is close to King without being part of an inner circle, and thus his telling of events involves little self-interest. In fact, like Smith, he has doubts about his selfhood, since his life's meaning appears so much tied to that of the leader. Moreover, they have an additional similarity in that the double sees Bishop as another Cain, one who cannot fit. The reason for this is that, despite his names, Matthew Bishop cannot be an unquestioning follower or part of a system of authority; the name Abel, according to Smith, means "one who refers all things to God" (66). The narrator, though devoted to King's cause, cannot simply accept what is taught; he must make it his own. Among the "Abelites" Smith includes all manner of ideologues: " 'Christians or Communists or Cultural Nationalists, but I call 'em sheep. Or zombies—that's what Malcolm X called the Nation of Islam, you know, after he broke away from Elijah, *his* surrogate daddy. There's not a real individual in the bunch. No risk-takers, Bishop. No iconoclasts. Nobody who thinks the unthinkable, or is cursed (or blessed) with bearing the cross of a unique, singular identity . . . except for him [King]' " (67).

The position stated here can be identified with that of Johnson, who, among other forms of expression, drew cartoons satirizing the Black Power movement and who later in the novel creates an exploitative nationalist in the style of Eldridge Cleaver who contemplates gas chambers for those who disagree with him.[3]

But it is equally important to note that Johnson's emphasis on the individual rather than the group is not a defense of American hyperindividualism. Rather, it operates within his essentially Buddhist perspective, which insists that each person must find "the Way" on his or her own terms. Thus it is that Smith spent a year as a Zen novice in Japan and continues to practice meditation and other spiritual arts. He in a sense tried to become an Abel, working hard to demonstrate to the priests that he could learn the rituals, the texts, and, more important, their meanings. He felt that he had arrived: " 'He led me down a hallway with wooden floors polished so brightly by hand that they almost gleamed, then he stopped in front of a bulletin board listing the names of the monks and laymen presently training at the temple. Mine was the last, the newest one there. I tell you, buddy, when I seen that I broke down and cried like a goddam baby. I was home. You get it? After centuries of slavery and segregation and being shat on by everybody on earth, I was *home*' " (97–98). In this moment Smith is doubly not an individual: first, he feels that he has become part of a spiritual community, taking his identity from them, and, second, he connects the experience to his race, those having experienced slavery and segregation.

Crucial to his development is his later enlightenment about the limits of "group-think." At the end of his year, he is called into the Roshi and told that he was wasting his time, even though his practice was perfect: " 'Only a Japanese could experience true enlightenment' " (99). This becomes his moment of enlightenment: " 'If anything, my year in the temple taught me what Gautama [the Buddha] figured out when he broke away from the holy men: if you want liberation, to be free, you got to get there on your own' " (99). Thus, the racism of monks provides a lesson very similar to that of their American counterparts: freedom must be gained for the self by the self.

But the paradox of this philosophy is that true freedom can be had only by giving up the self. Smith comes to this in two experiences: construction work on a rural church and an observation of King speaking. The labor in effect returns him to the life of the temple, in which work keeps the self located in the present moment, not focused on either past or future and thus not concerned with desire. As for the second experience, just as he had studied carefully Zen teachings, so the double studies King's talks and sources so as to perfect his role. But when it comes time to serve as the replacement, he cannot do so. Instead, he must stand in the wings and observe. What he understands is that this leader transcends selfhood: " 'His voice. . . . It feels when he's preaching like his words come from inside *me*, not outside—like he gives my soul a voice' " (142).

It is this point that reveals Johnson's real interest in King. What he sees in this Christian leader is a Buddhist spirituality much like his own. This civil rights leader moves beyond race and religion and American individualism to a plane of transcendent spirituality. Time after time in the novel, King is made to reflect attitudes and insights consistent with the author's perspective. One purpose of the double, then, is to specify this connection; King could not be shown to be consciously adopting such a position within the frame of historical fiction, so Smith is the device used to establish the parallels. Moreover, this underlying philosophy is shown to be fundamental to the leader's achievements. In the prologue, King thinks about his "deeper, esoteric message about freedom": "The gleaming keys he offered to the Kingdom made men and women who accepted his exoteric, surface-skimming political speeches shrink back once they saw the long-sealed door he was asking them to enter; they could not pass through that portal and remain as they were: white and black, male and female, Jew and Gentile, rich and poor—these were ephemeral garments, he knew, and could no more clear that entrance than a camel through a needle's eye. To gain the dizzying heights of the mountaintop the self's baggage had to be abandoned in the valley" (17). King also sees himself as walking a tightrope between material and spiritual worlds and remembers a moment of awakening from "the long, lurid dream of multiplicity and separateness" (82).

Though the language of these contemplations uses the figures of Christianity, it clearly reflects a larger spiritual frame of reference that incorporates self-sacrifice, not in the sense that Wideman condemns but in notions of transcendence. The irony is that they are refracted through the sensibility of a man caught up in a historical moment when political, social, and racial divisions are at their most intense. The point Johnson chooses, 1966, includes Vietnam protests, economic conflicts, debates within the civil rights movement, riots, and political violence, all of which King speaks to. But his very ability to see connections at the deepest levels is taken as a sign of his decreasing effectiveness. Advocates for each of the issues see the other problems as distractions from their concerns. King's skill at speaking for the silenced and oppressed of various groups is disruptive to both his supporters and his antagonists. Because others lack his insight, the work he feels he must do adds to the disorder rather than resolves it. Not even a sympathetic observer such as Matthew Bishop can grasp the full significance of his leader's efforts.

Another irony, then, is that Bishop (and through him readers of the novel) must learn King's meaning through the inferior expression of the double. Chaym Smith, as one who has not reached enlightenment but has a sense of the value of the quest, can point a direction that is intelligible to doubters like himself. He can be a cynical voice that rejects certain positions, while King must emphasize love and forgiveness. He can make use of dichotomies, such as Cain and Abel, black and white, while King must speak of unity. Because

Smith can, through his confrontational personality, bring Bishop to an understanding of aspects of the self that he has carefully suppressed, it is possible to grasp the difference that is King and still see its relevance to human experience. They represent two different versions of the Way, though they lead to the same place: "[I]f the prophet King had shown us the depths of living possible for those who loved unconditionally in a less than just universe engraved with inequality, and that only the servants should lead, then Chaym had in his covert passage through our lives let us know that, if one missed the Galilean mark, even the pariahs, the fatherless exiles, might sometimes—and occasionally—doeth well" (236).

This closing passage of the novel might well be taken as signal for hope, even an almost sentimental assertion that all of us have our roles, no matter how humble. But it is important to understand the limiting conditions of Bishop's remarks as an application to contemporary society. After all, they come at the time of King's death and the civil violence that followed, which have as historical parallel the beating of Rodney King and the consequent violence, which occurred at the time Johnson was working on this novel. If the great leader's death allows us to see him as the embodiment of love and justice, recent history would suggest that he and his disciples are seen by many as having failed to bring those qualities into social reality.

Another aspect of the narrative that conditions a hopeful reading is the implication that Chaym Smith is involved in FBI conspiracies to destroy King's power and perhaps King himself. While this cooperation appears to be coerced, it is of some importance to the government. And if Smith represents, through his spiritual insights, one version of the Way, then that Way must include susceptibility to intimidation and perhaps collaboration and betrayal. At best, it offers little indication that the pariahs can, in fact, "doeth well." Moreover, the novel's discussion about the possible players in the assassination, which suggests possible roles of the very powerful, may indicate Smith's significant involvement. The text plays with conspiracy and racial paranoia without being specific. But it is precisely such play that has apocalyptic overtones, since it implies that unknown forces are at work in shaping history and the social order. Against such forces, King and Smith can have little impact. Those who follow them, such as Bishop, lacking their insight, experience, and spritiual force, are even more helpless.

Finally, even if such speculations are false, what the narrator calls "ethnic ego" would be enough to destroy the "dream": "The Way of agapic love, with its bottomless demands, had proven too hard for this nation. Hatred and competition were easier. Exalting the ethnic ego proved far less challenging than

King's belief in the beloved community. We loved violence—verbal and physical—too dearly. Our collective spirit, the *Geist* of our era, had slain him as surely as the assassin's bullet that cut him down. We were all Cainites. And deservedly cursed. Did we not kill the best in ourselves when we killed King? Wasn't every murder a suicide as well?" (235–36). Because "ethnic ego" had been established earlier in the text as a part of the emergent militancy of blacks, as well as the patronizing language of whites, the condemnation is national rather than limited to a specific race. Moreover, "ethnic ego" would seem to be synonymous with the "identity politics" of the 1990s. But while this latter term has tended to be associated with racial and other minorities, it applies as well, in the narrative's rendering of it, to whites who seek to claim for themselves a version of minority status as victims of the nation's racial politics. Whether the argument is over multiculturalism, affirmative action, or the nation's "common culture," white claims of lost status serve as yet another articulation of ethnic ego.

The text concludes, then, in a moment of contradiction and perhaps paradox. On the one hand is the monumentalizing impulse of calling King "the best in ourselves." He is the emblem and model of human possibility; in addition, the meaning of that model would seem to be fixed outside of history. Thus, what we should do now is the same as what should have been done a quarter century earlier, regardless of changes in historical conditions. The point is reinforced when the "we" of the text are labeled "Cainites," which reinscribes a previously valorized term as an expression of opprobrium. It would appear in fact to align Bishop with "Abelite" discourse, in providing certainty about the "cursed" condition of all who created the conditions for King's death. "We" have reenacted the original sin and the crucifixion of Christ in the treatment of our own divine incarnation.

But the text also returns to Smith, the quintessential Cain:

"Her eyes swung up, searching my face. 'What about Chaym? Where do you think he is?' I dropped my gaze, watching my feet and those of the sinners in front of me. I thought hard. 'Everywhere. . . .' That seemed to satisfy her, and she smiled" (236). He is reclaimed so as to be Cain (in the text's original sense) and not Judas. His immanence in the world, which pleases Amy, is a kind of hope for all the "sinners." But it is a hope, not for transcendence or creation of a "beloved community," but for endurance of the fatherless in a fallen, perhaps hopeless, world. Because King and Smith are doubles, the monumentalizing of the one is always tempered by the historical presence of the other. We need to construct memorials to the ideal in order to change history, but we have to recognize our place in the history we change.

Toni Morrison can be seen as combining Wideman's image of human sacrifice with Johnson's concern with historical change, with the added fillip of gender's connection to race. In *Paradise*, she describes, as she often does in her work, the creation of an African American community. In this instance, however, she problematizes the invention of communal narrative by showing its oppressive and ultimately self-destructive effects. In doing so, she would appear to be challenging the ideological uses to which black history specifically and American history generally have been put.

The first chapter of the novel establishes the historical and ideological context for all else that happens. The rest of the book may be said to fill out the details of this introduction. It shows the men of the all-black town of Ruby engaged in their mission of hunting down and killing a group of women living in an isolated house known as the Convent. Their motive for this, never entirely made explicit, is to destroy the female "filth" (3) that is in some way threatening their community. As the men move through the house that was built as a gambler's mansion and later became a school where nuns taught Arapahoe girls "to forget" (4), they recall the history of their town and the reasons it must be so sternly protected.

That history is closely linked to myth in the versions that have survived. A group of former slaves heads west to establish a new life but meets repeated rejection along the way, including from other blacks. Their pariah status generates group solidarity that enables them to build a successful and self-sufficient community under difficult conditions. They become a band of the elect. At the center of the town is placed the Oven, with the cryptic message, "Beware the Furrow of His Brow." The story serves as an African American version of a number of national utopian narratives, most particularly the experience of the Mormons, in the incorporation of rejection, architectural symbol, and sacred text. These elements are central to the identity of the group and not merely accidents of history. They must be preserved at all costs because they are the keys to distinctiveness; without them, this would simply be another band of pioneers.

This history/myth also must come to terms with failure and change. In this case, the current dominant group has defined itself as the saviors of the original vision. When Haven began to decline with the Depression and World War II, a core determined to keep the dream alive. They did so by, in 1949, leaving Haven, taking with them the Oven, and creating a new community, Ruby. A key motivation was fear of the larger world: "Ten generations had known what lay Out There: space, once beckoning and free, became unmonitored and seething; became a void where random and organized evil erupted when and where it chose—behind any standing tree, behind the door of any house, humble or grand. Out There where your children were sport, your women quarry, and where your very person could be annulled; where congregations carried arms to church and ropes coiled in every saddle. Out There where every cluster of whitemen looked like a posse, being alone was being dead" (16).

What leads to the departure is not simply the racist environment but also the adjustments that have been made to live in that circumstance, what the men label the "grovel contaminating the town" (16). So the purpose is to return to origins, to the founding principles and values that history had confounded. Both the action and the narrative of it, in other words, are means of erasing history.

This first chapter also demonstrates the extent to which such efforts support a masculinist order. The present-time violence, set in 1976, is carried out by the leading men of the town. They have named themselves the New Fathers, since they replicated the journey and struggle of the original founders. The community is ordered according to their rules; as Deek Morgan says during a later meeting: " 'Nobody is going to mess with a thing our grandfathers built' " (85). To protect what was created, they wield all the economic, social, and political power, believing that they are the ones who truly understand the vision that was Haven and has now become Ruby.

It is a vision of safety and protection, but one that demands sacrifice: "The house he lives in is big, comfortable, and this town is resplendent compared to his birthplace, which had gone from feet to belly in fifty years. From Haven, a dreamtown in Oklahoma Territory, to Have, a ghosttown in Oklahoma State. Freedmen who stood tall in 1889 dropped to their knees in 1934 and were stomach-crawling in 1948. That is why they are here in this Convent. To make sure it never happens again. That nothing inside or out rots the one all-black town worth the pain" (5). Curiously, the selection of the Convent and its inhabitants as the evil ones who must be destroyed is not consistent with the history remembered, which suggests that economics more than morality produced Haven's decline: "Subsistence farming, once the only bounty a large family needed became just scrap farming as each married son got his bit, which had to be broken up into more pieces for his children, until finally the owners of the bits and pieces who had not walked off in disgust welcomed any offer from a white speculator, so eager were they to get away and try someplace else" (6). Declining possibilities based in part on success (at least at having children) is not clearly equatable to "stomach-crawling." Reference to 1934 clearly places the experience in the dust bowl and thus beyond the control of any community.

But to admit the power of impersonal forces in the narrative is to question the power and authority of those controlling Ruby. By constructing the past as the achievements of strong-willed men able to endure both natural and human hostility to their vision, the modern generation can put on the mantle of that experience by pointing to their parallel experience. Their success, then, is the result of comparable moral seriousness and individual virtue; their material prosperity is simply the expected reward of their righteousness. It is not an accident of the text that their views were shaped by service in World War II; those who remained behind and brought Haven to its lowest point were the weak and the female. History is conceived of as war, as a struggle of good and evil, of the elect and the damned.

If women are weak and potential contaminants ("detritus"), they nonetheless can be of use, particularly as sacrifices. The new town is named after the sister of Deacon and Steward Morgan, whose names imply both responsibility and materialism. Ruby had been weak during the journey to the new town; when she became seriously ill after arrival, the brothers sought medical care. None of the nearby facilities would admit black patients, and she died in a waiting room while, according to the story, the nurse attempted to locate a veterinarian. The town was then named Ruby, not only to honor her, but also to place the narrative of a sacrifice comparable to that of the Old Fathers at the heart of the communal consciousness. At the same time, however, the naming also is a reminder of the vulnerability of African American life, a weakness now forever associated with a woman.

The emerging problems of the town—family conflict, birth defects, spoiled weddings, venereal diseases, violence, disobedient children—seem to be primarily associated with women, and thus a cleansing sacrifice is needed. Given the perceived cause of the decline, the sacrifice should be female. So it is that the group of nine men enter the Convent to kill or drive off the women who live there.

Unlike Wideman and Johnson, who largely exclude blacks from blame for the "troubles" in their narratives, choosing instead to point to white responsibility, Morrison here locates responsibility within the African American community. She insists that the men of the town retain control through closed readings of the "texts" of the world. Their misreadings are symbolized by the debates throughout the novel over the actual words and meaning of the motto placed on the Oven. While the men insist that it originally read "Beware the Furrow of His Brow" and is a warning about the need for self-protection and moral order, others speculate that it might say "Be the Furrow of His Brow," implying the need for self-assertion, or "We Are the Furrow of His Brow," suggesting the need to accept responsibility for the problems of the town rather than putting it on others.

As the men proceed through the Convent on their murderous mission, they "read" this space created by women and do so in a way that validates their actions. All objects are taken as emblems of evil or of female "filth." It is not possible for them to imagine a world in which good women can live without men, and therefore it follows that these must be demonic creatures. Morrison devotes much of the remainder of the novel to the past and present experiences of these women, so as to offer alternative ways to understand the Convent, ways that the women of the town begin to grasp, though few of the men do.

A crucial question is why the men are willing to engage in a mini-holocaust in order to maintain the dubious purity of Ruby. After all, the women cannot be held responsible for appeals to civil rights or black nationalist activism that causes conflict between generations. These modern men are not likely to really believe that women seventeen miles away can produce birth defects.

Women of the town suggest two drives that run as deep as human history. Patricia Best, who has served as the town's unofficial historian, has to keep her effort private because silence largely pervades the recalling of the past; only the acceptable details are spoken. What she comes to understand is that the people of Ruby see themselves, in essence, as a separate race. Though the "rules" are unspoken, it is unacceptable to marry someone from outside the community, especially if that person is light-skinned. This is a response to the "Disallowing," when a mulatto town refused a place to the Old Fathers. A curse was placed on that community, and Haven, followed by Ruby, became endogamous. Purity of vision is symbolized by purity of blood. The very meaning of the town is thus linked to its hatred and repudiation of others. The special virtue of this group, its self-preservation, necessitates the Other as an absolute.

Moreover, Pat sees the New Fathers as having made a bargain with God. They would retain purity, and in exchange they would become immortal. She points out that no one has died in the town since Ruby. Only those who have gone elsewhere have died. By remaining unchanged, by refusing contact with the larger world, by insisting on purity, the men can believe that they have conquered death.

It then becomes clear why women threaten such a fantasy. Because it is (was) impossible to determine the identity of a baby's father with absolute certainty, it was always possible for women to "contaminate" the bloodlines. Moreover, given the seductive powers of women, it was not possible to guarantee that young men would marry or have children within the boundaries of the town. Finally, of course, in-group marriage eventually exaggerates genetic defects, resulting in problems with children blamed on the Convent women. In a community distrustful of outsiders and especially women, a group of women living without men and coming from places unknown to the townspeople can easily be read as an assault on everything Ruby is and means. They symbolize freedom, impurity, change, and ultimately death itself. Corruption of blood produced the mulattoes who rejected their ancestors; corruption of spirit produced the death of Haven; and claims of black freedom through civil rights and black power appear to be corrupting Ruby's next generation. Destroying the women, like destroying the Jews in the European holocaust, enables the killers to imagine an unchanging reality outside history.

What is important to Morrison's construction of her narrative is that she does not fall into the trap of the men of Ruby. The women of the Convent are not simply victims seeking unchanging self-enclosure, nor are they tempted to define themselves as a "race" based on their experiences. On the surface, their narratives would seem to follow the pattern of representation in contemporary black women writers, including ntozake shange, Alice Walker, Gloria Naylor, and Gayl Jones. Each of the women has suffered in some way from societal hostility. Mavis, whose twins died due to her momentary negligence, is made to feel guilty beyond what circumstances warrant. Gigi (Grace) is repeatedly deceived by men in her quest for wholeness. Seneca, abandoned as a child, practices self-mutilation. Pallas's boyfriend left her for her own mother. And Consolata, who is the connection to the nuns, was "kidnapped" by them and brought to the United States; she also experienced sexual abuse as a child. In each case, the problems have produced some form of madness: Mavis sometimes believes that her children are alive; Gigi is both promiscuous and exhibitionist; Pallas has no sense of identity; and Consolata has become alcoholic. Thus, sympathy for them is mitigated by their own flaws. The Convent is an imperfect community in which there is neither miraculous healing nor suppression of personal needs and desires. Their problems are sometimes denied but never seen as irrelevant. In this sense, they are an alternative to Ruby, though not a utopia. And it is perhaps because of the experimental nature of the women's world that it is seen as a danger to the town. Because some of the people of Ruby (both men and women) have been involved in some way with the Convent, they are aware of its difference. This difference, as Pallas puts it, is its "malelessness," which makes it a safe place for women. But if women can come from anywhere and create their own order, then the male-centered vision, history, and society of Ruby are rendered, if not meaningless, at least of limited significance.

Like the people of Ruby, the women of the Convent tell their stories, though not in the ritualized, self-righteous, congratulatory mode of the town. Instead, they use first dream-speech and then images to construct the metaphoric and physical realities of their experiences. But while their stories are ones of individual suffering, no one "owns" them:

> That is how the loud dreaming began. How the stories rose in that place. Half-tales and the never-dreamed escaped from their lips to soar high above guttering candles, shifting dust from crates and bottles. And it was never important to know who said the dream or whether it had meaning. In spite of or because their bodies ache, they step easily into the dreamer's tale. They enter the heat of the Cadillac, feel the smack of cold air in the Higgledy Piggledy. . . . Each one blinks and gags from tear gas, moves her hand slowly to the scraped shin, the torn ligament. Runs up and down the halls by day, sleeps in a ball with the light on at night. Folds the five hundred dollars in the foot of her sock. Yelps with pain from a stranger's penis and a mother's rivalry—alluring and corrosive as cocaine. (264)

Each woman also creates a "template" of herself on the floor of the cellar, which is the space in which the dreams are spoken. They begin to paint their stories on the images—the pain, the self-abuse, the fear. In doing so, they liberate themselves from their troubling pasts and their private obsessions. That which had been denied or silenced can be expressed through art, even if it cannot be spoken in words. A visitor to the house recognizes the effect on the women, without knowing the cause: "Then she might realize what was missing: unlike some people in Ruby, the Convent women were no longer haunted" (266).

Because the men of Ruby remain ghost-ridden, they must destroy the women. And their discovery of the painted cellar, with its "obscene" art, only deepens their hatred. The female body as a site of suffering cannot be meaningfully interpreted without implicating the viewers in its and their own history. While some of the women of Ruby interrupt the slaughter, it is not clear that the men ever grasp the significance of the painting or their own actions. Though Deacon Morgan performs a form of medieval penance by walking barefoot through the streets and seeking forgiveness through the new minister, his brother remains as arrogant and stern as ever. Lone, the eldest woman of the town, sees the end of the old Ruby but also the opportunity for a new beginning. The apparent deaths but magical disappearances of the women offer an apocalyptic moment: "He had actually swept up and received His servants in broad daylight, for goodness sake! right before their very eyes, for Christ's sake!" (298). But the hopefulness of this transfiguration is qualified by the impulse of the townspeople to explain away and suppress the actions of the men. The disappearance of the women, including the bodies of the ones known to be dead, permit the evasion of justice. Once again, women are sacrificed to protect the men of Ruby.

But Morrison does not leave that as the moralistic message of her text. After the town's rationalization, we are told of the appearances of the women to those they had known in their earlier lives. These visitations serve to reassure or trouble relatives who had caused the problems or had been also hurt by them. While these scenes can be taken as resolutions, they can equally be understood as ghostly visitations to those who have not yet come to terms with the past. Similarly, the novel closes with Consolata resting in the lap of Piedade, the woman who sings but does not speak. But the closing image is of a ship headed to port after being lost; the narrator says of the people on board: "Now they will rest before shouldering the endless work they were created to do down here in Paradise" (318).

If "down here" is the world of historical reality, then Paradise is the society that human beings create, and the creation of it will be "endless work." If Ruby cannot learn from its experience after such horror, then the effort needed to make a better world must go on and on. And if Ruby is in some sense the nation, the failure to confront the harsh realities of past and present doom it to repeated acts of human sacrifice. If the discourse of the present permits each element of the society, regardless of its privilege, to claim victim status, then delusion is always present and holocaust ever possible. One specific example exemplifies the relevance of the novel's meaning. In her recently renewed role as editor, Morrison put together a collection of materials on the Clarence Thomas–Anita Hill controversy.[4] What drew special attention was Thomas's claims that the attacks on him were a form of "high-tech lynching." This identification with historical violence enabled him to draw around himself the cloak of victimization and thereby evade the accusation of victimizer. Significantly, his rhetoric brought to his defense the band of white male senators who could self-righteously claim status as nonracists through their protective postures. What is suppressed in this ritual is the renewed sacrifice of a woman for the preservation of male power.

This incident is part of the larger pattern of a society that appears to engage history but does so only to limit its significance and to hide the bodies. Whether it is the commodification of Native American cultures or the selling of *Roots* (and its descendants) or the packaging of Afrocentrism as the true history of African Americans or the media productions of various feminisms and antifeminisms or the arguments of neoconservatives and neoliberals that

America's greatness is being compromised by the "tribalism" of multicultural-ists or the "cultural baggage" of outdated African American traditions, the objective is to gain and maintain privilege at the expense of the Other. Each represents a closing of the discourse of history instead of an opening of it to the expressions of true victims. But Morrison, like Wideman and Johnson, also insists that the denial of history is an act of fear, as well as oppression. The men of Ruby in fact know the damaging cost of confronting the fullness of the past and of the present. At some level they realize, as James Baldwin phrased it, "the price of the ticket." If the Anita Hills are not heard, if the black men in prisons, such as Wideman's son and brother, are not recognized, if the images created by Martin Luther King and Malcolm X are erased, sometimes through venera-tion, then the work will be endless, and Paradise will continue to be sought through human sacrifice.

Notes

Introduction

1. See Omi and Winant.

2. Recent popular history texts have framed the black past specifically in holocaust terms. See S. E. Anderson, Clarke, and Del Jones.

3. See Hollinger.

4. The foundational text for the study of abjection is Kristeva, but there have been many other studies on specific literary works since then, including a few on Toni Morrison, which will be cited in the chapter on *Beloved*.

5. The range of work in cultural studies is vast. A useful sample of that range can be found in During. The work of Stuart Hall, Paul Gilroy, and bell hooks has been especially important for African diasporic cultural studies.

6. On trauma theory, the following are relevant to this study: Aberbach, Caruth, Felman and Laub, and Horowitz.

7. See Lawrence Langer on the complexities and falsification of attempting to incorporate the incomprehensibility of the Holocaust within rational and moral discourse.

8. This is the meaning of historical narrative as it is articulated by Georg Lukács in *The Historical Novel*.

9. On the historical novel tradition and the problematics of the genre, see Budick, Kennedy and Fogel, Hutcheon, Juan-Navarro, Jacobs, Cowart, Wright, Foley, and Henderson.

Chapter One

1. Among the works informing this discussion are Dent; Ferguson et al.; Gilroy, *Black Atlantic*; Guerrero; hooks; Lubiano; Merelman; and Greg Tate.

2. For a discussion of the significance of racialized bodies, see Doyle.

3. See hooks, *Black Looks*; Morrison, *Race-ing Justice*; Collins, *Fighting Words*; Dent; and Greg Tate. For a somewhat different reading of the function of black cultural elements in American society, see Merelman.

4. The discourse of the neoconservatives is remarkably similar, regardless of discipline. See Crouch, *All-American Skin Game*; D'Souza; Herrnstein and Murray; Lefko-

witz; Loury; McWhorter; Sowell, *Race and Economics*; Shelby Steele; and Thernstrom and Thernstrom.

5. On postmodernism, literature, and history, see Attridge et al., Brooks, Cain, Dirks et al., Fairlamb, Francese, Hutcheon, Pocock, Saldívar, and White.

6. On the ethics of narrative, see Newton and Nussbaum.

7. See William Andrews for a detailed discussion of the form of the slave narrative.

Chapter Two

1. On the Holocaust and Jewish identity, see Cheyette and Marcus; Hirsch; Langer, *Holocaust Testimonies*; and Epstein. The meaning and impact of "black holocaust" are described in S. E. Anderson; Clarke, *Christopher Columbus*; and Del Jones.

2. See the introduction to Bal, Crewe, and Spitzer.

3. See especially Randall Kennedy.

4. D'Souza is a key text among those committed to repudiation.

5. On related aspects of female narratives, see Kubitschek, Awkward, McDowell, and Christian.

6. See especially the narratives of male writers, including Frederick Douglass and Moses Roper. For a general reading of these texts, see William Andrews.

7. For a discussion of how trauma is experienced, see Caruth, 16–18.

8. For a detailed discussion of this theme in Morrison, see Bouson.

9. See Van Alphen and Brison.

10. In this sense, Morrison is making the same complex point that Richard Wright did in *Native Son* when Bigger Thomas interpreted his act of murder as a act of creation. For other readings of Sethe's actions, see Baker-Fletcher, Heller, Holden-Kirwan, Randle, and Wyatt.

11. See Crouch, *All-American Skin Game*; Shelby Steele; and Sowell, *Civil Rights*.

12. See Moses, 21–25.

13. See Heller, Kubitschek, 165–77; Mbalia; Puri; Ryan; and Sale.

14. See Baker-Fletcher; Bouson; Crouch, "Aunt Medea"; Clemons; Thurman; and Walters.

15. See, for example, Angelo.

Chapter Three

1. On the complicated meaning of being a survivor, see Aberbach and Felman and Laub.

2. On the means by which repressed, traumatic experience is rendered, see Caruth; Horowitz; LaCapra, *Representing the Holocaust*; Tal; and Van Alphen.

3. One only has to consider what was presented as the "black canon" prior to approximately 1980: Frederick Douglass, W. E. B. Du Bois, Langston Hughes, Richard Wright, Ralph Ellison, James Baldwin, and LeRoi Jones. See also recent works by Angela Davis, Elaine Brown, and others on attitudes toward women in the civil rights

and black nationalist movements. Commentators such as Ishmael Reed have been vociferous in their attacks on the castrating effects of black women writers.

4. The "black men as endangered species" argument is a recent version of this. See Gibbs and Madhubuti.

5. See Brearly for a definition of the folk figure of the bad man.

6. This well may be an act of signifying on Alice Walker's *In Search of Our Mother's Gardens*.

7. See Baker, *Blues, Ideology, and Afro-American Literature*, 23–31.

8. See, for example, Madhubuti's poem "The Self-Hatred of Don L. Lee."

9. Herrnstein and Murray's *Bell Curve* is only the most notorious of recent commentaries on this point.

10. Ellis Cose has been the most prominent of recent commentators on the black middle class.

Chapter Four

1. See Christian; Kubitschek; McDowell, *"Changing Same"*; Mary Helen Washington; and Wilentz.

2. See McDowell, "Negotiating between Tenses."

3. See Rushdy, "Reading Mammy," and Davis.

4. One possible reading of this moment in the text as a site of struggle is that Dessa represents Williams herself and Rufel represents Styron. In this sense, Styron is creating a black figure useful for whites. Given the psychoanalytical approach of *Nat Turner*, an additional element of signifying, then, would be the image of the black mother in this conflict.

5. See Nora, 284–85.

6. Compare Christian, Kubitschek, and McDowell, "Negotiating between Tenses."

Chapter Five

1. The first major critical work to undertake a study of African American writing in psychoanalytic terms is Claudia Tate's *Psychoanalysis and Black Novels*.

2. Ann Douglas, in *Terrible Honesty*, with her image of "mongrel Manhattan," offers a reading of the city's culture at the time in similar terms.

3. For cultural and literary readings of the Renaissance, see Baker, *Modernism and the Harlem Renaissance*; Douglas; Huggins, *Harlem Renaissance*; Hutchinson; Lewis; Spencer; Wall; and Watson.

4. Much has been written on the social, cultural, and political experience of the Great Migration of the early twentieth century. Standard works include Campbell and Johnson, Crew, Griffin, Gossman, Harrison, Henri, Lemann, and Painter.

5. See Bell, "Blues People," and Stuart.

6. See Valerie Steele for a discussion of the gender implications of style in the 1920s.

7. Dreiser, Faulkner, Fitzgerald, and Hemingway, among the canonical writers, make similar connections between gender and violence during this period.

8. For discussions of this self-representation, see Claudia Tate, *Domestic Allegories*, and Carby.

9. See Morrison, *Race-ing Justice*.

10. See Gabriel.

11. See Horowitz.

12. Given Naylor's earlier work, such as *Women of Brewster Place* and *Linden Hills*, with its emphasis on the suffering of women, one can presume a similar audience for this novel.

13. This numbering would seem to be a play on folk numerology, since it is the seventh son who is special. In the context of the book's themes, this may be a subtle repudiation of the valorization of folk wisdom popular among contemporary African American writers, including Naylor herself in *Mama Day*.

14. Sanyika Shakur's *Monster* is the as-told-to story of an imprisoned gang leader.

Chapter Six

1. See Pauley, 201–2.

2. See hooks, *Yearning*, 57–64, on the effects of white male rape of black women on both the women and black men.

3. On cultural representations of the "underclass," see hooks, *Outlaw Culture*, 165–72.

4. That idealistic version may well be embodied by fellow Georgian Jimmy Carter, who was president when Andrews's first novel came out. But he was limited to one term, which was bounded by the much different Nixon/Ford and Reagan administrations. Thus, it could be argued that contemporary history was validating the author's point that idealism was the aberration.

5. See, for example, Haki Madhubuti's poem "The Self-Hatred of Don L. Lee."

Chapter Seven

1. For a detailed discussion of Johnson's philosophical position, see Little.

2. See especially Rushdy, "Phenomenology" and "Properties of Desire."

Chapter Eight

1. For a history of this mode of historiography, see Moses, esp. 1–17.

2. See Blassingame, *New Perspectives on Black Studies*; Ford; Hine; Huggins, *Afro-American Studies*; Van Deburg; and Walker.

Chapter Nine

1. For discussions of some of these discourses, see Rosenberg, Taylor-Guthrie, and Werner.

2. On the earlier experiences of the black family, see Gutman and Genovese. The

most famous commentary on contemporary black family structure is Moynihan, but his analysis still shapes much of neoconservative analysis of African American culture.

3. For analyses of these earlier works, see, Byerman, *Fingering the Jagged Grain*, 238–55; Warren; and Allen.

4. For the significance of the father in African American male narratives, see Dudley.

5. See especially Wideman, Morrison, and Gayl Jones.

6. See Byerman, "Angularity," 442.

7. See Gilroy, *Black Atlantic*, and Early, *Lure and Loathing*.

8. See Omi and Winant, 55–61.

9. On commodifications and reifications of black art, see Wallace, 118–31; Merelman; and Greg Tate.

10. See Byerman, "Angularity," Hernton, and Claudia Tate.

11. Compare *Absalom, Absalom!*, on which Forrest is signifying in this scene.

12. On Johnson's views on Buddhism, see Little.

Chapter Ten

1. It is postmodern in the sense that it challenges the conventions of the genre even as it enacts them. "The Beginning of Homewood," and thus the family, comes at the end of *Damballah*; the narrative is fragmentary rather than linear and involves absences and gaps, as well as repetitions; three of the key characters of the saga (Orion, Brother, and Albert Wilkes) are not members of the family; and the text (as in "Across the Wide Missouri") is sometimes self-reflexive.

2. Wideman discusses his rethinking of his relationship with black culture in interviews with Wilfred Samuels and Charles Rowell. This is also the central concern of James Coleman's book-length study of Wideman.

3. In addition to the Samuels and Rowell interviews, see the interview with Jessica Lustig.

4. See Brearly, 578–85, and Roberts, 174–86.

5. One representation of this image is Sanyika Shakur's *Monster*.

Chapter Eleven

1. These figures appear in other Wideman texts, suggesting their continuing significance. Mandela is mentioned in "All Stories Are True" and Ramona Africa in "Fever" and *Philadelphia Fire*.

2. For a view of how whites can be marked as black, see Morrison's comment on Bill Clinton in the 5 October 1998 *New Yorker*.

3. Johnson also targets Afrocentrists by having this same character distinguish the races as "sun people" and "ice people." See Welsing for full development of these concepts.

4. See Morrison, *Race-ing Justice*.

Bibliography

Aberbach, David. *Surviving Trauma: Loss, Literature, and Psychoanalysis*. New Haven: Yale University Press, 1989.

Adell, Sandra. *Double Consciousness / Double Bind*. Urbana: University of Illinois Press, 1994.

Adorno, Theodor. *Negative Dialectics*. Translated by E. B. Ashton. New York: Atheneum, 1973.

Agger, Ben. *Cultural Studies as Critical Theory*. London: Falmer Press, 1992.

———. *The Discourse of Domination: From the Frankfort School to Postmodernism*. Evanston, Ill.: Northwestern University Press, 1992.

Aistrup, Joseph A. *The Southern Strategy Revisited: Republican Top-Down Advancement in the South*. Lexington: University Press of Kentucky, 1996.

Allen, Jeffrey Renard. "Blood Bastards: *The Bloodworth Orphans* and the Psychology of Form." In *Leon Forrest: Introductions and Interpretations*, edited by John G. Cawelti, 166–83. Bowling Green, Ohio: Bowling Green State University Popular Press, 1997.

Anderson, Benedict. *Imagined Communities: Reflections on the Origin and Spread of Nationalism*. London: Verso, 1983.

Anderson, S. E. *The Black Holocaust for Beginners*. New York: Readers and Writers, 1995.

Andrews, Raymond. *Appalachee Red*. 1978. Athens: University of Georgia Press, 1987.

———. *Baby Sweet's*. 1983. Athens: University of Georgia Press, 1988.

———. *Rosiebelle Lee Wildcat Tennessee*. Athens: University of Georgia Press, 1988.

Andrews, William. *To Tell a Free Story: The First Century of Afro-American Autobiography, 1760–1865*. Urbana: University of Illinois Press, 1986.

Angelo, Bonnie. "The Pain of Being Black." *Time*, 22 May 1989, 120–21.

Arac, Jonathan, ed. *Postmodernism and Politics*. Minneapolis: University of Minnesota Press, 1986.

Asante, Molefi Kete. *The Afrocentric Idea*. Philadelphia: Temple University Press, 1987.

———. "Racism, Consciousness, and Afrocentricity." In *Lure and Loathing: Essays on Race, Identity, and the Ambivalence of Assimilation*, edited by Gerald Early, 127–43. New York: Penguin Press, 1993.

Attridge, Derek, et al., eds. *Post-Structuralism and the Question of History*. Cambridge: Cambridge University Press, 1987.

Awkward, Michael. *Inspiriting Influences: Tradition, Revision, and Afro-American Women's Novels*. New York: Columbia University Press, 1989.

Baker, Houston, Jr. *Black Studies, Rap, and the Academy*. Chicago: University of Chicago Press, 1993.

——. *Blues, Ideology, and Afro-American Literature: A Vernacular Theory*. Chicago: University of Chicago Press, 1984.

——. *Modernism and the Harlem Renaissance*. Chicago: University of Chicago Press, 1987.

Baker-Fletcher, Karen. "Fierce Love Comes to Haunt." *Commonweal*, November 1987, 631–33.

Bal, Mieke, Jonathan Crewe, and Leo Spitzer, eds. *Acts of Memory: Cultural Recall in the Present*. Hanover: University Press of New England, 1999.

Baldwin, James. *Going to Meet the Man*. New York: Dial, 1965.

——. "Stranger in the Village." *Notes of a Native Son*. Boston: Beacon Press, 1955.

Bell, Bernard W. *The Afro-American Novel and Its Tradition*. Amherst: University of Massachusetts Press, 1987.

——. "Blues People in a Jazz World." *The World and I*, July 1992, 378–85.

Bhabha, Homi. *The Location of Culture*. London: Routledge, 1994.

Bjork, Patrick Bryce. *The Novels of Toni Morrison: The Search for Self and Place Within the Community*. New York: Peter Lang, 1994.

Blassingame, John W. *The Slave Community: Plantation Life in the Antebellum South*. New York: Oxford University Press, 1972.

——, ed. *New Perspectives on Black Studies*. Urbana: University of Illinois Press, 1971.

Bouson, J. Brooks. *Quiet As It's Kept: Shame, Trauma, and Race in the Novels of Toni Morrison*. Albany: SUNY Press, 2000.

Bradley, David. *The Chaneysville Incident*. New York: Harper and Row, 1981.

Brearly, H. C. "Ba-ad Nigger." In *Mother Wit from the Laughing Barrel: Readings in the Interpretation of Afro-American Folklore*, edited by Alan Dundes, 578–85. Englewood Cliffs, N.J.: Prentice-Hall, 1973.

Brison, Susan J. "Trauma Narratives and the Remaking of the Self." In *Acts of Memory: Cultural Recall in the Present*, edited by Mieke Bal, Jonathan Crewe, and Leo Spitzer, 39–54. Hanover: University Press of New England, 1999.

Brooks, Linda Marie, ed. *Alternative Identities: The Self in Literature, History, Theory*. New York: Garland, 1995.

Brown, Elaine. *A Taste of Power: A Black Woman's Story*. New York: Pantheon Books, 1992.

Budick, Emily Miller. *Fiction and Historical Consciousness: The American Romance Tradition*. New Haven: Yale University Press, 1989.

Burton, Angela. "Signifyin(g) Abjection: Narrative Strategies in Toni Morrison's

Jazz." In *Toni Morrison*, edited by Linden Peach, 170–93. New York: St. Martin's, 1998.

Byerman, Keith E. "Angularity: An Interview with Leon Forrest." *African American Review* 33.3 (1999): 439–50.

———. *Fingering the Jagged Grain: Tradition and Form in Recent Black Fiction*. Athens: University of Georgia Press, 1985.

Byrd, Rudolph P., ed. *I Call Myself an Artist: Writings by and about Charles Johnson*. Bloomington: Indiana University Press, 1999.

Cain, William, ed. *Reconceptualizing American Literary / Cultural Studies: Rhetoric, History, and Politics in the Humanities*. New York: Garland, 1996.

Campbell, Daniel M., and Rex Johnson. *Black Migration in America: A Social Demographic History*. Durham: Duke University Press, 1981.

Caponi, Gena Dagel, ed. *Signifyin(g), Sanctifyin', and Slam Dunking: In African American Expressive Culture*. Amherst: University of Massachusetts Press, 1999.

Carby, Hazel. *Reconstructing Womanhood: The Emergence of the Afro-American Woman Novelist*. New York: Oxford University Press, 1987.

Carr, Leslie G. *"Color-Blind" Racism*. Thousand Oaks, Calif.: Sage, 1997.

Caruth, Cathy. *Unclaimed Experience: Trauma, Narrative, and History*. Baltimore: Johns Hopkins University Press, 1996.

Cawelti, John G., ed. *Leon Forrest: Introductions and Interpretations*. Bowling Green, Ohio: Bowling Green State University Popular Press, 1997.

Cheyette, Bryan, and Laura Marcus. *Modernity, Culture, and "The Jew."* Stanford: Stanford University Press, 1998.

Christian, Barbara. *Black Women Novelists: The Development of a Tradition, 1892–1976*. Westport, Conn.: Greenwood, 1980.

Clark, Keith. "Re-(W)righting Black Male Subjectivity: The Communal Poetics of Ernest Gaines's *A Gathering of Old Men.*" *Callaloo* 22.1 (1999): 195–207.

Clarke, John Henrik. *Christopher Columbus and the Afrikan Holocaust: Slavery and the Rise of European Capitalism*. Brooklyn: A&B Publishers, 1994.

———, ed. *William Styron's Nat Turner: Ten Black Writers Respond*. Boston: Beacon Press, 1968.

Clemons, Walter. "A Gravestone of Memories." *Newsweek*, 28 September 1987, 74–75.

Coleman, James W. *Blackness and Modernism; The Literary Career of John Edgar Wideman*. Jackson: University Press of Mississippi, 1989.

Collins, Patricia Hill. *Black Feminist Thought: Knowledge, Consciousness, and the Politics of Empowerment*. New York: HarperCollins, 1990.

———. *Fighting Words: Black Women and the Search for Justice*. Minneapolis: University of Minnesota Press, 1998.

Comfort, Susan. "Counter-Memory, Mourning and History in Toni Morrison's *Beloved.*" *LIT: Literature Interpretation Theory* 6.1–2 (1995): 121–32.

Connor, Steven. *Postmodernist Culture: An Introduction to Theories of the Contemporary*. 2nd ed. Cambridge, Mass.: Blackwell, 1997.

Cose, Ellis. *The Rage of a Privileged Class*. New York: HarperPerennial, 1993.

Cowart, David. *History and the Contemporary Novel*. Carbondale: Southern Illinois University Press, 1989.

Crew, Spencer. *Black Life in Secondary Cities: A Comparative Analysis of the Black Communities of Camden and Elizabeth, N.J., 1860–1920*. New York: Garland, 1993.

Crouch, Stanley. *The All-American Skin Game; or, The Decoy of Race*. New York: Pantheon, 1995.

——. "Aunt Medea." *New Republic*, 19 October 1987, 38–43.

Darling, Marsha. "In the Realm of Responsibility: A Conversation with Toni Morrison." *Women's Review of Books* 5 (March 1988): 5–6.

Davis, Angela Yvonne. *Angela Davis: An Autobiography*. New York, Random House, 1974.

Davis, Kimberly Chabot. "Postmodern Blackness: Toni Morrison's *Beloved* and the End of History." *Twentieth Century Literature* 44.2 (1998): 242–60.

Davis, Mary Kemp. "Everybody Knows Her Name: The Recovery of the Past in Sherley Anne Williams's *Dessa Rose*." *Callaloo* 12.3 (1989): 544–58.

DeHay, Terry. "Narrating Memory." In *Memory, Narrative, and Identity: New Essays in Ethnic American Literatures*, edited by Amrijit Singh et al., 26–44. Boston: Northeastern University Press, 1994.

Dent, Gina, ed. *Black Popular Culture*. Seattle: Bay Press, 1992.

Diedrich, Maria, Henry Louis Gates Jr., and Carl Pedersen, eds. *Black Imagination and the Middle Passage*. New York: Oxford University Press, 1999.

Dirks, Nicholas B., et al., eds. *Culture / Power / History: A Reader in Contemporary Social Theory*. Princeton: Princeton University Press, 1994.

Dixon, Melvin. "The Black Writer's Use of Memory." In *History and Memory in African-American Culture*, edited by Genevieve Fabre and Robert O'Meally, 18–27. New York: Oxford University Press, 1994.

Douglas, Ann. *Terrible Honesty: Mongrel Manhattan in the 1920s*. New York: Farrar, Straus, and Giroux, 1995.

Doyle, Laura. *Bordering on the Body: The Racial Matrix of Modern Fiction and Culture*. New York: Oxford University Press, 1994.

D'Souza, Dinesh. *The End of Racism: Principles for a Multiracial Society*. New York: Free Press, 1995.

Du Bois, W. E. B. *The Souls of Black Folk*. Chicago: A. C. McClurg, 1903.

Dudley, David L. *My Father's Shadow: Intergenerational Conflict in African American Men's Autobiography*. Philadelphia: University of Pennsylvania Press, 1991.

During, Simon. *Foucault and Literature: Towards a Genealogy of Writing*. London: Routledge, 1992.

——, ed. *The Cultural Studies Reader*. London: Routledge, 1993.

Dyson, Michael Eric. *Race Rules: Navigating the Color Line*. New York: Vintage, 1997.

Early, Gerald, ed. *Lure and Loathing: Essays on Race, Identity, and the Ambivalence of Assimilation*. New York: Penguin Press, 1993.

——. *Tuxedo Junction: Essays on American Culture.* Hopewell, N.J.: Ecco Press, 1989.

Easthope, Antony. *Literary into Cultural Studies.* London: Routledge, 1991.

Elkins, Stanley M. *Slavery.* Chicago: University of Chicago Press, 1959.

Epstein, Helen. *Children of the Holocaust: Conversations with Sons and Daughters of Survivors.* New York: Putnam, 1979.

Fabre, Genevieve, and Robert O'Meally, eds. *History and Memory in African-American Culture.* New York: Oxford University Press, 1994.

Fairlamb, Horace L. *Critical Conditions: Postmodernity and the Question of Foundations.* Cambridge: Cambridge University Press, 1994.

Felman, Shoshana, and Dori Laub. *Testimony: Crises of Witnessing in Literature, Psychoanalysis, and History.* New York: Routledge, 1992.

Ferguson, Russell, et al., eds. *Out There: Marginalization and Contemporary Cultures.* Cambridge: MIT Press, 1990.

Fischer, Roger A. "Ghetto and Gown: The Birth of Black Studies." In *New Perspectives on Black Studies*, edited by John W. Blassingame, 16–27. Urbana: University of Illinois Press, 1971.

Foley, Barbara. *Telling the Truth: The Theory and Practice of Documentary Fiction.* Ithaca: Cornell University Press, 1986.

Ford, Nick Aaron. *Black Studies: Threat-or-Challenge.* Port Washington, N.Y.: Kennikat Press, 1973.

Forrest, Leon. *Divine Days.* New York: Norton, 1993.

——. *Relocations of the Spirit.* Wakefield, R.I.: Asphodel Press, 1994.

——. *Two Wings to Veil My Face.* 1983. Chicago: Another Chicago Press, 1988.

Fossett, Judith Jackson, and Jeffrey A. Tucker, eds. *Race Consciousness: African-American Studies for the New Century.* New York: New York University Press, 1997.

Foulke, Gyasi A. *The Real Holocaust: A Wholistic Analysis of the African-American Experience, 1441–1994.* New York: Carlton Press, 1995.

Francese, Joseph. *Narrating Postmodern Time and Space.* Albany: State University of New York Press, 1997.

Friedlander, Saul, ed. *Probing the Limits of Representation: Nazism and the "Final Solution."* Cambridge, Mass.: Harvard University Press, 1992.

Gabriel, John. *Racism, Culture, Markets.* New York: Routledge, 1994.

Gaines, Ernest. *A Gathering of Old Men.* 1983. New York: Vintage, 1992.

——. *A Lesson Before Dying.* New York: Knopf, 1993.

Gates, Henry Louis, Jr. *The Signifying Monkey: A Theory of Afro-American Literary Criticism.* New York: Oxford University Press, 1988.

——, ed. *Black Literature and Literary Theory.* New York: Methuen, 1984.

Gates, Henry Louis, Jr., and Cornel West. *The Future of the Race.* New York: Vintage, 1996.

Genette, Gérard. *Narrative Discourse: An Essay in Method.* Translated by Jane E. Lewin. Ithaca: Cornell University Press, 1980.

Genovese, Eugene D. *Roll, Jordan, Roll: The World the Slaves Made*. New York: Vintage Books, 1976.

Gibbs, Jewelle Taylor, ed. *Young, Black, and Male in America: An Endangered Species*. Dover, Mass.: Auburn House, 1988.

Giddings, Paula. *When and Where I Enter: The Impact of Black Women on Race and Sex in America*. New York: William Morrow, 1984.

Gilroy, Paul. *Black Atlantic: Modernity and Double Consciousness*. Cambridge, Mass.: Harvard University Press, 1993.

———. *Small Acts: Thoughts on the Politics of Black Cultures*. London: Serpent's Tail, 1993.

Goldberg, David Theo. *Racial Subjects: Writing on Race in America*. New York: Routledge, 1997.

———. *Racist Culture: Philosophy and the Politics of Meaning*. Oxford: Blackwell, 1993.

———, ed. *Anatomy of Racism*. Minneapolis: University of Minnesota Press, 1990.

Gossman, Lionel. *Between History and Literature*. Cambridge, Mass.: Harvard University Press, 1990.

Gray, Paul. "Something Terrible Happened." *Time*, 21 September 1987, 75.

Griffin, Farah Jasmine. *"Who Set You Flowin'?": The African-American Migration Narrative*. New York: Oxford University Press, 1995.

Guerrero, Ed. *Framing Blackness: The African American Image in Film*. Philadelphia: Temple University Press, 1993.

Gunn, Giles. "Approaching the Historical." In *Reconceptualizing American Literary / Cultural Studies: Rhetoric, History, and Politics in the Humanities*, edited by William Cain, 59–72. New York: Garland, 1996.

Gutman, Herbert. *The Black Family in Slavery and Freedom, 1750–1925*. New York: Vintage, 1976.

Hare, Nathan. "What Should Be the Role of Afro-American Education in the Undergraduate Curriculum?" In *New Perspectives on Black Studies*, edited by John W. Blassingame, 3–15. Urbana: University of Illinois Press, 1971.

Harris, Norman. *Connecting Times: The Sixties in Afro-American Fiction*. Jackson: University Press of Mississippi, 1988.

———. Rev. of *Beloved*. *Minnesota Review* 30 (1988): 190–95.

Harris, Trudier. *Fiction and Folklore*. Knoxville: University of Tennessee Press, 1991.

———. "On *The Color Purple*, Stereotypes, and Silence." *Black American Literature Forum* 18.4 (1984): 155–61.

Harrison, Alferdeen, ed. *Black Exodus: The Great Migration from the American South*. Jackson: University Press of Mississippi, 1991.

Hartman, Geoffrey H. *Holocaust Remembrance: The Shapes of Memory*. Cambridge, Mass.: Blackwell, 1994.

Heller, Dana. "Reconstructing Kin: Family, History, and Narrative in Toni Morrison's *Beloved*." *College Literature* 21.2 (1994): 105–17.

Henderson, Harry. *Versions of the Past: The Historical Imagination in American Fiction*. New York: Oxford University Press, 1974.

Henri, Florette. *Black Migration: Movement North 1900–1920: The Road from Myth to Man*. New York: Anchor Press, 1976.

Hernton, Calvin C. *Sex and Racism in America*. New York: Grove Press, 1965.

Herrnstein, Richard J., and Charles Murray. *The Bell Curve: Intelligence and Class Structure in American Life*. New York: Free Press, 1994.

Hill, Herbert, and James E. Jones Jr., eds. *Race in America: The Struggle for Equality*. Madison: University of Wisconsin Press, 1993.

Hine, Darlene Clark. *The State of Afro-American History: Past, Present, and Future*. Baton Rouge: Louisiana State University Press, 1986.

Hirsch, Marianne. "Projected Memory: Holocaust Photographs in Personal and Public Fantasy." In *Acts of Memory: Cultural Recall in the Present*, edited by Mieke Bal, Jonathan Crewe, and Leo Spitzer, 3–23. Hanover: University Press of New England, 1999.

Hodgson, Godfrey. *More Equal than Others: America from Nixon to the New Century*. Princeton: Princeton University Press, 2004.

Holden-Kirwan, Jennifer L. "Looking into the Self that Is No Self: An Examination of Subjectivity in *Beloved*." *African American Review* 32.3 (1998): 415–26.

Hollinger, David A. *Postethnic America: Beyond Multiculturalism*. New York: Basic, 1995.

Holloway, Karla F. C. *Moorings and Metaphor: Figures of Culture and Gender in Black Women's Literature*. New Brunswick: Rutgers University Press, 1992.

Holt, Thomas. "Introduction: Whither Now and Why?" In *The State of Afro-American History: Past, Present, and Future*, edited by Darlene Clark Hine, 1–10. Baton Rouge: Louisiana State University Press, 1986.

Holton, Robert. *Jarring Witnesses: Modern Fiction and the Representation of History*. New York: Harvester Wheatsheaf, 1994.

hooks, bell. *Black Looks: Race and Representation*. Boston: South End Press, 1992.

——. *Outlaw Culture: Resisting Representations*. New York: Routledge, 1994.

——. *Yearning: Race, Gender, and Cultural Politics*. Boston: South End Press, 1990.

Horowitz, Sara R. *Voicing the Void: Muteness and Memory in Holocaust Fiction*. Albany: State University of New York Press, 1997.

Howe, Stephen. *Afrocentrism: Mythical Pasts and Imagined Homes*. London: Verso, 1998.

Huggins, Nathan. *Afro-American Studies*. New York: Ford Foundation, 1985.

——. *Harlem Renaissance*. New York: Oxford University Press, 1971.

Hutcheon, Linda. *A Poetics of Postmodernism: History, Theory, Fiction*. New York: Routledge, 1988.

Hutchinson, George. *The Harlem Renaissance in Black and White*. Cambridge, Mass.: Harvard University Press, 1995.

Jacobs, Naomi. *The Character of Truth: Historical Figures in Contemporary Fiction*. Carbondale: Southern Illinois University Press, 1990.

Jameson, Frederic. *The Political Unconscious: Narrative as a Socially Symbolic Act*. Ithaca: Cornell University Press, 1981.

Johnson, Charles. *Being and Race: Black Writing Since 1970*. Bloomington: Indiana
University Press, 1988.
——. *Dreamer*. New York: Scribner, 1998.
——. *Middle Passage*. New York: Atheneum, 1990.
——. *Oxherding Tale*. New York: Grove, 1984.
Jones, Charles E., ed. *The Black Panther Party (reconsidered)*. Baltimore: Black Classic
Press, 1998.
Jones, Del. *Black Holocaust*. Philadelphia: Hikeka Press, 1992.
Juan-Navarro, Santiago. *Archival Reflections: Postmodern Fiction of the Americas*.
Lewisburg: Bucknell University Press, 2000.
Kekeh, Andreé-Anne. "Sherley Anne Williams' *Dessa Rose*: History and the
Disruptive Power of Memory." In *History and Memory in African-American Culture*,
edited by Genevieve Fabre and Robert O'Meally, 219–27. New York: Oxford
University Press, 1994.
Kelley, Robin D. G. *Yo' Mama's Disfunktional: Fighting the Culture Wars in Urban
America*. Boston: Beacon Press, 1997.
Kellner, Douglas. *Critical Theory, Marxism, and Modernity*. Baltimore: Johns Hopkins
University Press, 1989.
Kennedy, J. Gerald, and Daniel Mark Fogel, eds. *American Letters and the Historical
Consciousness: Essays in Honor of Lewis P. Simpson*. Baton Rouge: Louisiana State
University Press, 1987.
Kennedy, Randall. "My Race Problem—and Ours." *Atlantic Monthly*, May 1997, 55–
66.
Kinder, Donald R., and Lynn M. Sanders. *Divided by Color: Racial Politics and
Democratic Ideals*. Chicago: University of Chicago Press, 1996.
King, Nicole R. "Meditations and Mediations: Issues of History and Fiction in *Dessa
Rose*." *Soundings* 76.2–3 (1993): 351–68.
Kristeva, Julia. *Powers of Horror: An Essay on Abjection*. New York: Columbia
University Press, 1982.
——. *Strangers to Ourselves*. Translated by Leon S. Roudiez. New York: Columbia,
1991.
Kubitschek, Missy Dehn. *Claiming the Heritage: African-American Women Novelists and
History*. Jackson: University Press of Mississippi, 1991.
LaCapra, Dominick. *Representing the Holocaust: History, Theory, Trauma*. Ithaca:
Cornell University Press, 1994.
——. *Soundings in Critical Theory*. Ithaca: Cornell University Press, 1989.
Lane, Christopher, ed. *The Psychoanalysis of Race*. New York: Columbia University
Press, 1998.
Langer, Lawrence L. *Admitting the Holocaust: Collected Essays*. New York: Oxford
·University Press, 1995.
——. *Holocaust Testimonies: The Ruins of Memory*. New Haven: Yale University Press,
1991.

——. *Preempting the Holocaust.* New Haven: Yale University Press, 1998.

Lefkowitz, Mary. *Not Out of Africa: How Afrocentrism Became an Excuse to Teach Myth as History.* New York: BasicBooks, 1996.

Lemann, Nicholas. *The Promised Land: The Great Black Migration and How It Changed America.* New York: Knopf, 1991.

Levine, George, ed. *Aesthetics and Ideology.* New Brunswick: Rutgers University Press, 1994.

Levine, Lawrence W. *Black Culture and Black Consciousness: Afro-American Folk Thought from Slavery to Freedom.* New York: Oxford University Press, 1977.

Lewis, David L. *When Harlem Was in Vogue.* New York: Knopf, 1981.

Little, Jonathan. *Charles Johnson's Spiritual Imagination.* Columbia: University of Missouri Press, 1997.

Loury, Glenn C. *One by One from the Outside In: Essays and Reviews on Race and Responsibility in America.* New York: Free Press, 1995.

Lubiano, Wahneema. *The House That Race Built: Black Americans, U.S. Terrain.* New York: Pantheon, 1997.

Lukács, Georg. *The Historical Novel.* Translated by Hannah Mitchell and Stanley Mitchell. Lincoln: University of Nebraska Press, 1962.

Lustig, Jessica. "Home: An Interview with John Edgar Wideman." *African American Review* 26.3 (1992): 453–57.

Madhubuti, Haki R. *Black Men: Obsolete, Single, Dangerous?* Chicago: Third World Press, 1990.

Maier, Charles S. *The Unmasterable Past: History, Holocaust, and German National Identity.* Cambridge, Mass.: Harvard University Press, 1988.

Mailer, Norman. *Advertisements for Myself.* New York: Signet, 1959.

Mathieson, Barbara Offutt. "Memory and Mother Love: Toni Morrison's Dyad." In *Memory, Narrative, and Identity: New Essays in Ethnic American Literatures,* edited by Amrijit Singh et al., 212–32. Boston: Northeastern University Press, 1994.

Mayer, Jeremy D. *Running on Race: Racial Politics in Presidential Campaigns, 1960–2000.* New York: Random House, 2002.

Mbalia, Doreatha Drummond. *Toni Morrison's Developing Class Consciousness.* Selinsgrove: Susquehanna University Press, 1991.

McBride, Dwight A. "Speaking the Unspeakable: On Toni Morrison, African American Intellectuals and the Uses of Essentialist Rhetoric." In *Toni Morrison: Critical and Theoretical Approaches.* Edited by Nancy J. Peterson, 131–52. Baltimore: Johns Hopkins University Press, 1997.

McDowell, Deborah E., *"The Changing Same": Black Women's Literature, Criticism, and Theory.* Bloomington: Indiana University Press, 1995.

——. "Negotiating between Tenses: Witnessing Slavery after Freedom: Dessa Rose." In *Slavery and the Literary Imagination,* edited by Deborah E. McDowell and Arnold Rampersad, 144–63. Baltimore: Johns Hopkins University Press, 1989.

McDowell, Deborah E., and Arnold Rampersad, eds. *Slavery and the Literary Imagination.* Baltimore: Johns Hopkins University Press, 1989.

McWhorter, John H. *Losing the Race: Self-Sabotage in Black America.* New York: Free Press, 2000.

Meier, August, and Elliott Rudwick. *Black History and the Historical Profession, 1915– 1980.* Urbana: University of Illinois Press, 1986.

Merelman, Richard M. *Representing Black Culture: Racial Conflict and Cultural Politics in the United States.* New York: Routledge, 1995.

Michaels, Walter Benn. *Our America: Nativism, Modernism, and Pluralism.* Durham: Duke University Press, 1995.

Mikics, David. "Postmodernism, Ethnicity, and Underground Revisionism in Ishmael Reed." In *Essays in Postmodernism,* edited by Eyal Amiran and John Unsworth, 295– 324. New York: Oxford University Press, 1993.

Morrison, Toni. *Beloved.* New York: Knopf, 1987.

——. *Jazz.* New York: Knopf, 1992.

——. *Paradise.* New York: Knopf, 1998.

——. *Playing in the Dark: Whiteness and the Literary Imagination.* Cambridge, Mass.: Harvard University Press, 1992.

——. "Portraits of Loneliness, and a Writer's Response." *New Yorker,* 12 October 1998, 68.

——. "Talk of the Town." *New Yorker,* 5 October 1998, 31–32.

——. *Tarbaby.* New York: Knopf, 1981.

——. "Unspeakable Things Unspoken: The Afro-American Presence in American Literature." *Michigan Quarterly Review* 28.1 (1989): 9–34.

——, ed. *Race-ing Justice, En-gendering Power: Essays on Anita Hill, Clarence Thomas, and the Construction of Social Reality.* New York: Pantheon Books, 1992.

Moses, Wilson Jeremiah. *Afrotopia: The Roots of African American Popular History.* Cambridge: Cambridge University Press, 1998.

Moynihan, Daniel Patrick. *The Negro Family: The Case for National Action.* Washington, D.C.: Department of Labor, 1965.

Myrsiades, Kostas, and Linda Myrsiades, eds. *Race-ing Representation: Voice, History, and Sexuality.* Lanham, Md.: Rowman and Littlefield, 1998.

Naylor, Gloria. *Bailey's Cafe.* New York: Harcourt Brace Jovanovich, 1992.

——. *Mama Day.* New York: Houghton Mifflin, 1988.

Newton, Adam Zachary. *Narrative Ethics.* Cambridge, Mass.: Harvard University Press, 1995.

Nora, Pierre. "Between Memory and History: *Les Lieux de Mémoire.*" In *History and Memory in African-American Culture,* edited by Genevieve Fabre and Robert O'Meally, 284–300. New York: Oxford University Press, 1994.

Nussbaum, Martha C. *Poetic Justice: The Literary Imagination and Public Life.* Boston: Beacon Press, 1995.

Omi, Michael, and Howard Winant. *Racial Formation in the United States: From the 1960s to the 1990s.* 2nd ed. New York: Routledge, 1994.

Otten, Terry. *The Crime of Innocence in the Fiction of Toni Morrison.* Columbia: University of Missouri Press, 1989.

Outlaw, Lucius T. *On Race and Philosophy*. New York: Routledge, 1996.

Page, Philip. *Dangerous Freedom: Fusion and Fragmentation in Toni Morrison's Novels*. Jackson: University Press of Mississippi, 1995.

Painter, Nell Irvin. *Exodusters: Black Migration to Kansas after Reconstruction*. New York: Knopf, 1977.

Parish, Peter J. *Slavery: History and Historians*. New York: Harper and Row, 1989.

Pauley, Garth E. *The Modern Presidency and Civil Rights: Rhetoric on Race from Roosevelt to Nixon*. College Station: Texas A and M University Press, 2001.

Peterson, Nancy J. " 'Say Make Me, Remake Me': Toni Morrison and the Reconstruction of African American History." *Toni Morrison: Critical and Theoretical Approaches*. Edited by Nancy J. Peterson, 201–14. Baltimore: Johns Hopkins University Press, 1997.

Pocock, J. G. A. *Politics, Language, and Time: Essays on Political Thought and History*. New York: Atheneum, 1973.

Puri, Usha. "Convergence of History and Feminism in Toni Morrison's *Beloved*." *Indian Journal of American Studies* 24.2 (1994): 89–96.

Randle, Gloria T. " 'Knowing When to Stop': Loving and Living Small in the Slave World of *Beloved*." *CLA Journal* 41.3 (1998): 279–302.

Reed, Ishmael. *Writin' Is Fightin': Thirty-Seven Years of Boxing on Paper*. New York: Atheneum, 1988.

Rhodes, Chip. *Structures of the Jazz Age: Mass Culture, Progressive Education, and Racial Discourse in American Modernism*. London: Verso, 1998.

Roberts, John W. *From Trickster to Badman: The Black Folk Hero in Slavery and Freedom*. Philadelphia: University of Pennsylvania Press, 1989.

Robinson, Armstead L., et al., eds. *Black Studies in the University: A Symposium*. New Haven: Yale University Press, 1969.

Rosenberg, Bruce A. "Leon Forrest and the African-American Folk Sermon." In *Leon Forrest: Introductions and Interpretations*, edited by John G. Cawelti, 115–26. Bowling Green, Ohio: Bowling Green State University Popular Press, 1997.

Rowell, Charles H. "An Interview with John Edgar Wideman." *Callaloo* 13.1 (1990): 47–61.

Rushdy, Ashraf H. A. "Daughters Signifyin(g) History: The Example of Toni Morrison's *Beloved*." *American Literature* 64.3 (1992): 567–97.

——. "Fraternal Blues: John Edgar Wideman's Homewood Trilogy." *Contemporary Literature* 32.3 (1991): 312–45.

——. *Neo-Slave Narratives: Studies in the Social Logic of a Literary Form*. New York: Oxford University Press, 1999.

——. "The Phenomenology of the Allmuseri: Charles Johnson and the Subject of the Narrative of Slavery." *African American Review* 26.3 (1992): 373–94.

——. "The Properties of Desire: Forms of Slave Identity in Charles Johnson's *Middle Passage*." *Arizona Quarterly* 50.2 (1994): 73–108.

———. "Reading Mammy: The Subject of Relation in Sherley Anne Williams' *Dessa Rose*." *African American Review* 27.3 (1993): 365–89.

Ryan, Judylyn S. "Spirituality and/as Ideology in Black Women's Literature: The Preaching of Maria W. Stewart and Baby Suggs, Holy." In *Women Preachers and Prophets through Two Millenia of Christianity*, edited by Beverly Mayne Kienzle and Pamela J. Walker, 267–87. Berkeley: University of California Press, 1998.

Saldívar, José David. *The Dialectics of Our America: Genealogy, Cultural Critique, and Literary History*. Durham: Duke University Press, 1991.

Sale, Maggie. "Call and Response as Critical Method: African-American Oral Traditions and *Beloved*." *African American Review* 26.1 (1992): 41–50.

Samuels, Wilfred D. "Going Home: A Conversation with John Edgar Wideman." *Callaloo* 6.1 (1983): 40–59.

Shakur, Sanyika. *Monster: The Autobiography of an L.A. Gang Member*. New York: Penguin, 1994.

Shull, Steven A. *American Civil Rights Policy from Truman to Clinton: The Role of Presidential Leadership*. Armonk, N.Y.: M. E. Sharpe, 1999.

Simpson, Andrea Y. *The Tie That Binds: Identity and Political Attitudes in the Post–Civil Rights Generation*. New York: New York University Press, 1998.

Singh, Amrijit, et al., eds. *Memory, Narrative, and Identity: New Essays in Ethnic American Literatures*. Boston: Northeastern University Press, 1994.

Sollers, Werner, and Maria Diedrich, eds. *The Black Columbiad: Defining Moments in African American Literature and Culture*. Cambridge, Mass.: Harvard University Press, 1994.

Solomon, Barbara H., ed. *Critical Essays on Toni Morrison's Beloved*. New York: G. K. Hall, 1998.

Sowell, Thomas. *Civil Rights: Rhetoric or Reality?* New York: W. Morrow, 1984.

———. *Race and Economics*. New York: D. McKay Co., 1975.

Spencer, Jon Michael. *The New Negroes and Their Music: The Success of the Harlem Renaissance*. Knoxville: University of Tennessee Press, 1997.

Stampp, Kenneth. *The Peculiar Institution: Slavery in the Ante-Bellum South*. New York: Vintage, 1956.

Steele, Shelby. *The Content of Our Character: A New Vision of Race in America*. New York: HarperPerennial, 1991.

Steele, Valerie. *Fashion and Eroticism: Ideals of Feminine Beauty from the Victorian Era to the Jazz Age*. New York: Oxford University Press, 1985.

Steinberg, Stephen. *Turning Back: The Retreat from Racial Justice in American Thought and Policy*. Boston: Beacon Press, 1995.

Stone, Albert E. *The Return of Nat Turner: History, Literature, and Cultural Politics in Sixties America*. Athens: University of Georgia Press, 1992.

Stuart, Andrea. "Blue Notes." *New Statesman and Society*, 1 May 1992, 39–40.

Tal, Kalí. *Worlds of Hurt: Reading the Literatures of Trauma*. Cambridge: Cambridge University Press, 1996.

Tate, Claudia. *Domestic Allegories of Political Desire: The Black Heroine's Text at the Turn of the Century.* New York: Oxford University Press, 1992.

——. *Psychoanalysis and Black Novels: Desire and the Protocols of Race.* New York: Oxford University Press, 1998.

Tate, Greg. *Flyboy in the Buttermilk: Essays on Contemporary America.* New York: Simon and Schuster, 1992.

Taylor-Guthrie, Danielle. "Sermons, Testifying and Prayers: Looking Beneath the Wings in Leon Forrest's *Two Wings to Veil My Face.*" In *Leon Forrest: Introductions and Interpretations,* edited by John G. Cawelti, 216–32. Bowling Green, Ohio: Bowling Green State University Popular Press, 1997.

Thernstrom, Stephan, and Abigail Thernstrom. *America in Black and White: One Nation, Indivisible.* New York: Simon and Schuster, 1997.

Thurman, Judity. "A House Divided." *New Yorker,* 2 November 1987, 175–80.

Van Alphen, Ernst. "Symptoms of Discursivity: Experience, Memory, and Trauma." In *Acts of Memory: Cultural Recall in the Present,* edited by Mieke Bal, Jonathan Crewe, and Leo Spitzer, 24–38. Hanover: University Press of New England, 1999.

Van Deburg, William L. *New Day in Babylon: The Black Power Movement and American Culture, 1965–1975.* Chicago: University of Chicago Press, 1992.

Veeser, H. Aram, ed. *The New Historicism.* New York: Routledge, 1989.

Wachtel, Paul L. *Race in the Mind of America: Breaking the Vicious Circle between Blacks and Whites.* New York: Routledge, 1999.

Walker, Alice. *In Search of Our Mothers' Gardens: Womanist Prose.* San Diego: Harcourt Brace Jovanovich, 1983.

Walker, Clarence E. *Deromanticizing Black History: Critical Essays and Reappraisals.* Knoxville: University of Tennessee Press, 1991.

Wall, Cheryl A. *Women of the Harlem Renaissance.* Bloomington: Indiana University Press, 1995.

Wallace, Michele. "Negative Images: Towards a Black Feminist Cultural Criticism." In *The Cultural Studies Reader,* edited by Simon During, 118–31. London: Routledge, 1993.

Walters, Colin. "A Ghostly, Terrifying Tale of Lives in Slavery." *Insight,* 12 October 1987, 60–61.

Warren, Kenneth W. "Thinking Beyond the Catastrophe: Leon Forrest's *There Is a Tree More Ancient Than Eden.*" In *Leon Forrest: Introductions and Interpretations,* edited by John G. Cawelti, 152–65. Bowling Green, Ohio: Bowling Green State University Popular Press, 1997.

Washington, Elsie B. "Talk with Toni Morrison." *Essence,* October 1987, 58, 136–37.

Washington, Mary Helen. Introduction to *Black-Eyed Susans: Classic Stories by and about Black Women.* New York: Anchor, 1975.

Watson, Steven. *The Harlem Renaissance: Hub of African-American Culture, 1920–1930.* New York: Pantheon, 1995.

Welsing, Frances Cress. *The Isis Papers.* Chicago: Third World Press, 1991.

Werner, Craig. "Leon Forrest and the AACM: The Jazz Impulse and the Legacy of the Chicago Renaissance." In *Leon Forrest: Introductions and Interpretations*, edited by John G. Cawelti, 127–51. Bowling Green, Ohio: Bowling Green State University Popular Press, 1997.

West, Cornel. *Race Matters*. Boston: Beacon Press, 1993.

White, Hayden. *Tropics of Discourse: Essays in Cultural Criticism*. Baltimore: Johns Hopkins University Press, 1978.

Wideman, John Edgar. *Cattle Killing*. Boston: Houghton Mifflin, 1996.

——. *Damballah*. New York: Avon, 1981.

——. *Hiding Place*. New York: Avon, 1981.

——. *Sent for You Yesterday*. New York: Avon, 1983.

Wilentz, Gay. *Binding Cultures: Black Women Writers in Africa and the Diaspora*. Bloomington: Indiana University Press, 1992.

Williams, Sherley Anne. *Dessa Rose*. New York: William Morrow, 1986.

Wilson, Carter A. *Racism: From Slavery to Advanced Capitalism*. Thousand Oaks, Calif.: Sage, 1996.

Wright, Andrew H. *Fictional Discourse and Historical Space*. New York: St. Martin's Press, 1987.

Wyatt, Jean. "Giving Body to the Word: The Maternal Symbolic in Toni Morrison's *Beloved*." *Publications of the Modern Language Association* 108.3 (1993): 474–88.

Young, Robert. *White Mythologies: Writing History and the West*. London: Routledge, 1990.

Young-Bruel, Elizabeth. *The Anatomy of Prejudices*. Cambridge, Mass.: Harvard University Press, 1996.

Zavarzadeh, Mas'ud, and Donald Morton. *Theory, (Post)Modernity, Opposition: An "Other" Introduction to Literary and Cultural Theory*. Washington, D.C.: Maissoneuve Press, 1991.

Index

Trauma theory, 28, 203 (intro., n. 6)

Two Wings to Veil My Face (Forrest), 24, 138–46; storytelling as theme in, 138; as patriarchal narrative, 138–39; structure of, 139; Sweetie Reed as narrator in, 139; as revision of womanist narrative, 143–44; orphans as theme in, 144; multiple voices in, 145

Vidal, Gore, 22

Walker, Alice, 11, 15, 23, 39, 40, 46, 50, 54, 58, 68, 69, 76, 87, 88, 89, 93, 118, 125, 146, 147, 151, 198, 205 (chap. 3, n. 6); *Meridian*, 15; *The Color Purple*, 40, 56, 58, 76, 103, 144; *Possessing the Secret of Joy*, 76; *In Search of Our Mothers' Gardens*, 76, 205 (chap. 3, n. 6); *The Third Life of Grange Copeland*, 88

Walker, Clarence, 21, 128

Walker, Margaret, 36, 54, 97; *Jubilee*, 54, 97, 107, 128

Washington, Booker T., 140

West, Cornel, 46, 181; *Race Matters*, 181

Wideman, John Edgar, 6, 10, 11, 23, 45, 46, 68, 125, 127, 157–75, 179, 180– 88, 194, 196, 201, 207 (chap. 9, n. 5; chap. 10, n. 2; chap. 11, n. 1); *All Stories Are True*, 11, 170; *Damballah*, 68, 158, 164, 170, 171, 174; *Fatheralong*, 157, 174; theme of patriarchy in, 157– 58; relationship of fiction and autobiography in, 158; *Hiding Place*, 158, 170, 171, 174; relationship of history and fiction in, 159; as gatherer of stories, 160; "Lizabeth: The Caterpillar Story," 162–63, 164; "Daddy Garbage," 163–64; "Across the Wide Missouri," 166–67; *Brother and Keeper*, 170; role of brother in writing of, 170; "All Stories Are True," 171; "Solitary," 171, 174; "Tommy," 171–74; "Fever," 181. See also *Cattle Killing*; "Damballah"; Homewood trilogy; *Sent for You Yesterday*

Williams, Sherely Anne, 8, 27, 54–64, 68, 107, 108, 205 (chap. 4, n. 4). See also *Dessa Rose*

Winant, Howard, 7, 13, 203 (intro., n. 1), 207 (n. 8)

Womanism, 54, 67, 76, 88, 89

Woodson, Carter G., 19

Wright, Richard, 47, 97–98, 204 (n. 10); *Native Son*, 47, 170